W9-AGX-364

SEX, GENDER & SEXUALITY

The Author

Dr Tracie O'Keefe, DCH, BA, N-SHAP Adv Dip Thp MCRAH is a Clinical Hypnotherapist, Psychotherapist and Counsellor at the London Medical Centre in Harley Street. She is currently in post-doctoral studies with the American Institute of Hypnotherapy. Tracie is also studying the cross-over between biology and psychology with the Open University.

Her practice involves helping people with many forms of identity and body dysmorphic disorders. She is a member of the British Association of Counselling, Institute of Complementary Medicine, Central Register of Advanced Hypnotherapists, Gender Trust, Harry Benjamin International Gender Dysphoria Association, and a patron of Gendys Network and TransEssex.

As well as being a practitioner, Tracie also lectures internationally on sex, gender and sexuality and is the author of *Trans-X-U-All: The Naked Difference* and *Investigating Stage Hypnosis*. She regularly takes part in television and radio discussions on sex, gender, sexuality, hypnosis and psychotherapy.

Katrina Fox (Editor) is a freelance journalist and editor, and the co-author of *Trans-X-U-All: The Naked Difference*.

This book is dedicated to:

All the sex, gender and sexuality diverse people across the globe who are empowering themselves by speaking up, organising education, persuading, campaigning, and planting their feet firmly in the world.

It is also dedicated to the victims of the 1999 Bank Holiday hate bombing in Soho, the heart of London's gay community, in which three died and several others lost limbs.

SEX, GENDER & SEXUALITY

21st Century Transformations

Dr Tracie O'Keefe DCH

Edited by Katrina Fox

Published by:
Extraordinary People Press
1B Portman Mansions
Chiltern Street
London W1M 1PX
Tel. 0207 935 4490
Fax. 0207 486 5998
E-mail katfox@easynet.co.uk
Website http://easyweb.easynet.co.uk/~katfox/

First published 1999

British Library Cataloguing-in-Publication Data
A catalogue record for this book is available from the
British Library

ISBN 0 9529482 2 2

Printed in Great Britain

Distributed in the UK by Turnaround

SEX GENDER AND SEXUALITY ARE
FLUID CONCEPTS

Can science, knowledge and understanding be developed to suit our needs, or should we suit our needs according to our perceived limitations?

By the same author:

**Trans-X-U-All: The Naked Difference
(with Katrina Fox 1997)**
ISBN 0 9529482 0 6

**Investigating Stage Hypnosis
(1998)**
ISBN 0 9529482 1 4

Published by Extraordinary People Press

CONTENTS

Acknowledgements   viii

Preface   ix

1   **Myths and Prejudices**   1

2   **Sex**   28

3   **Gender**   56

4   **Sexuality**   70

5   **The Science of Truths and Non-Truths**   88

6   **The Development of the Pan-identity Model**   100

7   **The Stories**   118

8   **Papers and Articles**   169

9   **Papers by Dr Tracie O'Keefe DCH**   212

Afterword   317

Bibliography   319

Resources   334

Dr Tracie O'Keefe: Talks & Lectures   345

Index   351

Acknowledgements

First of all let me thank all those people who bought my first book, *Trans-X-U-All*, whose enthusiastic responses motivated me to share more of my learnings with the world. Also a big thank you to the many professionals in the field who are willing to listen, look and learn.

Thanks to:

Joe and Josephine public, who constantly throw up members of the human race who astound me with their common sense and tolerance, and humble me with their acts of kindness.

My clients over the years who have taught me that I have a great deal to learn and they have a great deal to teach me about the diversity of humanity.

Those who consented to give interviews and contribute pieces to this book. They have written about things which are very personal to them and sometimes in doing that I know they have had to do great deal of soul searching.

Alice Purnell, nurse counsellor, for her medical technical assistance.

Special thanks to:

Gerald Franklin, my research assistant, who tirelessly filed, cut, pasted, fetched, carried and patiently organised the material that we used to form the text and body of the book and many of my papers.

Katrina Fox, my partner, editor and adviser of how far I should shout from the rooftops, how to dot my i's and cross my t's, and with whose help I speak more clearly.

Preface

Sex, gender and sexuality are my business – they are what I know, and I can safely say that I am considered an expert in those fields. Yet even I can recognise that I have so much more to learn and hope to impart to you that every person we meet has something to teach us about themselves. The pan-identity wheel of sex, gender and sexuality is an old concept, but I endeavour to present it to you in a way you can more easily understand.

Times, laws, medicine, psychology, philosophy, social order and acceptance are changing as we go into the new millennium, which means that we all have to move onto a new plateau of understanding about the people around us.

Those in this book who tell us about their more unusual identities are to be commended for their bravery in attempting to educate us, in a world that can often be hostile to them.

The new categories of individuals who identify as having more than one sex, neither sex, or belonging to the third sex have a great deal to contribute to our own debates about how we view ourselves. If, like me, you are fascinated or curious about the human condition then READ AND ENJOY!

Dr Tracie O'Keefe DCH May 1999

1

Myths and Prejudices

A few years ago a retired school mistress sailed into my consulting room asking to speak to me about a very personal and confusing matter. "Look here," she said, pointing to a page in a women's magazine. "Everywhere I look there are articles on this female orgasm thing. Well I've taught children for 50 years, got a PhD in mathematics and shot down aeroplanes during the Second World War, but I've never been married."

Nervously and perplexed she poked the article continually with her right forefinger. "Can you tell me what it is and how to do it?"

After two hours of explaining to her the anatomy of the female genitals, how each part works, what it is for, where to apply pressure with what, why, when and with whom, she went away with her first owner's manual.

Two weeks later she re-entered my office thrilled about the first orgasm that she had purposely experienced. Not only did she tell me that it was something she was going to experience again and often, but also that such mysteries had never been explained to her before. "You know when I was young it was not permitted to talk about anything to do with those parts of the body. In fact I don't think I ever heard the word sex until I left home and even now I certainly can't imagine that my parents had ever done it."

When considering how to start this book I decided to ask lots of people what the concepts of sex, gender and sexuality meant to them. The answers I got back were wildly different from everyone and no two people had the same views or understandings. Even among those who came from similar families, backgrounds and educations had different perceptions of the composites of identity, which varied enormously.

Gemma, 26, married, mother of three: "Isn't gender something to do with those people who dress up? You know we did sex education at school but it was all condoms and diagrams or was it diaphragms?"

I guess the most profound conclusion I drew from my research was that for as many people as there are in the world, there are individual theories to match their life experiences. None of those theories are either right or wrong, but just simply different ways of looking at our own life patterns and what we observe about others.

A sexual health adviser I once taught at a seminar said: "In my day people were just happy doing it with their wives and husbands. I don't understand what all this promiscuity is about, but of course I would get fired if I said that at work."

Another thing I discovered was that the public in general do not break down the way they relate to their sex, gender and sexuality experiences into manageable and understandable components. Therefore I thought it an exciting project for me to put forward a systematic and easy way for each of us to understand ourselves and others. I cannot tell you that what I am writing is purely original work because it is simply my own distillation of the sex, gender and sexuality concepts that have formulated in the world at the end of the 20th and beginning of the 21st century.

Danny, a gardener: "I would like to understand more of those things. Wouldn't anyone? But it always seems to be tied up with radical politics and I get lost after a while."

Over the years I have studied sex, gender and sexuality, both as professional in the healthcare sector and in a personal context. I never cease to be surprised by the lack of understanding that the medical, psychological and social care sectors have of these concepts too.

A doctor once telephoned me with a patient who he was referring to me with sex and gender identity problems.

"This patient is unsure whether they are a man or a woman and I have to tell you Dr O'Keefe, I've never had one like this before. We do have some friends who are gay, but of course, my wife and I are perfectly normal."

I hope in sharing my knowledge, that has also developed along the way in the writing of this book, and the views of the contributors, it enriches your understanding of what is possible through the diversity of nature, sexualisation and socialisation. Alongside this I shall hope to seed many potted philosophies that will bear fruit upon the rich meadows and oases of your lives.

Sheepishly, and with an air of embarrassed curiosity, my 74-year-old mother asked me: "Now you're a lesbian, which one gets on top?"

In the Victorian times sex was never mentioned in polite society and such discussions were generally deemed filthy and improper. After the Second World War an air of propriety of what was right and wrong continued for a while in the West amid social insecurity. I guess a world of such magnitude will always breed paranoia about the differences that can sometimes seem alien to our own individual maps of the world.

However, to cite the Victorian times as the only perpetuators of such closeted sexual climates would be a mistake. Any threat to the normality (statistical average) of living can induce a public feeling of not wanting to recognise differences or accept other people's way of life.

The British government for many years kept a register of known homosexuals, believing them to be security threats to the nation. So did Russia, the US, South Africa, Australia, New Zealand along with many other countries, and some still do.

Of course it would also be easy to keep dragging the old victim of religion out into public kicking and screaming that there is only one true way, and to nail it to the cross as the perpetrator of prejudice. But I know, and you know, that politics and politicians are as much to blame for the unevenness of human sexual rights in the world as the good book, whichever one you are reading.

Coincidentally, before sitting down to write this I have just read a newspaper report on the Vatican's concerns about the rise in other religions, birth control, unmarried mothers and homosexuality. All this from a religion where many priests and nuns sleep with each other and that once had a pope who was a woman dressed as a man and had a child out of wedlock.

And then of course there is the family with its dynamics of incestuous power games that not only saves the good and the outcasts, but also condemns them to eternal damnation according to the direction of the wind and the day of the week.

Grandmother 1985: "What do you mean your brother's wife wants to be a lorry driver? But she is a woman so she must stay at home and look after the children. It's the only natural thing to do, isn't it?"

It is estimated that one in approximately every 200-300 children are born with genitals that are different from the average Joe or Josephine. These are often never talked about within the family or society, and advice that is open and honest has not, over the years, been clearly given by the medical profession.

The course of action taken by many doctors has been to perform surgery to bring the appearance of these people's genitals cosmetically in line with what is perceived as normal. This is often done without the person's or their family's permission and can damage the genitals so that there is little sexual sensation left.

An intersexed friend commented: "Where unauthorised surgery is performed on any other part of the body, the surgeon would be sued and fired from his position. However, because it is sexual organs they get away with inflicting their own views of normality on those of us who are born different."

In total the three components of sex, gender and sexuality are only some of the many profiles of identity that make up the overall picture and value of a person, but they can be used by harbingers as slingshots, as well as being worn as badges of pride. Other labels may be family, cultural identity, religious assimilations, national pride, being a member of a profession or anything that a person needs to identify themselves in order to quantify their value in the world.

Aunt Mary: "Do you know I am from the town and we did not have any animals so some 60 years ago I wasn't very knowledgeable about nature. When I got married at 22 and had my first child, I thought it came out of the belly button until he was actually born. I was in shock for weeks afterwards, because no one in those days ever mentioned anything to do with those taboo parts of our bodies. Yes I can laugh about it now, but at the time the surprise of how I gave birth was more profound than the birth itself and I thought I had done it wrong."

Years ago people would talk about delivering children in very secretive, code-like metaphors. Children would be told they were they were brought by the stork, in the midwife's little black bag or left under a gooseberry bush. In mentioning anything associated with the sexual act or organs, no direct linguistic connection would be made and reference to sexual behaviour in society would generally be avoided at all costs.

Of course there were always sectors of many societies who had their Bohemian and avant-garde ways, who spoke about sex with an almost blasé air, but in general, people were forbidden from discussing such things.

There are still millions of people, including doctors, therapists, psychologists, and psychiatrists all over the world who find it too difficult or embarrassing to talk openly about the experiences of sex, gender and sexuality. The silence is always driven by lack of knowledge, which causes fear.

The Divination and Demonisation of Sex, Gender and Sexuality

*All the world's a stage and all the men and women
merely players*
(Shakespeare)

Throughout history the attractions and battles of the sexes, power struggles of sex and gender conflicts, scenarios of lovers, and fashionability of sexualities have created deities, emperors and queens, but also often cast the innocent into eternal damnation. Cleopatra and Mark Anthony, Romeo and Juliet, Adam and Eve, Caligula, Mary Magdalene, Henry VIII, Caravaggio, Casanova, Oscar Wilde, Virginia Woolf, Edward Windsor and Mrs Simpson, Orlando, Linda Lovelace and Leslie Feinberg all evoked conflict and empathy among their peers when following their chosen course of love, lust and lifestyle.

Ancient civilisations and cults were often devoted to the Earth Mother or the Great Goddess who had been worshipped for tens of thousands of years. The central axis of these cultures was the mystical and magical worship of fertility, sexuality and the death and rebirth cycle. The interaction of the essence of male and female was the central focus of mysticism and philosophy. Their understanding of the biological dynamics of reproduction was limited.

Palaeolithic and Neolithic societies imagined a profusion of spirit-like deities to explain human existence and procreation. They regarded sexual intercourse as the most powerful of all acts, revered, and in which they would enter into the realms and forces of the gods and goddesses, often depicted by the symbolism of animal forces to represent fertile, ethereal or brutal alter-egos.

The Great Goddess was all powerful, heavy or many breasted, and Neolithic cults depicted her as being associated with the symbolism of snakes which portrayed eternal life and reincarnation. Later, in the emergence of patriarchal cultures the snake symbol was taken over to symbolise male potency and the phallus. The Great Goddess was seen as the giver of life itself, and sacrifices of food, animals and even humans were offered to her to ask for her favours and fertility. Her magical ability to produce life gave her an omnipotent and omniscient status and male influences were secondary in her world.

In later civilisations she became the Greek goddesses Demeter, Rhea, Aphrodite, Potnia, Selene, Pallas Athena; the Amazonians saw her as Gaia and Cybele; Babylonians as Astarte and Ishtar; and the Egyptians encapsulated her as Isis and Hathor. Mythologically she was described as the Star of the Night, Lady of the Night, Dark Goddess, Black Virgin. In Hebrew terms she was transmuted into the gentler Hebrew spirit which is feminine and then into the Christian Holy Spirit, Greek Pneuma, and Gnostic Sophia. In the East she was the Hindu goddesses Prana, Kali, Shakti, Dakini and Durga.

She had a macabre side too, which coincided with the lunar cycle when she was feared and associated with death, disintegration and evil darkness. This shadow side would strike fear in the hearts of even the bravest warriors. The second face of Eve emerged: the archetypal shadow side who was all powerful, awe inspiring, to be revered, worshipped and to whom a person prayed for compassion. With the emergence of patriarchal cultures, tales of slaying the dragon symbolised masculine triumph over the uncontrollable, powerful feminine by the masculine.

The Great Goddess or Earth Mother was often linked through sexual favours with divine prostitution, who granted sex and offspring through her almighty fertility. Yet more than that she was the goddess, queen warrior, granter of favours, the divine whore as well as the virgin and keeper of innocence. Her downfall came as travelling armies spread across the world conquering other civilisations and men, more adapted for war, traversed their concepts of womb-like origins. The masculine power of the one male god emerged, engendering the female servile, dangerous and full of lustful temptation to be resisted.

Pagan religions, from prehistory onwards, derived from legends, were connected to the earth through rituals and beliefs that surrounded the birth/death/rebirth cycle of nature. Since paganism has been handed down through folklore, and little written record was left behind, it is difficult for us to judge the gender structures of these early sects and cults. There were Cornish, Manx, Celtic, Breton, Pick, Scandinavian and Germanic influences of cultures who worshipped many gods both male and female, and sometimes polygamy was practised. In some sects they worshipped primarily male gods like Odin, god of war, and some were male-dominated cultures.

In Ireland the goddess Brigit was prevalent, who was also connected with Kilda-Kele, which was a word meaning "harlot"; such goddesses have been linked by scholars with the Indo-European goddess Kali. Secret sisterhoods centred around Celtic goddesses existed, similar to the Vestal Virgins of ancient Rome and Sibyls of Greece. To say that these were matriarchal cultures would not necessarily be true, but because their deities were heavily based around Mother Earth, this could have had considerable bearing on gender power structures. Females are considered divine and magical in pagan cultures and men cannot take the goddess role but females can take both.

Today paganism is greatly on the increase in the modern world as it is a very mix-and-match religion that you can literally make up as you go along, even though the priests and priestesses are often very highly trained in the ways of their own sects. Goddesses may be taken from any culture such as Egypt, Rome, Mesopotamia or early paganism to represent affiliation with any idealism. Native American cultures and their religions now come under the banner of paganism and have very similar godlike structures in the way they introduce animal characterising elements into their gods like the stag, bear or snake gods. This also includes Druids and the Wisecraft or Witchcraft as it is called, that may also have a herbalist basis.

In polarity worship the balance of the male and female is sought as a means of power and perfection. However, exclusively male or female iconoclastic orders may exist and this can make it a very suitable religion for gay people or those who are less gender or sexuality stereotyped. In polarity witchcraft, however, there can be an element of homophobia in some sects and a lack of tolerance of people who are sex, gender and sexuality fluid.

The Aboriginal societies were founded on the concepts of the characteristics of the universal feminine, surrounding the central respect for the earth which Aborigines refer to as Mother Earth. They have a great respect for nature and their families. Although feminine characteristics such as receptivity, mutability, interrelatedness and diffusion are paramount, the universal masculine also reveres limitation, order, structure, and definition.

Known as the oldest culture in the world, the Aborigines, with between 40,000 and 150,000 years of history, had retained their own unique gender structure until the Europeans landed at the end of the 18th century. It was perfectly natural for them to wander around naked in their hot climate, unfettered by artificially constructed ideas about inappropriate displays of genitals. The separateness of the sexes was not so much imposed, but naturally occurring, where women and men had their own spaces, as well as times when they came together. They were a hunter-gatherer set of tribal societies with applicable sex and gender concepts. Women and men could have separate gatherings, songs, rituals, stories and paintings that were exclusive to each sex.

White Europeans, however, in an attempt to civilise the Aborigines to Western ways, separated the children into males and females. They were imprisoned in missionary-type schools and taught Christian values that linked shame and sex in the same breath. This was also a way of preventing the Aborigines breeding or reclaiming their lands, and obsessive efforts were made by missionaries to try and rid the perceived savages of their so-called devil-like religions.

Judeo-Christianity attempts to place men in an elevated position of moral correctness, not to be contaminated by the lure and folly of women who achieve respect only when they are devoid of sexuality. The adulation of the

Virgin Mary constantly pushes women towards denial of their sexual powers and gender independence, subservient in service of the almighty, who is identified as male. Purity is based on an individual being separated from carnal knowledge and in spite of being in possession of sexual intimacy of any kind.

Christianity has tried to stereotype all women, keeping them devoid of intelligence, reason, or responsibility. The only exceptions to this are nuns who were to become the brides of Christ, withholding themselves from the sexuality of men. However, many nuns in pure sexual frustration, turned to lesbianism in order to relieve their unnatural abstinence.

The Vatican intensely dislikes birth control and the power it gives to women to determine their own fate and size of family. Catholicism is a male-dominated institution which constantly proposes that women have no sexuality of their own. Women's impurity is seen as a weapon to lure or withhold sex in an attempt to control the gender hierarchy and power structure that has existed in previous matriarchal cultures.

Origen (185-253 CE) was prominent among the Alexandrine church philosophers and he was one of the principle formulators of early Christian theology. He believed and disseminated the idea that all women were daughters of Satan and inherently manifested with eternal sin. Origen castrated himself "for the kingdom of Heaven", and was involved with one of the earliest Christian sects of castrated males in 250 CE. It is important here not to confuse the behaviour of these men with Skopsy Syndrome (see p113), with people who identify as having Sex and Gender Dysphoria, because the basic intention and driving behaviour is different.

At the time of writing this book, the catholic church was still playing the game of controlling the world's sex life by prohibition, releasing a report from the Vatican claiming that homosexuality was linked to paedophelia. The reasoning behind this report had no scientific basis or substantiated considerations but was rooted in prejudice that ignored ethnological studies by sociologists, anthropologists, psychologists, medics and psychiatrists that suggested the contrary. It is even more strange to think that the catholic church could take such a view in light of the fact that a large number of its priests are gay men. One of the factors in determining these priests' sexuality is that they are prevented from marrying, and since many men keep their sexual encounters between themselves secret, it is easier for the priests to appear celibate.

If we look at the origins of catholic priests' celibacy, it is easy to see that the Vatican distorted the need to be pure for materialistic reasons. In the Middle Ages the church was giving its priests property and lands, but upon their deaths their children were claiming inheritance rights, and the church was losing out. So it decided it would be more cost effective and profitable if they deemed that their priests were prohibited from getting married or having sex. The church began to shun the bastards of priests and demonised the women who bore their children as harlots and whores.

While the fall from grace of Adam and Eve only seems to go to a thousand years before Christ, as they ate the fated apple and tasted impure carnal desires, different cultures had other creation stories. Ancient Egyptian versions of the origins of the world saw man and woman as being in transcendental unity, which was parted in creation into two separated entities. The act of trying to become one again was seen as a divine and essential function of human relationships and sexual expression.

The early Christian movement of Gnosticism saw Adam and Eve as being equal both in sexuality, gender responsibility and power sharing. However, the Gnostics' theology, with its heavily mystical elements, was rejected by Constantine when Christianity was embraced around the 4th century AD. According to Gnostic texts, when the water was divided from the land, heaven and earth were created, and seven androgynous rulers were produced to govern the regions of heaven. Eros came into being and was androgynous with fine masculine elements being fire from the light and feminine characteristics coming from the blood of the virgin.

Hindus have fundamental belief systems that are transcendental in nature. The mythological god Vishnu visits the earth and blesses a womb of flesh with his presence. Vishnu is often depicted with his goddess consort Padma, also called Lotus or Lakshmi, reclining on a cosmic bed of serpents. He is seen with a serpent running up his back which signifies his sexual energy and virility. The primal male energy is manifested in purusha which is pure light and the female prakriti that is impregnated by the light and gives birth. Lovemaking is frequently depicted throughout Indian art in paintings, sculptures, scriptures, folklore and dance.

Women can be seen as magical and mysterious, holding the quality of all that is not definite, tangible or real, although reality cannot come into being without them. They can be loved but never altogether trusted because they always have unknown qualities. Women are seen as being beautiful and life giving, with a threat of also being all powerful like the Earth Mother that has lived on from earlier and more primal religions.

Far from being shy of sex the Hindus have the Kama Sutra, an instructive book of lovemaking in the Sanskrit literature written between 100 and 300 AD by the Hindu sage Vatsyayana. It instructs on sexual positions, etiquette, expectations and ways to reach the divine state of unity when the male and female essences once again unite their bodies.

Sex is seen as being a process of transcending the physical self to divine states of ecstasy and as an out-of-body-experience. Tantric practices were derived from Hindu archetypes of the male/female relationship, with the lovemaking being a part of the god and goddess concepts. During tantric sex magical qualities of union are aimed for through ritual nakedness, mudras (positions of lovemaking), mantras (sounds and repeated phrases), yantras (visual equivalent of a mantra), and breathing exercises. In Shiva cults their god was shown as hermaphroditic, symbolic of the male and female differences that seek to unite.

Tantric sex has been found to be threaded intermittently in early Christian, Gnostic, Jewish and many Western cultures throughout the centuries. Permissibility of such practices has survived but has often been lost as puritanical pressures were brought to bear on individuals to cease their actions or leave the cultures.

In India Hijra are castrated males who dress, live and behave as females, presiding ceremoniously over weddings and family gatherings, giving their blessings, which are highly valued. Their curses are also greatly feared and they are paid for services and revered as holy and powerful. Many, however, live scorned lives working as prostitutes in the poor ghettos between religious engagements. Although culturally these individuals arrive at their castrated status through execution of Skopsy Syndrome many are now identifying as transsexuals and seeking surgery. Perhaps it may be a case that many who were sex and gender dysphoric or curious sought out Hijra cults as a best poverty-laden option to living as males.

In Asia sons are more prized for their abilities to go out into the world and earn a living, particularly as their success is seen as a guarantee for the parents against poverty in old age. Women, in reality, are not highly prized nor have any real gender power in politics or economics. Hindu cultures tend to have great problems with poverty and India is fast becoming the most populated country in the world. Marriages are generally arranged in order to further the good fortunes of the families bringing together their wealth. Young girls from poor families are often sold into prostitution at 12 years of age if their fathers have no money for dowries and children as young as five can be seen on the streets of major cities begging and trading sex for food or money.

In Buddhism, which came out of the Hindu religion, the central female goddess power is known as Kundalini (the serpent energy), also referred to as Candalini. She is their version of Kali who is to be worshipped, revered or feared. She is fiery, powerful, the initiator of men's sexuality, mys-

13

tical and all giving, being the intellectual encapsulation of the Earth Mother theme.

In China for the past three and a half thousand years women have been considered to be without intellectual status or great worth, only in relation to their husbands, masters, lovers or male family members. They were cobbled, which meant their ankles were broken and tied together so that they could not run away and remained as servants in the home. At the beginning of the revolution, during the long walk across China, women believed that communism would free them from the shackles of their history so that they would be considered equal. This did not transpire as after Mao Tse Tung took power women failed to become key intellectuals, political components in government or ambassadors for their civilisation. Today in China, female children are often left in orphanages, secretly killed or sold to foreigners for adoption.

Sexual or gender freedom does not exist for women in the Muslim world; they are considered to be without higher reasoning, devoid of morality and their sexuality a threat to society. The women themselves are brainwashed into thinking that they are being protected from the unwanted ravages of rapists and philanderers by being covered up in veils and imprisoned in their homes. It is still common practice in the Muslim world to buy and sell women even though this may go under the disguise of arranged marriages.

In parts of the Muslim world homosexuality is prohibited by law, with penalties as severe as death, although it is common for Muslim men to have sex together in secret. This is more prevalent when it comes to older men having sex with young boys who are live-in lovers or prostitutes from poorer foreign countries. In some countries it is considered natural for young men to sleep together until they become married.

Lesbianism is not so prevalent in Muslim communities because of the enormous repression that women live under. Not only do they have a fear of being subject to their husband's wrath for not being his sole partner, but they also fear economic hardship if their husband rejects them or turns them out. Many Muslim women are subject to physical violence by their husbands or public stoning. Women's fate is so controlled by men in the Muslim world that it is almost impossible for them to even begin to perceive the concept of personal freedom.

According to the culture, homosexuality has been considered tolerably natural, abhorent or even normal. Many societies, however, choose not to acknowledge the presence of homosexuality within their public awareness. They prefer it to be an unrecognised activity. Although nearly all males may have experienced some man-to-man sexual encounters and many women have had lesbian encounters, a conspiracy of silence prevails. This double standard castigates those who openly carry out such lifestyles. Fluidly sex, gender and sexuality people tend to gather in subcultures in ghetto areas where other demonised members of society bond to facilitate safety in numbers.

The writer Virginia Woolf was both public and reclusive about her lesbianism in the 1920s onwards, feeling that she wanted people to respect her life choices, but at the same time being afraid that she would be seen as a public enemy. Quentin Crisp became a British personality of the late 20th century when he wrote about his life and loves as a gay man. His story told about the persecution and violence he had suffered at the hands of homophobic lynch mobs. In an age of gay rights he was also held up as an icon for the way he had been out, proud and outrageous in public about his sexuality.

Medicalisation of sex, gender and sexuality

As imperialism spread across the globe throughout Victorian times the biological exploration of sex grew with the continuous mapping out of modern medicine. At times the primitive understanding of the mechanisms of the mind and body led to barbaric forms of treatment to deal with common conditions. Hysterectomies were beginning to be performed with a view that they would cure diagnosed neurotic pathologies in women. Unmarried mothers were considered to be mentally ill, and could be locked away in institutions for the rest of their lives, simply for having a child out of wedlock. The knowledge that the medical establishment gathered on biology was, however, closely guarded and the common people were kept in the dark about the functions of their own anatomy.

Gender interpretations of the Victorian era were strictly male dominant and women were not considered intelligent enough to be in possession of great knowledge. More than that it was considered improper for women to be educated in anything other than domesticity and they were thought to be an adjunct of the male identity. There was no stigma attached to a male not being married, but unmarried women, unless employed in domestic service or teaching, were considered to be undesirable, wayward and immoral.

Heavily influencing the 20th century was Sigmund Freud (1856-1939), a medical doctor in Vienna, who with his misinterpretation of mythological metaphors, developed psychoanalysis and associated much of sexuality with pathology. His ideas about mental illness often being based in sexual repression and incidents of early sexual abuse were at the least a product of his time, personal history, and possible remnants of his own sexually repressed background. Many of his ideas about the pathology of human behaviour may have been influenced by his studies at the Salpêtrière, which was an asylum in Paris, where he studied with the French neurologist Charcot. His ideologies obsessed the 20th century, compounding the negativity that Europeans and their colonies associated with sexual freedom and exploration.

The medicalisation of sexuality mostly came about through Freud publishing his works on psychoanalysis, proposing that sexuality was heavily based in early traumatic childhood experiences. He proposed that many of his patients had been molested as children, but then on the threat of ruin through law suits, he decided to abandon that theory as too dangerous. His contribution towards investigating human behaviour was still no less than profound, and he was certainly a catalyst in reinvigorating the open discussion of sexuality. The pathologising of behaviour, however, due to the patients' early childhood experiences, bore little fruit and his patients spent many years in therapy trying to get to the bottom of their problems that he had often invented for them.

Henry Havelock Ellis (1859-1939), an English doctor, published several volumes of the *Studies in the Psychology of Sex* between 1896-1928 which proved so controversial that the first volume was banned. In 1894 he published *Man and Woman*, a book in which he attempted to present a balanced view of homosexuality and bisexuality. He campaigned for early sex education, birth control, an end to concepts of illegitimacy, the right for unmarried couples to live together without persecution, the right to divorce, and the repeal of laws against homosexuality.

Richard von Krafft-Ebing (1840-1902), a forensic psychiatrist, published *Psyhopathia Sexualis*, in German in 1886, an enormous collection of cases of sexually unusual behaviours. Because much of his work was done with criminals he cited these behaviours as being deviant and associated with varying forms of insanity. He was responsible for coining the phrases sadism and masochism.

Magnus Hirschfeld (1868-1935), a German psychiatrist, was one of the few highly sympathetic clinicians to specialise in homosexuality. He also founded the first journal of sexual pathology, which was a publication for open discussion of the field of sexology. He determined and defined the difference between homosexuality and transvestism, also being involved in the first experiments in treating transsexualism, which in those days was not recognised as a separate condition.

Albert Freiherr von Schrenck-Notzing (1826-1929) was a psychiatrist who published his work on trying to cure homosexuality by hypnosis and taking men on trips to brothels. The standard medical term at the time for homosexuality was "contrary sexual instinct".

Ivan Petrovich Pavlov (1849-1936), a Russian experimental physiologist received a Nobel prize in 1904 for his work on conditioned responses. Although the application of his stimulus-response in behavioural training has been applied in successfully treating a number of sexual dysfunctions, such as premature ejaculation, retarded ejaculation, vaginismus and inorgasmia, it has also been cruelly used to try to change people's sexual orientation. Many clinicians have tried to cure people of their sexual orientation by showing patients pictures of sex objects of desire and then administering stimuli such as electric shocks. In the long term this rarely works and tends to cause the subjects a great deal of emotional distress.

Carl Jung (1875-1961), the son of a Swiss pastor, completed his medical and psychiatric training which led him to Freud who influenced him greatly. However, after a falling out with Freud, Jung came into his own as a great scholar, believing that Freud's view of sexual impulses and libido were unbalanced, reductionist and limiting. Jung studied the cross-cultural interpretation of spiritual sex and sexuality which led him to the concept that not only was bisexuality quite natural but that it was cultural influences that prohibited its development.

Margaret Sanger (1879-1966) was America's pioneer campaigner in the field of birth control, writing and speaking throughout her life on the need for women to be in control of their own bodies. Sanger, on opening her first birth control clinic in Brooklyn, New York, was arrested, but went on to organise the first world population conference in Geneva in 1927.

Marie Stopes (1880-1958) was a palaeobotanist, who lectured at Edinburgh University and founded the British movement for women to be in control of contraception and have the right to abortion. Between them Sanger and Stopes changed the ideas of millions of women throughout the world and therefore changed much of the gender power balance by helping women learn to be in control of their own fate.

William Reich (1897-1957), an Austrian, met Freud while still at medical school and became one of Freud's most devoted assistants, working with him in the new science of psychoanalysis. He opened sex clinics in Vienna and Berlin. In 1942 he published his major work, *The Discovery of The Orgone: The Function of the Orgasm*. He was a man greatly misunderstood in his time and was dissociated from the mainstream of psychiatry. His colleagues and the law hounded him and suspected him of being involved in sex rackets, which led to him being tried and convicted and dying in jail in 1957. It was not until the 1960s that Reich's ideas – that the orgasm was a natural build up of energy – were accepted and embraced.

Alfred Charles Kinsey (1894-1956), who began his career as a zoologist, became famous for the work he did collecting thousands of statistical pieces of information about ordinary Americans' sex lives. In 1942 the state of Indiana supported Kinsey's establishment of the Institute of Sexual Research at the university. His publications *Sexual Behaviour in the Human Male* (1948) and *Sexual Behaviour in the Human Female* (1953), based on 10,000 interviews, demystified much of the common misunderstanding about sexuality in the English-speaking world. The profusion of homosexual and lesbian experiences among heterosexual people was a shock to the climate of the times which was generally homophobic.

There has been a great deal of controversy centred around Kinsey's work as some of it was with paedophiles. Many scientists believe that in order to be an observer he allowed and did not sufficiently dissuade perpetrators from abusing children. This raises questions on the ethics of research in that should a researcher intercede when they believe their subjects are in danger, and would that then corrupt the true nature of the research? By not intervening is the researcher then encouraging the subject to continue or compound that behaviour? With paedophilia it is understandable that society would be distressed by some of Kinsey's research; but if the same set of circumstances were applied to the study of other sexual behaviours would the scientist be contaminating the research with their own moral transference?

The laboratory work of Dr William H Masters, a gynaecologist with a keen interest in endocrinology, and his assistant and wife Virginia E Johnson, built on the work of the Kinsey reports, which was made possible by a shift in public opinion. Their publication *Human Sexual Response* (1966) suggested that males' sexual performance was in no way connected to the size of their penis, there was no such thing as a vaginal orgasm, and that women had no need to rest after orgasm, unlike men. Even though they suggested that the vaginal orgasm did not exist, their studies had a sociocultural basis that generally expected women to be inorgasmic anyway.

In 1959 Masters and Johnson began to apply their observations to people in sex therapy clinics for couples and concentrate on impotency and frigidity. Many of the techniques that Masters had learned from his early studies with prostitutes were developed and used in the treatment of sexual inadequacies. Their work *Human Sexual Inadequacy* (1970) became a standard work for sex therapists.

John Money PhD (1921 to date), who received the 1985 American Psychological Society's Distinguished Scientific Award, has to be considered one of the greatest researchers in human sex, gender and sexuality in the 20th century. His exploration of psychoendocrinology led to a catalogue of publications on the variation in behaviour that occurs due to hormonal or chromosomal differences in humans.

A New Zealander by birth, Money became a psychology graduate at Harvard University in America in 1948. Before and since his PhD he was fascinated by intersex conditions and the social presentation of sex performance, describing it as gender role. His studies of unusual sexualites have also earned him considerable respect in the wider field of medicine, psychology and sociology, as well as him taking a populist public role in educating the public as to the differences in human sexual behaviour. Professor of Medical Psychology at John Hopkins University School of Medicine and Hospital, Money has been internationally acclaimed for his clinical work and research. With several books to his name and more than

300 papers, his work is recognised as being ground-breaking and inspirational.

The book *Venuses Penuses: Sexology Sexosophy and Exigency Theory* was a milestone in helping sexologists to view the human condition as a continuum rather than a polarity male and female experience. As a psychologist he understood the great empowerment of the diversity of descriptive language in the field of sexology and the tenuous temporary reality by which we all live our lives. Much of his work has been around dispelling the mythology of misleading information concerning human sexual behaviour that was left over from the puritan and Victorian eras.

He has, at times, been viewed by many sex liberationists as seeing the diversity of human sexuality as being normal and abnormal, but in that instance I believe that some of his work has often been misunderstood. We must also remember that his work, like the rest of us, is always subject to the understandings and acceptability of the social constructs of his time.

Harry Benjamin MD (1885-1986), was an endocrinologist whose high profile work with transsexuals led him to be a pioneer in the field of Sex and Gender Dysphoria. This was the field he spent the last 30 years of his career in from 1948 to 1978. One of his major conclusions was that psychoanalysis was a complete waste of time with the severely sex and gender dysphoric who identified as transsexuals. The best treatment, he concluded, was hormonal and surgical intervention to give the individual the external appearance of the sex they psychologically believed they were or should have been.

While his work was controversial to mainstream medicine and psychiatry, often being accused of succumbing to the delusions of effeminate homosexual men, he stood his ground and formed the Harry Benjamin International Gender Dysphoria Association. This organisation can be said to be the world's leading forum for the sharing of knowledge and clinical research in the field of Sex and Gender Dysphoria. His book *The Transsexual Phenomenon* (1966) was a classic in the field and paved the way for many international hospitals to add gender units to their overall clinical services. During my research, one of the most recurring themes about Benjamin that pops up is that the patients and academics who knew him personally remember him as being a very kind man who was a marvellous listener and communicator.

In the 1960s the first generation after the Second World War grew up and a sexual revolution took place in the Western world. For a large part the birth control pill changed the choices of women, allowing them to be more permissive without getting pregnant. In other words they could have the sexual freedom men had always had without having to carry the biological consequences of getting pregnant. The gender balance of who did what, where and when also changed in society as freedom of choice was suddenly extended to half of the human race who, previously, could be condemned to servitude through unwanted pregnancies. Sexuality also began to be considered more of an area of exploration and less of a no-go zone for the common person.

Since the 1960s the communication revolution has taken place and the dissemination of information about how different people live has had a profound impact on our thinking of empathic ways of living together. The way medicine has conspired to pervert the development of sex within the medical model has been and continues to be reviewed and replaced with new knowledge. Gender studies are causing all our histories to be rewritten as more people are now included in many countries' bill of rights. Sex, gender and sexuality minorities are no longer content to hide in corners and be persecuted by bigots, religious maniacs, and politicians looking for scapegoats.

Masculinity studies are now emerging as cultural changes have wiped out many of the traditional roles that men have had in society for so many centuries. It has been realised that feminism alone cannot redress the imbalances between the sexes. Men's rights and rituals have, in many ways, also been decimated by the industrial society.

Many men are not quite sure of their role in society, how to vent aggression in an acceptable way and how to balance both their masculine and feminine natures.

When we study the interpretation of sex, gender and sexuality it is essential to consider that as we trace the development of cultures, theologies, philosophies, and other disciplines, that our time references and individual perspectives are taken into the picture and change it. Concepts of what makes a male, female or anything else from the physiological point of view are dependent upon sociocultural interpretation. Gender performance even changes from village to village, never mind cross-culturally. Sexuality is inexorably linked with philosophical guidelines, rules and transgressions, and not just a process of interpretation of the sexual direction of the libido.

While I have looked at the diverse spirituality, history and reality of sex, gender and sexuality, this work is not attempting to record the whole sequential antecedents of those three concepts. Such a work is far beyond many books, never mind my humble review. The cultures, societies and religions that I have written about are also incredibly diverse and within their boudoirs there are also many dissenters and evolutions that, due to space, I have been unable to mention. However, I hope the reader will take on board the general idea that we are all continuously both right and ill-informed, at the same time, when we think we understand human behaviour within the larger concept of humanity.

A truly open scientific mind could never categorically state that it had pinned down static definitions of any of the three concepts of sex, gender or sexuality, because that would not allow for human development and change. Neither could anyone say that other people's definitions may be intrinsically wrong, because such observations may come from a position of different enlightenment and no one, metaphorically speaking, has the patent on ideas.

The emergence of women's liberation, gay rights and the global transgender movement has further generated a monumental revision of the war of the sexes, which has been running since time immemorial. Many cultures are having to confront their own demons in the shape of revising outdated sex, gender and sexuality stereotypes. At times, for those cultures, it has been very painful to admit that for such a very long time they have been behaving barbarically in a way that both suggests and confides in hypocrisy.

The divination and demonisation of sex, gender and sexuality looks set to run and run and the curtain calls for repeat performances will never end. History has taught us that our social order and the knowledge we need to function as a species are formed by our actions and in response to our needs. As humans we have always needed gods and devils both in the spiritual world and on earth, and anyone of us for many reasons could fall prey to the fashion of our time. Whether that particular group of individuals choose to suffer or are defenceless against attack will have a direct bearing on how they shape their own future.

Puritans of any culture cite those who are sex, gender or sexuality different as enemies of society because it suits their political needs. They may even believe that they are purging the world of evil and wrong-doing in order to make it a better place for their communities and children. Practices like Tantric yoga, which originated in matriarchal societies, retained much of the intellectual balance between the sexes and appreciation of the differences. However, all cultures have their aspirations and taboos which always change from street to street and house to house.

Into this arena I must now throw the gauntlet of modern medicine and the art of science that not only cures but kills. The dogma that masquerades as the truth, the real truth and the truth above all other truths. The clipboards and pencils that compose and judge comparative quantitative medicine which we use to both liberate and imprison our bodies, behaviours and minds. The medicine that changes laws, proves the point of the day and promises to be authoritative in moments of self and social doubt.

One of the profound enlightenments of the 20th century has been the abdication of some of the Newtonian concepts which depict that things can be measured to exactitudes. Instead we need to consider the proliferation of Einstein's understanding that science and life are according to time and space ratio, and for each of us it can be different.

Not only have we divinated and demonised our concepts of sex, gender and sexuality in the past, and present, but will also repeat it all again in the future

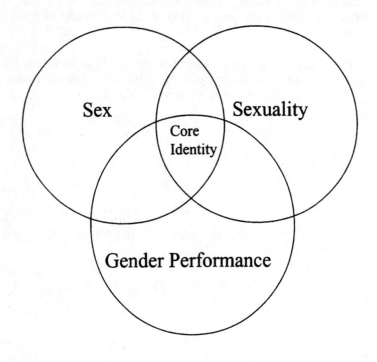

Sex

Sexuality

Core
Identity

Gender Performance

SEX, GENDER
& SEXUALITY

2

Sex

A person's physical sex can never be a matter of certainty and is always a process of dynamic development. We all start life as physiologically female and then some foetuses, around seven weeks, if the genetic switch, SRY (Sex-determining Region Y) gene is activated, and under the influence of hormones, go on to develop as predominately male. The male sperms have only half their number of chromosomes that intend to join up with the female egg, which also has half the number of chromosomes, to make a whole genetic code. Half of the sperm are Y chromosomes indicated and the other half are X. According to which one breaks through into the egg, this designates whether the foetus will be male or female.

The female egg is always X so it could end up after fertilisation as XX for the female foetus or XY for the male. However, nothing in nature is ever that simple and we now know that many variations on this theme can occur as will be seen later. Bits can be broken off genetic codes or added on in order to create humans who are less or more than male or female.

Even though females are generally XX and males XY chromosomes it is possible experimentally to create the reverse to be true. It was shown in experiments with the killifish (see p38) that dramatic genetic differentials could be achieved and that an organism will still be able to breed. Humans also have other genetic formulations that can cause dramatic differences in physiology or may be undetected. For these reasons chromosome testing cannot be relied on to determine a person's overall sex.

At puberty we start to get secondary physical characteristics such as pubic, facial and body hair, glandular and muscular development, ovulation and sperm production, as well as fantisisation and the desire for sex, which can more clearly define our biological sex. In old age the orchestration of the reproductive processes becomes much less pronounced than it was during our breeding years. Little old men and women, like children, look far more alike than they did in their breeding years.

At the critical time when the foetus is only seven weeks old the gonads develop into either ovaries or testes and the hormones they produce influence developments still further. However if the foetus is exposed to abnormal amounts of female or male hormones, certain toxic chemicals, or nutritional influences a female can develop, externally appearing as a male and vice versa. Such imbalances may be due to the foetus's or the mother's production of hormones.

Exposure to cross-sex hormones can change the appearance and function of the foetus, child or adult, at any time during life. This simple fact also contributes to the hypothesis that sex is never a permanent constancy and its status always fluctuates.

As a species we are profuse breeders but that is only a small part of the life cycles we now live. In our more primitive form this was the sole purpose of our existence as a species and the whole of the living process was centred around reproduction. Human beings, however, are now developing physiologically to have perhaps only a third to a fourth of their life cycles taken up with the breeding, rearing and nurturing process. Many creatures have a very short lifespan centred around the breeding process and then expire, but humans no longer have to function that way. Modern medicine has extended the life, intellect, and abilities to achieve beyond the simple reproductive process.

So why do so many of the breeders judge the non-breeders by their own standards, castigating those who choose not to conform to the evangelical call of the womb and seed?

Testosterone?

Many people choose to hang on to the concept of the modular nuclear family, its values and beliefs that often attempt to destroy social and physiological diversity, which it can see as a threat. Herein lies the roots of predatory ignorance that perpetuates persecution of those people who are different: the intersex, transsexuals, transgenderists (see p110), transvestites, androgynes (see p111), sinandrogynes (see p111), gays and lesbians, people with Thalidomide or Downs Syndrome, the short, obese, deaf, and mentally and physically differently configured.

Don't laugh because testosterone may well be one of the reasons

Everyone is subject to a cacophony of hormones, all of which are created for different reasons and each causing physical, psychological and emotive reactions. It would be logical to assume that hormones such as testosterone perpetuate aggression and defensive mechanisms in all of us. Territory is everything to the surviving individual and any perceived threat will elicit a defensive reaction.

I was on television recently with a person who held strong religious convictions, who insisted on demonising me when I suggested that there were, in fact, many kinds of sexes.

The truth is that most people do not know that one in every 200-300 people are born different than the average Joe and Josephine. Their reproductive organs, genetics or secondary physical characteristics are other than clearly defined as male or female as any midwife, obstetrician or sexologist can verify. They can often go undetected in society, with even the individuals themselves being unaware that they have intersex qualities. These people have in the past been described as abnormal but they should now politically be referred to as having a different sex than bipolar male or female.

Many variations of human sex can occur in genetics, genitalia, endrocrinologically or psychologically. Some of these conditions are rare, some are common, but what has been even rarer is for them to be discussed or talked about openly in our societies, where difference is often viewed with hostility.

Sex Determining Characteristics

Primary determination of sex happens at birth when the doctor or midwife looks at the genitalia and announces whether the infant is a boy or a girl, according to whether it has a penis or vagina. In cases where the genitalia is ambiguous the declaration may be put off until later or the child may be registered as the wrong sex. Children with ambiguous genitalia are often operated on to turn them into girls but the danger with this is that it can damage the erogenous zones that give sexual feelings. Many surgeons, under pressure from the Intersex Society of North America, have now conceded to wait until the child is old enough to decide what sex they would like to be.

It is possible to have a girl with what appears to be a penis and a boy with what appears to be the physical genital characteristics of a girl.

Secondary bodily characteristics are the way the body may appear. Some females develop to look more muscular and masculine than others and may be atypical of the biological sex type. There are boys who appear to be physically very feminine. Males generally have more body hair than females but if we compare races, that may not always apply. While this can be due to many physical things happening in their bodies, we must remember whether a person's face or body looks female or male can again very much depend on racial traits or social interpretation.

The third sex determining factors can depend on ancillary reproductive structures present within the physiology. Examples of this are a boy growing breasts or a girl not developing them due to hormonal activities or even environmental poisoning. There are also internal reproductive sexual characteristics associated with each sex.

Gonadal sex is the fourth classification by which a child is sexed. Generally girls have two ovaries and boys two testes. It is also possible to have a boy who has ovaries buried within his body, and girls to have testes. In very rare cases a child may have one of each. Infertility, however, is high in this group but not necessarily conclusive. Some of these characteristics can be hidden and never known until an examination discovers the nature of the condition.

Fifth brain sex needs to be considered because some males have more female-shaped brains and the reverse is also true. The size of each part of the brain varies from sex to sex and person to person and some men have female brain characteristics while some women have more male brain characteristics. This can be seen through the published work of Gooren and Gorski, who have both identified behaviour-determining regions of the brain that are related to concepts of sex.

The sixth sex determinate is hormonal since these are the chemicals that induce in us the physical and mental characteristics that are associated with male and female. It can be either the hormones we produce within our own bodies, or the hormones we are exposed to in the womb or our living environment. Certain chemicals we encounter in our everyday lives actually have masculinising or feminising effects upon us; these can also include toxins or the foods we eat.

Seventh sex determination occurs when a genetic test is done and people are categorised as XY for males and XX for females; however, that can only ever be a generality. Many people do not fit into these genetic categories and cross-sex genetics is a possibility.

Eighth sex determination is psychological because people do indeed identify as having a psychological sex. Here we must also introduce philosophy because that must never be separated from psychology as perceptions are always influenced by all parties involved. When a person talks about feeling or thinking like a particular sex, or not a particular sex, then since it is a subjective experience, we must allow the person the right to clarify their own experience.

So if people are profoundly and constantly convinced

they are or should have been a particular sex and wish to be treated as that sex it is cruel to do otherwise. Realigned intersex and transsexual people are the purest example of cross-sex identification. Since Decartes' separation of the mind and body concepts there has been a bias toward the physical and a tendency to impoverish the necessity to include the importance of the psychological in the human experience.

Self-perceived fantasy sex is the ninth determining characteristic and this can occur during the sexual act or in normal waking consciousness. It is very common for people of one sex to have fantasies about being another sex and while this has often been ignored it is a very important part of psychological make-up. For some people this is their secret pleasure; for others it can be highly disturbing and a cause of great anxiety. However, during the sexual act it is common for many people to fantasise about being made love to or making love as another sex, which does not necessarily leak into their non-sex lives.

The tenth determination of sex is spiritual, which is another category that has been largely been ignored over the past few hundred years. To become esoteric about a person's spiritual aspect of self demands a separate consideration other than psychological because the world is largely populated by people who follow religious convictions. Experientially it is sometimes difficult to quantify what is sanctioned as a person's sense of spiritual self or sex but we all have a sense of self that is other than existential.

The eleventh sex determination factor can be said to be social sex because some people who may belong to one sex in other categories may fulfil the social role of another sex. This is also behavioural and could include work, family role, the way they dress or performance of body language; again, in assessing this the caveat of social interpretation must be considered.

The twelfth determination is the historical sex ie the social sex by which the child was raised. This can also pertain to the social sex of a previous identity that seems inappropriate to the sex by which the person now identifies. Although a person may be one sex or of ambiguous sex, they may have been socialised as a different sex and forced into gender roles that were not of their free choosing. For some this may not cause them any difficulties in the area of sex or gender identity later in life; however, for others this can be a role which they feel they were forced to comply with against their will.

The thirteenth sex determination is cosmetic sex, which is the presenting sex that has been achieved after an individual has undergone hormone and surgical intervention. This can happen with intersex groups who choose to present themselves as a sex that is other than may be indicated by other sex determining factors or they may have been assigned a cosmetic sex. Transsexuals, transgenderists, androgyne and sinandrogyne groups also undergo transition to represent themselves as the destination cosmetic sex or non-sex.

The law is the fourteenth sex determinant in that if a child has been registered as a particular sex, in many cultures that can be changed on application to the relevant authorities. Some countries, such as the UK, however, have been adamant that the birth certificate is a historical document and cannot be changed, but this attitude does an enormous amount of damage to the lives of those people. A person's physical sex is part of their core central identity that ultimately needs to be determined by a number of factors. The person should have the right to have the registration of their sex altered if those factors are later reconfigured. To deny that to a person is no less than abuse of human rights that is often driven by religion, over-zealous morality, and ignorance.

Legal determination of sex must never act on its own but must be guided by the other disciplines of medicine, psychiatry, psychology, philosophy, sociology, and anthropology.

Fifteenth sex determination is communication and linguistic in that the use of engendered language has profound effects on our own self-concepts and the way other people interact with us. It is important for me as a hypnotist who spends much of my time studying the use of human communications to draw the reader's attention to the immense power that pronouns, adjectives and miscommunications can have on the human experience. Some people want to be called he, she, or in certain cases neither.

Sex Variation

To anyone, the words *abnormal* or *congential abnomalities* in the English language can often carry with them an interpretation of moral or social judgement, even though it is simply referring to someone being other than the statistical average. Again the use of the word *deformed* when referring to those people who are born sexually ambiguous is far from correct, since no one's sex is set in stone. A better and more considerate use of language could be kinder. People's sex characteristics can be variant since the official classification of a person's sex needs to be made up of at least the 15 previous categories.

When we talk about the intersex conditions it can refer to the formation of the genitals that are neither typically male or female. Since we all begin as female that would mean that the formation of the genitals became confused. A series of combinations could show that the clitoris has grown larger than in the standard girl and has developed as a small phallus. It could also mean that there are testicles instead of ovaries or vice versa and the testicles may be external or internal. There can be many reasons for this happening, which can be either genetic, hormonal, environmental or due to malformation of other organs within the child. Since the testicles and ovaries start as the same basic organs then it is easy to understand why a result can be genital or gonadal ambiguity.

Masculinisation of the Female Foetus & Feminising of the Male Foetus

This variation in development can be due to gonad dysfunction in the foetus or the mother host. The mother may have a naturally occurring hormone imbalance during

Sex

pregnancy due to the presence of disease, cancer, poly-cystic ovaries, an overactive adrenal gland or ingested female or male hormones. We also need to consider that different women have different hormone levels which can vary due to diet, exercise, body type, exposure to environmental toxicity, drug abuse or hereditary endocrine dysfunction.

The foetus itself may also have a natural genetic variability which has an effect on its development. As we have discovered, genetics are not a black and white affair in the differentiation of male or female body types.

Androgen Insensitivity Syndrome (AIS) (Testicular Feminisation)
The foetus started genetically as a male (XY chromosomes), but in these individuals there is an inability to respond to the male sex hormones. The child is born with what appears to be female genitalia because the male genitalia did not develop. The penis is absent. The male testicles are present internally so the child is gonadally male. The testes may need to be removed due to there being a high risk of future cancers.

Normal amounts of male and female hormones are present, but the individual is not sensitive to male hormones so develops externally resembling a female. Menstruation does not commence during adolescence and vaginoplasty may be required to extend the vagina which is only a pouch. If given female hormones at puberty these XY women do develop breasts but they cannot produce ova so are infertile. In some studies this has been identified as an inherited condition with some people.

46XX Virilising Adrenal Hyperplasia (Adreno Genital Syndrome)
In 46XX babies a form of hermaphroditism occurs when the adrenocortical gland overproduces masculinising hormones at the time of differentiation of the genitalia and the brain. There can be an overdeveloped clitoris which resembles a penis, and the labia look like an empty scrotum.

36

There will be a vagina and ovaries. Often the child grows a female body type but may have some masculine secondary sexual body characteristics.

This can be a dangerous condition because the body is unable to retain salt and water, causing weight loss, dehydration, low blood sugar and shock. It is essential to treat this condition medically. Severe cases can be spotted early in life. Milder cases can cause the onset of early puberty in boys, and delayed menstruation, hair growth and infertility in girls.

Mayer-Rokitansky-Kuster-Hauser (MRKH-46XX)

This syndrome is similar to AIS in that the vagina and vestigial mullerian (internal) structures are not properly formed. The girl has typical 46XX genetic coding, without any apparent genetic deficiencies.

Turner's Syndrome

These girls grow to have short stature, often have a webbed neck and are usually sterile, having been born without complete ovaries or testes. Some can have genome type XO and others can have mosaic chromosomes which are a combination of XO and XX and can even be a variation of XY. Other people who have this syndrome may have 45 chromosomes instead of the usual 46. Girls who are born with Turner's Syndrome do not have the ability to procreate since germ cells are not present in the ovaries. Sometimes these children are educationally slow. If stature is very small there may also be heart defects.

46X Females

There are females who are born with simply one X on their chromosomal chains. A form of Turner's syndrome.

XYY Males

This group of males have an extra Y chromosome and have been cited in newspapers as having a propensity to be mentally unstable, aggressive and with a tendency towards violence. Some theorists have suggested that this group of men have a tendency to be highly strung and reactionary, often leading to them falling foul of the law and ending up in prison. The problem with these studies is that they were done on prison populations and did not consider the general public.

47XXY Males – Klinefelters Syndrome
This group of males have a 47 chromosome configuration of one or more extra X chromosomes and are often not identified until adolescence when they may begin to grow breasts. By the onset of puberty they are often tall and eunuch-like with long limbs, but sometimes have a tendency to obesity. The small testicles are almost always sterile with atrophy of the spermatic tubules (shrinkage of the tubes carrying sperm). While Money (1986) has referred to instability of the nervous system, sometimes retardation and at other times superior intelligence, insufficient studies of this group have been carried out to validate such hypotheses across the general populations. The incidence of this condition may be as high as one in every 500 males.

In fact there seems to be a range of Klinefelter presentations – the common factor being small testes with sometimes a tendency to change primary and secondary sexual characteristics.

XX Males
Emil Witschi at the Basel Laboratory in Switzerland set up an experiment where the XX (female genome type) larvae of the killifish were exposed to male hormones. This produced an XX fish that was able to breed as a male. XX males do exist in humans who have inherited a tiny part of the Y chromosome from their fathers. Although they develop as male they are genetically fundamentally XX.

5-Alpha-reductase (5-AR) Deficiency
This is a type of male pseudo-hermaphroditism which results in what appears to be a female-to-male transition at puberty. The male foetus normally produces testos-

terone during gestation, but in order for normal development to take place the tissue must have the enzyme 5-
Alpha-reductase to convert it into dihydrotestosterone. If
the foetus is (5-AR) deficient then the child is born with
what appears to be a clitoris, labia and a small vagina.

At puberty the testes produce more testosterone and the
body begins to respond so development takes place as the
testes drop into the labia/scrotum, and the apparent clitoris grows to more resemble a penis. The child often
develops a masculine muscular body.

Ovo-testes

Sometimes the gonad can be a mixture of ovary and testes
producing both eggs and sperm in some cases. Such tissue may need to be removed due to the possible threat of
future cancers.

Gonadectomy

While there is concern that the gonads of many members
of the intersex are in danger of becoming cancerous this is
unlikely to happen before the person becomes an adult.
Therefore it may be more advantageous to allow the person to grow sufficiently to make their own decision before
any such surgery takes place.

One of the reasons for this is to allow natural production of hormones which is preferable to hormone replacement therapy.

Fused labia

In some pseudo-hermaphroditic girls there may be an
over-developed clitoris and labia which are fused together
leaving a minimal or absent opening to the vagina. In
these cases the child may be mistaken for a boy or be classified as being of undetermined sex.

Feminisation of Males Due to Genital Damage.

Some males during their lives may suffer damage to their
genitalia through accident or testicular cancer. In cases of
physical damage through accident, surgical repair or reat-

tachment of the penis may be attempted.

One option that has been practised on very young children is that they have had vaginoplasty and then been brought up as girls. Some of theses cases have been successful but others were left with the desire to return to living in their original gender roles and may apply to doctors to masculinise them through hormones and surgery.

Testicular Cancer

In the case of testicular cancer removal of the testes is sometimes necessary. One of the treatments has been administration of female hormones.

This can cause the individual great psycholgical difficulty and later there may be a need to reinitiate testosterone treatment – or have any developed breast tissue surgically removed.

Mechanical Failure of the Renogenital, Intestinal or Reproductive Systems

Some people, due to an accident or disease, suffer a failure or chronic difficulty with their body systems. This can leave them with deep feelings of sexual inadequacy, unattractiveness, or confusion about sex, gender or sexuality.

Polycystic Ovaries

Many women with polycystic ovaries suffer hirsutism (hair growth) of the face and body which may cause them to feel very unfeminine. Thyroid problems may also be prevalent in this group of women. The hair can be removed by laser or electrolysis treatment and sometimes brief counselling may be appropriate.

Pseudo Menses

This is when one or more ovaries are hidden or obscured and start reacting to monthly or bimonthly cycles. The person will feel pain and discomfort often because this ovulation and exodus of such material is prevented from leaving the body due to lack of fallopian tubes, womb, cervix or vagina.

Masculinisation through the Administrat[ion] Steroids in Females

The administration of medication to fight cance[r] conditions, or to enhance athletic perfomance ca[n] masculinising effect upon females. This can ofter[n] distressing for them. They grow facial and body [hair,] voice may drop and they may become very muscu[lar tak-] ing on the appearance of a male body type. This c[an] lead to extended bouts of depression which can b[e resolved] through counselling.

Congenital Virilising Adrenocorticism (CVA)

These boys may have an abnormal prenatal hormo[nal his-] tory, and could also be receiving an excess of andro[gen] hormones from their own adrenocortical glands. Earl[y vir-] ilisation occurs which needs to be suppressed by cor[tisone] treatment to allow puberty to develop at the correct tim[e.]

Premature Puberty Due to a Malfunction in the Pituitary

In some cases puberty can occur as young as four or five years old if the brain has developed lesions in the pituitary/hypothalamus which in turn can initiate an early onset of secondary sexual characteristics and behaviour. Unless this is medically diagnosed the child can be isolated because of their indulging in inappropriate sexual activity. Should shame and overt social denigration be aimed at these children, severe psychological dissociation from normal sexual activity can occur. These conditions can be treated with appropriate medications.

Uro-genital Sinus

Small cul-de-sac, pouch-like vaginal opening that has no depth and does not lead to a female reproductive system.

Acromegaly

This is a rare disease where there is a tumour to the anterior of the pituitary gland which causes enlargement of bone stucture, especially hands, feet and lengthening of

41

atures. In some cases there is a virilising effect, if
s within the first 10 years of life when gigantism
ur.

Exstrophy

a very rare and serious condition that occurs when
information for forming the abdomen, intestines
italia is present but gets muddled up. A child can
n without some organs and the stomach and
es may not be enclosed by the abdomen but be
g outside the body. Sometimes there is no anus,
r or genitalia and the infant will need immediate
ving surgery to rectify this condition.

is is not simply an intersex condition so the surgeon
suggest repair to the abdomen wall and rearing the
d as a girl, particularly as it is often surgically the only
tion. Phalloplasty is very difficult. However, once again
e individual should have the right to determine their
own sex and gender wherever possible. This decision
should be left open until the child feels they are old
enough to choose.

Bifid Scrotum

This is when the scrotum has not developed properly, is
empty, and appears to be divided into labia. Combined
with an under-developed penis this can give the illusion
that the child has female genitalia when it may in fact be
a male.

Hypospadic Male

A congenital defect which affects approximately one in
every 300 males where the opening of the urethra is situated undeneath the penis. The scrotum may be small and
the penis under-developed and malformed.

The appearance of these genitalia may lead to doubt
about the sex of the child and some boys have been mistaken for girls.

A urologist will be required to operate to enable the boy
to urinate standing by various surgical interventions.

42

Idiopathic Adolescent Gynaecomastia
The development of breasts in what appears to be a male, including swelling and pigmenting of the areola and some breast tissue. These boys are thought to have normal pre-natal and prepubescent hormonal history which may become atypical at puberty. A bilateral mastectomy using the double ring through the nipple, keyhole method with liposuction will give the best cosmetic reconstruction.

Hypertrophied Clitoris
The clitoris is enlarged and may extend to beyond the labia. An operation called a recession has often been per-formed to shorten the clitoris in order to make it appear average. This operation has often left many people without a great deal of sensitivity and is no longer considered eth-ical unless it is elective surgery.

As well as variations in physical development there can be other practices:

Male circumcision must be considered, although it is a man-made stiuation. It is important because it can be an abuse of human rights when it is thrust upon young chil-dren by some religions, without their permission. Biological males who later seek sex and gender realign-ment surgery are often short of penile skin when it comes to creating penile inversions.

Female circumcision is thrust upon some females in dif-ferent cultures, particularly in Africa. The philosophy is that this takes away sensation from the clitoris, so stops women straying sexually. What also tends to happen is that the vagina may be sewn up so that sexual intercourse cannot take place until after the woman's wedding when it is then sliced open.

Castration by removal of the testicles happens in some countries as a punishment or as a control mechanism for sex crimes including rape, child molestation or sodomy. Chemotherapy is also used in the same way through the forced administration of drugs. There is no doubt that unless this is a treatment that is requested by the person, then to perpetrate such actions is abusive and inhuman.

Hysterectomies were one of the most barbaric surgical scandals of the 20th century. These were often performed by male surgeons when women had other alternatives. In Canada and elsewhere Downs Syndrome and other women had a hysterectomy to prevent "subnormal children" being born.

This fell into the scope of the dreadful eugenics movements of the 19th and early 20th century. Many women described feelings of being raped by the medical system, having lost some of their natural ability to produce female hormones, and their sense of femininity.

John Money's Criteria for Intersex

Money (1986) set out seven categories of physical hermaphrodites:

1. Female pseudo-hermaphrodites with hyperadrenocorticism

Clitoral enlargement but not excessive, could be a single urogenital orifice or in rare cases penile urethra and fused empty scrotal sack. This development can carry on after birth and continue to masculinise the person. Gonads and chromosomes are female.

2. Female pseudo-hermaphrodites with phallus, ovaries and normal mullerian structures

Either singular urogenital orifice with penis-like clitoris or penis-like clitoris with an auxiliary urethra. Development is entirely feminine and reproduction possible.

3. True hermaphrodites with both testes and ovarian tissues

Three possibilities which are: A. One ovotestis plus one ovary or testis B. Two ovotestes. C. One ovary, one testis. Externally these children exhibit a real diversity of ambiguous genitalia.

4. Male pseudo-hermaphrodites with well defined mullerian organs

Possibilities are a fully formed penis with urethra, one or both testes being cryptorchid. One testis may be atrophic.

One testicle often herniates into the groin with the muller-ian structures.

5. Simulant females with feminising testes

External genitals are completely normal. The vagina is a blind pouch. Testes are present instead of ovaries. There is often often the complete absence of pubic hair. The testes should not be removed because they are producing oestrogen.

6. Cryptorchid hypospadic males with feminising testes

Present is a phallus that is variably larger than a clitoris. A blind vaginal pouch is present. This group develops as feminine at puberty but may not necessarily be very feminine.

7. Cryptorchid hypospadic males

These have a blind vaginal pouch and phallus only slightly larger than a clitoris. Variation cannot be predicted.

Since children are not cast in dyes in factories, each case must by considered on its own merits and physical variations will occur on these themes. Added to that is advanced knowledge that we are now gaining in the field of genetics and endocrinology. Once again I shall say that John Money's contribution to modern-day sexology has been no less than profound but on the point of normalistion he has fallen foul of the sex, gender and sexuality movements.

He suggested that it should be the aim of the obstetrician or paediatrician to settle the sex of an hermaphroditic baby once and for all, within the first few weeks of life, before establishment of the gender role gets advanced. This is no longer considered the correct thing to do because the only person who should have the right to permanently settle a person's sex is that person.

Genetic testing is neither normal nor mandatory in general medicine for sexation. Many minority pressure groups and human rights organisations are very afraid of the ways in which the collecting of genetic identification could be used or abused. This is none so clear as to when some people who are suspected of committing criminal offences, are given the option of either being charged with the crime or giving a sample of their DNA in exchange for a caution. Unfortunately this then leaves them on police genetic registers without ever having been found guilty or innocent of any crime, and since they may be vulnerable or afraid of the system, it allows their privacy to be put at risk. Insurance companies may also try to test for potential genetic variations which they think are likely to lead to claims for medical bills or early death.

On showing the manuscript for this section of this book to an intersex person, they offered the following comments:

"The difficulty with defining an individual on the basis of chromosomes 45 and 46 to the exclusion of other endocrinological, biological and social considerations is that it can have a very adverse effect upon the person's self-concept. This can then result in severe psychological consequences. Indeed the use of the terms *male foetus* and *female foetus* can cause difficulty in the minds of those who have intersex conditions.

"This and other sex anomalies raises fundamental questions about the notion that Y=boy. Many General Practitioners of medicine have caused great distress to female patients by telling them, arbitrarily that they are men because they have AIS. As you can see, the way the medical professions have interpreted the data surrounding masculinising effects of genetic material contained within the Y chromosome, as being an indication of empirical 'maleness' can if anything do more harm than good.

"When discussing the XX-XY paradigm I feel it best that the presence or lack of chromosomes indicates *probability* of maleness or femaleness, not an empirical male or empirical female – which is why the conditions you have discussed are confusing to most professions, they being seen as deviations rather than the results of clinical probabilities."

Professor Hughes, a paediatrician at the University of

Cambridge, has said that there certainly is an increase of intersex conditions and we have to address the problem of why that may be happening. He comments that this has been noticed by the scientific communities throughout the world and the fact that the environment may be changing could be an important factor.

Philip Ramsey, a British consultant paediatric urologist, has spoken out about how children need to be aware of any sexual genital differences that they may have. This empowers the child to face any future in an informed way that can help them to be more positive about their identities. He does, however, say that many children due to their backgrounds are unable to cope with the full facts of their intersex conditions. Education and openness is obviously the way forward in every walk of life but most of all during sex education in schools.

The intersex categories also need to include conditions such as transsexualism and androgyne identities. The argument of free intention being responsible for these conditions is no longer scientifically valid and such people should not be treated by science, the law or society as inferior males or females.

Certainly incidents of intersex seem statistically to be on the increase and it is not yet clear whether there are genetic markers that can identify those foetuses that could develop intersex conditions or people who are carriers of the conditions. Since it is now becoming evident that many animals are being found with intersex conditions, societies are beginning to wake up to the idea that it may be due to environmental toxicity. However, we must also be aware that the numbers we presently see may be natural and that it is only as we increase our statistical observations of nature that we become aware of its diversity.

It has been common practice among paediatricians and paediatric urologists to operate on children to create surgical females when ambiguity is genitally and gonadally present. This can no longer be accepted practice, and the intersex communities are now urging those doctors to wait, whenever possible, for the child to determine what sex they want to be and whether they want those operations. Many intersex patients have stepped forward in the 1990s and publicly stated their dissatisfaction with the way they have been treated, having had operations that they felt they did not actually want and which had caused damage to their genitalia and lives.

If a child has been socialised as one particular sex and then it becomes apparent that they are not physically that sex they may still want to carry on to define themselves as that sex. On the other hand they may wish to adjust their gender role and have surgery and hormone treatment to define themselves as another sex. It must ultimately, whenever possible, be the child's decision made before puberty arrives and secondary sexual characteristics have developed or not, as with the case of hormonal or gonadal deficiencies.

Not only do physically intersex children need to be treated prior to puberty but so do transsexual children who define their sex via psychological and behaviour differentiation.

With the assistance and care of doctors, psychologists and philosophical considerations, all persons should always have the right to ultimately determine their own sex.

Diamond and Sigmundson issued the following guidelines for raising individuals with ambiguous genitalia:

"Rear as male:

XY individuals with Androgen Insensitivity Syndrome (AIS) (Grades 1-3)

XX individuals with Congenital Adrenal Hyperplasia (CAH) with extensively fused labia and a penile clitoris

XY individuals with Hypospadis

Persons with Klinefelter Syndrome

XY individuals with Micropenis

XY individuals with 5-alpha or 17-beta reductase deficiency

Rear as female:

XY individuals with Androgen Insensitivity Syndrome (AIS) (Grades 4-7)

XX individuals with Congenital Adrenal Hyperplasia (CAH)

with hypertrophied clitoris
XX individuals with gonadal dysgenesis
XY individuals with gonadal dysgenesis
Persons with Turner's Syndrome"

While these are reasonable guidelines, we must always consider social, psychological, religious, and family orientation when advising people how to bring up their children. What is most important is that the clinicians and carers involved with such people fully educate the parents of these children and the children themselves about their condition. This will allow, within the availability of medical care, people to have the highest number of choices humanely possible about their own identities. However, in passing on Diamond and Sigmundson's guidelines, I urge the reader to be most careful that they do not emphasise the exclusivity of maleness or femaleness, but promote the validity of every other form of sex, gender and sexuality identity.

This section of the book does not attempt to be a definitive medical guideline to intersexuality, but a general heightening of awareness of the complexity and diversity of human physiology. You, the reader, may go deeper into the world of the intersex by cross-referencing many of the resources on the Internet, which include support groups that have close associations with the leading medics in this field.

Body Fascism

We are all, at times, thinking and doing body fascism naturally to a certain extent; it is a natural process of comparing and measuring our experiences against other people's. We know what we know and do not know – like and do not like. Measuring our life experiences against other people's life experience allows us to orientate ourselves and evaluate the world we live in. When this process of comparison becomes out of context in the social environment and causes offence to others it then becomes the unacceptable behaviour of body fascism.

As children we learn by experience who is comfortable

and profitable to be around and who to associate with danger, indifference, or lack of personal gain. Our parents and mentors also give to us a set of ideas about who they perceive as having loss or gain qualities, possibly adding to or distracting from our own levels of comfort or personal growth. From these basic set of ideas we then make our own computations about what is the correct or incorrect body form, looks, stature, colour, facial features, level of health or any other physical characteristics belonging to other people that promote or distract from our own life experience.

Such judgementalism is a natural part of our psychological processes, but we often make those judgements unconsciously, based upon prejudice or preferences that ignore the inducement of pleasure or injury to others. Phrases like too tall, short, fat, thin, Asian, Caucasian or loud spring to mind when we think of how certain individuals dictate what others should be like. Other prejudices talk about people who have large hands, tiny feet, deep voices, sweet smells, or are unable to hear, speak or see. Body fascism can extend to how many earrings a person wears or whether they decorate their bodies with make-up, tattoos, body paints or change the shape of their bodies through surgery or other methods.

In some cultures being perceived as fat is a sign of prosperity, wealth and success; in others it is an insult and cause for offence. In certain tribes the bigger the lips a woman has the more beautiful she is considered, even to the point of stretching those lips far beyond their natural proportions using templates. Tattoos are sometimes used to identify individuals of a certain culture, caste or even as outcasts or criminals; these markings may sometimes be done without the person's permission or even against their will.

Every one of us has tried to change our bodies to fit physical stereotypes at times. That may include dieting, working out, having surgery, or covering our grey hairs with tint. Inevitably we will fail at some of those tasks at some time during our lives and we can remember those experiences and how uncomfortable it was to be considered a loser due to the process of comparison.

There is a constant bombardment by the media and certain political and social groups to force us to conform physically to what might be put forward as the ideal human form. Further still we are constantly comparing our own performances against what we were, could have been, or might be in order to validate our lives.

How we come to be what we physically are, is to a large extent, out of our conscious control and due to our genetic determination. Therefore to exhibit prejudice against someone for their uncontrollable physical characteristics is less than what might be considered humane in a reasonable and fair society. Often we do it in order to help ourselves feel superior and less vulnerable but that in itself is insufficient reason to cause harm or injury to others. Each of us can constantly monitor the intention of our own body fascism in order to treat others with the greatest of respect, and inevitably guarantee when it is our turn to meet stereotype standards, our individuality is to be praised not castigated.

Sex Dysmorphobia

There are many forms of dysmorphobia, which is technically a fear of or unhappiness and discomfort with one's body and the condition can also be known as Body Dysmorphic Disorder (BDD). Some people develop a hatred of their looks, believing that they are ugly and unattractive which causes them to be reclusive and unable to interact socially. This is an illness that causes an individual to continually compare themselves against others and be dissatisfied with the results.

I have encountered fashion models, actors and actresses who have suffered from something I term as mirror disease, which is when they are constantly looking in the mirror to assess their looks. In an industry where looks are everything and a person is picked out of a line-up like cattle at the market it is very easy for someone to develop and compound intense feelings of rejection. To term this as narcissism would not be true because it is insecurity brought on psychologically, by constantly comparing the worth of a person's body to the perceived value of other people's looks.

Anorexia and bulimia are also forms of dysmorphobia which may have psychological roots in childhood experiences and trauma or dysfunctional body chemistry. The major problem with such diseases is that the sufferers are very suggestible people who introject underlying social messages that their body mass is disfiguring. In a world where the icons of our society are often stereotypes, like catwalk models or movie stars who are showered with great attention and million of pounds, and where praise is heaped on unusual body shapes, the majority of us get messages that says any body shape diversity which steers away from those perceived icons is undesirable.

The fashion industry is much to blame for the spread of dysmorphobia because the images they present are mostly unattainable for the average person, and that, after all, is part of their marketing ploy to make people buy their products. There is also something much more sinister going on here and that is the desexualisation of women by a male-dominated industry which disempowers women's sexuality by presenting images of them with reduced sexual features. Unfortunately the women in the fashion industry also collude with this desexualisation of the female body in order to succeed.

An extremely rare form of dysmorphobia is fetishistic amputeeism where an individual finds sexual arousal in the partial or whole amputation of their own or other people's limbs.

Sex Dysphoria is about being uncomfortable with your physical sexual characteristics and is therefore is a form of dysmorphobia. For diagnostic validation it is irrelevant whether this is divided into a physical or psychological disorder as neither is less right or wrong than the other. For treating the dysmorphobia of intense Sex Dysphoria it is, however, important to assess to what extent this discomfort has taken place and whether it is likely to disappear with psychotherapy or chemicotherapy.

It must be remembered that Sex Dysphoria is not the same as Gender Dysphoria because the latter is the performance of biological/social sex or sexuality type. Some people choose to take the transsexual, transgendered or the intersex sex confirmation route because they have either Sex Dysphoria or Gender Dysphoria, or both.

Sexuality Dysphoria is yet again something different because it is a person's unhappiness with their sexuality concept and behaviour, and should never be confused with Sex or Gender Dysphoria, although in some cases all three can be present.

To some extent we are all intersex

In helping someone who wishes to change their body's sexual characteristics we must, as clinicians, also take a leap of faith and go beyond the concepts of dysmorphobia, entering into the realms of philosophy and human rights. A clinician must learn to appreciate that people have the right to change their bodies if they simply have a desire to do so and do not necessarily have to have a desperate need.

Each person should have the right to define themselves as they so wish as long as they do no harm to themselves and others.

Medicine, psychology, philosophy, sociology and law making can never be removed from human rights and neither should those disciplines work in isolation. Corrective plastic surgery and medical technology is now available for the individual to be able to define themselves as they so wish. Many clinicians who have helped people redefine their physical selves have been accused of pandering to the delusions of the unstable, colluding with their patients and giving in to physical and gender elitism. In attempting to banish sex, gender or sexuality elitism, however, we must replace it with a different form of the very same.

In 1999 a Canadian transsexual, who was born a biological female, won the right to have the sex changed on his birth certificate to male after having undergone medical and surgical procedures. While this seemed a victory to the gender freedom movement, it was, in actual fact, in a way, a retrograde step. The problem is that the court required the transsexual male to undergo the construction of male sex organs in order to change the stated sex on the birth certificate.

What happened here was that the court re-enforced one set of bad laws with another since a person's sex can only truly be determined by considering a variety of different criteria and should not be restricted to the genitalia or any other singular factor. Reductionist medical or legal criteria cannot take into account the kind of philosophical adjunctive elements of the human experience. There are many criteria which make up the overall self-determined sex of anyone, and only that person has the right to make such a proclamation.

As I always tell all my clients who undergo a metamorphosis of their bodies to realign their identities to what they believe they should be:

I don't walk a mile in your shoes

Sex by Self Assessment

1.	Genital Sex
2.	Body Characteristics Sex
3.	Ancillary Sex Functions
4.	Gonadal Sex
5.	Brain Sex
6.	Hormonal Sex
7.	Chromosomal Sex
8.	Psychological Sex
9.	Fantasy Sex
10.	Spiritual Sex
11.	Social Sex
12.	Historical Sex
13.	Cosmetic Sex
14.	Legal Sex
15.	Linguistic Sex

People have the right to assess their own sex status

3

Gender

...is a game people play

Gender is a pattern of behaviours that are based around our natural biological sex initially in order to assist the breeding process and facilitate the structure of our societies. We do gender...it is a performance and a process of signalling to other people what is happening in and around sex, and what our sexuality might be. Further it is an indication to others as to whether we are available for breeding or recreational sex and what particular kind of sex we might be interested in.

Gender, however, is culturally based so it cannot be a clear set of signals that are universal because as we pass from one society to another, a different set of signals may be needed to communicate the same meaning. But some gender signals can be universal, built in our brain hardware, like certain ways of walking, body language and speech patterns. There are also sets of signals that may be specific to one society that may not exist in another social order. Within societies, different classes or subculture groups may also have different sets of signals that they perform.

Further down the systemic scale may be family gender signals or couples' private gender indicators in one-to-one situations. Gender information being put out by a person can change according to their mood and the environment in which they find themselves or what kind of person they are communicating with.

Gender is also built a great deal around class and the permissibility of certain kinds of behaviour that are amiable or limited to a particular type of people. In the Arabic and some Eastern countries women have a very low-class status based almost solely around facilitating the preferential breeding of male children. They are doing the gender of the servile female who must conform to the wishes of the dominant male.

In Britain there has been a thousand years of feudal rule and in general the majority of women are still doing the gender of the servile breeder, even though they are a large part of the wage-earning population. The English have always been in denial of their inequalities of the gender class system, pretending to the rest of the world that they are the very foundations of modern democracy and fairness. But according to a 1998 *Women in the Workplace* survey by the Institute of Personnel and Development, only 5 per cent of company directors in Britain were women.

In Russia, women were supposedly liberated from the shackles of breeding and domination by men during the revolution and the job market was supposedly open to them. The propaganda was put forward that Karl Marx believed we are all sociologically equal, but how many Russian women Premiers have there been whose partners stayed at home looking after the children?

In China, female children are considered to have no great value and are often left in orphanages or killed. Men are perceived as stronger, higher wage earners and a better prospect to provide for their parents as they get old. To have too many female children is considered a curse upon the family fortunes.

The role of gender becomes particularly interesting when we look at cultures such as the Inuits; when the early explorers arrived in the most northern parts of the planet, they found that every third female child took on the role of a male. Due to the harsh environment it was believed that there would be too many girls and it would upset their survival prospects. The third girl behaved as a male, took a wife, got her pregnant by having her sleep with a visiting male, had a family, and was not considered a lesbian. A reverse scenario can be found in the south seas area when faffini males take on the role of women.

In different cultures it can be common practice for one sex to temporarily or permanently take on the gender role of another in order to carry out rituals, entertainment or facilitate social needs. Doing gender separately from sex and sexuality can be seen among the male and female impersonators in the entertainment world. A person's gender representation changes during the performance but their biological sex or sexuality do not alter in any way. The character of Dick Whittington in pantomime is generally a young woman dressed in male clothing. All the audience is aware she is playing the part, but her embrace with the leading lady is not considered anything but pretending to be heterosexual.

The Pantomime Dame is another entertainment character that is generally played by a very obvious male dressed in female clothes with accentuated make-up. Everyone is pretending he is a Dame but no one really believes it and the base belief about his sex and sexuality is never questioned.

Men have often dressed as females during pagan fertility rights and it has never implied that they want to be women, just that they are focusing on female energy. Males often take on surrogate social roles of females in single-sex prisons, having sex with other men, partaking in pecking order activities based on degrees of masculinity, but they might not be considered gay, just accommodating heterosexuals, even though the activity they are carrying out is homosexual.

Gender cannot be satisfied by dividing it into simply male or female because as a society becomes more sophisticated, sex becomes largely recreational and the great spectrum of human behaviours are more recognised or allowed to flourish. Again we come back to the gender class system where the emergence of gender is based upon what a society becomes accustomed to or not.

In many Native North American cultures, before the Europeans arrived, children were observed as they grew up and allowed to choose their own gender roles in society. Some boys would stay at home, keep house, do bead work and follow the roles which the Europeans associated as only women's business. Girls that showed a desire to hunt or do battle would take on the gender role of mainly male activities. This did not necessarily mean that those people were seen as sex or sexuality different.

Since we are all doing gender automatically and encouraging certain kinds of gender specific behaviours in others, to some extent, it operates invisibly out of our conscious awareness. Over the period of our lives we have ingested certain concepts presented to us by our parents, teachers, philosophers, and rulers, as well as images from books, theatre, television and films. These ideas have led us to believe, often quite falsely, that there is a narrower range of gender behaviour that is acceptable and normal.

The fairytales and stories we tell our children are full of templates of gender stereotypes that we are instilling in them to induce specific behaviours from them. It is the knight that kills the dragon and the maiden who is weak and in distress. She can only be rescued by the stronger more intelligent male who will protect her from the evils of the world providing she remain true only to him.

Female children are placed in behavioural chastity belts to encourage them not to do certain behaviours. I remember being at school in the early 1960s, when girls were expected to be either secretaries, cooks, teachers or in extraordinary circumstances a doctor, but never generally expected to be strong and know the intellectual answers. Men were placed on pedestals, from which they would eventually tumble into disgrace for portraying human frailty. Weakness in men was and still is in most cultures considered bad or a sign of not being a whole man.

In other words we have been brainwashed into believing that gender issues are black and white or shades of grey. In reality they are none of those things because, as far as social order is concerned, gender is only what you create it to be.

One of the greatest myths around gender was that the father of a new-born child deserved a fat cigar after the birth. It was a symbol of his success and a celebration. The bigger the cigar the better representation of the symbolic size of his manhood and gender statement about himself. No mention was made at that time that smoking kills or that on a biological sensory basis it takes away the oxygen from his blood system that he needs as an essential part of the production of happy hormones.

So is gender only fallacy and a product of our age?

One answer to that would be yes, because our gender performances are socially specific. The gender statements and reactions we make with our behaviour would be different if we were elsewere with a group of other people. This is, of course, true to every kind of sex, gender, and sexuality expression because everyone we interact with has certain tolerance levels for our varied behaviours that we are aware of both consciously and unconsciously.

Another answer would be no, because on a micro-systemic level gender exists stable for short times within the constructs of all societies. Traditionally some jobs could only be done by men because they demand a particular kind of physical strength that women in general do not have. However, when women are left to their own devices they can get the same job done in a different amount of time through ingenuity. Nothing in our society today is dependent on brute force since our mechanical sophistication has surpassed the general need for a worker to rely purely on human strength. So the natural dependence of gender being performed as an extension of biological sex-based roles is weakened by the mechanical world.

We are also no longer dependent on brute force for our social structures being upheld by men's strength. The law is now being kept in a different way through the application of mechanical violence and deterrents, sophisticated detection of crime and technological monitoring of individuals from cradle to grave. War is not a matter of pure violence, instead being dependent on technological and economical superiority, and fanatical persistence.

Women being dependent on men's strength to protect them from competitive males or predators has, to some extent, been broken. Women may now protect themselves and be violent against others on their own through the redistribution of power due to the modern application of technology. The 20th century changed the order of sex and gender that had been upheld since the beginning of time.

A gun can make a very small and lethal hole in a very large attacker; Agent Orange kills and money talks a very old language

Women in general, however, have strong childrearing instincts and skills that cause them to act differently from men. During the gestation and rearing of their children their emotional composition causes them to remain closer to their lair, seeking to nest, creating a cosseted and safe environment for their offspring. These behaviours can never change for women as they will never think like men because at the end of the day biology determines much of the ways our minds work. But over and above those biological determinants the structure of social order and gender performance all over the world is now changing.

Throughout recent times the white man has relied on violence and fraternities to keep women in oppressed positions. They have also relied on violence to control and oppress other groups such as blacks, Jews and homosexuals, ruling by fear.

In the past these groups behaved according to their oppressors' expectations, as did women doing gender in order to safeguard their young and be protected by the stronger male of our species. That is all changing now and men have no other choice but to change with it as power becomes more evenly distributed between the variety of different gender roles that are being played out.

As gender roles are based on sexual rituals, social expectations and construct, breeding is no longer reliant solely on the bi-polar male and female gender stereotypes. Science can now produce human beings from a bottle without the nicety of a mother or father but just a single cell to clone from. Initially you would think that this could end sex and gender difference but it is more likely to allow freedom to create more. It can always be remembered that although humans, to a large extent, do conformity they biologically and sociologically seek individuality.

The British popstar Boy George in the 1980s was cited in the popular press as being a gender bender because he wore make-up and less male stereotype clothes. The fact that he was gay was something the press were unable to exploit because it was not an issue for him. He was clearly male and declared that he wished to be nothing else but a gay man. However, the press had a field day because of the flamboyant visual image he presented in a largely macho, male-dominated society.

The greatest gender liberator for women has undoubtedly been birth control and the right to have abortions. That has given women not only the choice of when to have children and the responsibility that goes with them, but also the choice not to have them. These abilities to choose have contributed to women's ability to separate their gender roles from their biological sex.

Men have, for many thousands of years, been able to sire their offspring, go away and have sex for pleasure and then only do the gender role of husband or parent if and when it suited them. Let's face it there are many women out there raising children on their own in this world, but how often do you find a father in that position? Many societies accept that a lot of fathers will walk away from that gender role, seeing it as manly, but when women do this they are demonised as whores, heartless and evil. For them to not want to do the gender role of mother is seen as more unacceptable than the irresponsible father.

The gender role for men is starting to change now as many choose to stay at home and look after the children while their female partners go out and earn a living to provide for the whole family. As women break away from the stereotypical gender roles that their mothers and grandmothers performed, they are gathering academic respect, political power and financial freedom. The male partners of those women are now often needing to rely on the female for their daily financial needs, which puts men in a more vulnerable position.

For some of those men this is too difficult for them to do; they find it too nerve-wracking to be subject to the good nature and will of their female spouses who are the major wage earners. They see it as the scenario of the Black Widow spider who eats her mate after she has mated with him. For other men in that position who have found that the job market is offering jobs only to their female partners, it is a very humiliating experience. However, if the situation was reversed and the female partners were unemployed they would not expect them to be humiliated.

Since the large majority of the structure of our modern world is mainly city-based dwellings we are no longer so dependent on whether it will be a good harvest or not. What is important now to an individual is that they are a wage earner and can then have the buying power that money gives them. This is what is perpetuating the power change in our society in that women now have their hands on much more of the wealth. We are also in the age of the double wage earner where both partners go out to work in order to facilitate their financial needs, which further redistributes the power base that is derived from a currency-based economy.

For some men the change in the gender roles from the old male-female bipolar model is very threatening. Men need to feel dominant and not threatened in order to perform sexually. The pressures facing them in modern society, with the newly engendered, liberated female are seen by many of them as demasculinising. A lot of the world's men do not want power transfer by gender diversification to take place because they have had all the male privileges for such a long time. The new gender performances are not only threatening to take away much of men's economic power but also women's dependence on men too.

A British male psychologist gave a lecture in London in the mid 1990s and declared that the increase in the female population would result in more lesbianism.

!...?

Yet couples continue to get married in droves with high expectations of what kind of satisfaction that union will bring. Divorce, on the other hand, is just as good a business to be in as more and more couples find that they are too cramped in the constraints of those traditional marriages. Few men want demanding, liberated wives, and many women will not play the older gender game or put up with men trying to fit them into the roles that their grandmothers performed.

Many couples prefer to simply live together so that the gender power game can remain more negotiable and adjustable. It seems for many that marriage is the kiss of death to their relationship when they begin to feel locked into playing out the traditional roles of man and wife. Though when couples have been married for many years the power sharing generally becomes more even and that may be because they are past the competitive breeding ages. The laws often do not protect women economically if those long-term relationships break up, and they are left without the protection of pensions or investments.

Into the 21st century new female super-heroines will continue to emerge as one of the most popular and fast-growing images. On television Xena, Warrior Princess kicks and punches her way to righteousness by helping the poor be protected from their exploiters. The role has taken on fully the violence of men with no excuses that she is a barbaric, murderous woman whose past was that of an exploiter too. Yet even in her repentance, under the cloak of traditional male behaviour, she is able to kill and continue killing with gratuitous violence in the name of righteousness.

Xena's rescuer comes in the form of her sidekick, Gabrielle, who is the essence of the feminine, and does not kill unless absolutely necessary to survive. Since this series is shown worldwide it is interesting to note that it is the feminine within the feminine that rescues Xena from moral depravation and not the masculine which has been the traditional plot for the last few millennia.

Another television female hero of note is Buffy, the Vampire Slayer, who fights the evil demons of dark forces that emerge from the depths of hell. She is a 16-year-old girl who also uses violence to defeat the mainly male archetypal vampire and monsters who seek to enslave the world.

The actress Sigourney Weaver, who played Ridley in the *Alien* films of the 1980s and 1990s paved the way for the new age of the female violent super-heroine. Her countless sequels of swashbuckling fighting with aliens in space changed the way Hollywood viewed women and their power to be strong and dependable. Feminism in the disguise of entertainment enthralled men into believing that it was her male side and tenacity that they wanted to see, as both actress and viewer bonded together against a common enemy from outer space.

I must state here that I do not think violence is the path to gender diversity, with one group being superior over another. What is true though is that the ability of one group to protect itself against the violent and unreasonable behaviour of another group is a major key to gender freedom. Positive female gender role icons such as the Israeli Prime Minister Golda Meir, Mo Mowlam, Madeleine Albright and Mother Teresa do appear on the surface to be peace-makers, but let us not forget, it is the strong arm of the law – domestic or international – that supports these women's power in society.

Gender then is a game but it is now a game that is also available to a greater diversity of players. Socio-cultural interpretations of sex and sexuality through gender performance is now more open to gay people. Playing the femme or butch lesbian, the macho or effeminate gay male is being replaced by the increasingly non-identified homosexual. In the 21st century it is going to be harder to tell who is gay and who is not because the gender game now allows heterosexual men to dress more colourfully, show feminine traits and flirt with homosexuality. Women, on the other hand, have been dressing as men since the introduction of slacks during the Second World War.

It was even chic in the 1990s to be a lesbian in Hollywood, or at the very least to suggest bisexuality. An actress just had to pretend not to be too heterosexual, doing more liberal gender performance. When Ellen Degeneres came out on TV as a lesbian it caused a shock, not because she was tomboyish but because she had such a feminine girlfriend, who had previously played the Hollywood scene as a straight woman.

Margaret Thatcher as Prime Minister of England played the gender game by being referred to in Europe as the Iron Lady, as she refused to allow her sex to be a way in which she could be bullied in the European Common Market. The popstar Madonna played the gender game by not allowing her publicly declared bisexuality to stop her career, and then going on to be a single mother.

The popstars Elton John and George Michael played the gender game for many years, pretending to their fans that they were heterosexuals in order to keep their market share of the record business. Before them, John Wayne, the American movie star, made a career of playing roles which personified an unrealistic masculinity that appealed to both women's and men's fantasises of how masculine a man could get.

The emergence of transsexual and transgender politics has produced new performance roles as different from each other as stereotypical male or female. The transvestite gender role is very different from those that are performed by the transsexual or even the transgendered person. The politics, social performances, economic power bases, and opportunities are as diverse among the newly sophisticated transglobal transgenerations as they are between the evolving feminist or men's movements.

Intersex and androgyne politics forces gender non-conformity to go one step further by demanding that these groups are not forced to conform, not only to the bipolar male or female gender roles, but also to the trans-stereotypical roles. So we can no longer presume a person's gender role, but enquire after and assess a gender performance, that within it gives a realm of information about how we should react to that individual to afford them maximum respect and equal opportunity to contribute to society.

In performing, reading and writing about gender roles I like to remember one of the immortal phrases of my old drama teacher, Madame Von de Hyke:

What are we today then?

Gender performance not only changes from place to place, sex to sex, sexuality to sexuality and class to class, but is also age dependent. Older people have greater gender and economic power than younger people, but old people have less than both.

Men have had more gender power than women but now that is changing and men find themselves for the first time in thousands of years, since matriarchal religions were suppressed, subject to female gender power.

Gay men's gender power in old China was not an issue before the white man came, but homosexuals are now singled out, finding themselves having to invent gay politics to reclaim their sex and sexuality since the white man partly destroyed their culture. Gay politics in America, Australia, and Europe find that gay men's gender power is threatened by the rise of the right wing once again, which only relentless campaigning can keep at bay.

Lesbian gender power is still a long way behind gay men's as they carry their history of being women with them. This has caused the lesbian movement to be less politically strident than the gay men's movement over the years, because they have been economically, educationally and politically deprived.

The gender power bases of transsexual, transgender, anydrogyne and transvestite politics are very new, even though in the Bay area of San Francisco it was happening in the 1960s. In many countries, however, there is no gender recognition for this group of people as they are seen as an abomination against God or mentally ill.

When a gender group has no recognition within a society it is impossible for them to carry out any form of gender performance that is liberal or unrepressed, like women in Iran, gay men in Turkey, lesbians in the White House, transsexuals in Brazil, androgynes in societies at large. Gender repression always means that the opressor is performing gender superiority and believing they are benefiting from their performances. This scenario can never be anything less than an abuse of human rights and in the greater picture detracts from the richness of human experience.

I shall reply here to Germaine Greer, the 1960s radical feminist, who in her 1999 book, *The Whole Woman*, commented that I had proposed to do away with the bipolar male/female gender system. She found it hard to imagine how a transsexual's life could make sense without the bipolar M/F gender system.

First of all I shall agree with her that she probably does find it hard to imagine diversity...her chapter that commented on people who had overcome Gender Dysphoria was no less than a vicious attack on a group of individuals who have attempted to do the best with their lot in life.

Secondly I have never proposed the extinction of the categories male and female, simply suggested that an extended model of sex, gender and sexuality identity can lead to a greater understanding of the whole human race.

Thirdly, but not least, I invite Dr Greer to consider that bashing one sector of society, intellectually or otherwise, does not in any way validate the experience of other oppressed groups.

It is is the duty of all in an equal and humanitarian society to ensure that their neighbours have gender freedom to contribute fully to that society

In March 1999 a landmark judgement was made in Britain when two Pakistani women were granted political asylum because it was considered too dangerous for their personal safety to return to Pakistan. The decision was made on the basis of their gender power inferiority in Pakistan and that in their country they were in danger of the kind of violence and oppression that would not happen to men.

While there had been cases before where people in such situations were granted tolerated asylum rights, this was a precedent that gave them full political status. The year before, a transsexual in another country was granted political asylum for the same reasons. The principle being applied here levels the playing field against persecution through race, creed, colour, religion, sex, gender, sexuality or political views.

I want to leave the reader with a positive note at the end of this chapter that gender freedom is on the way for all, but if I did that I would be a fool, and you would think me a liar. I just had a telephone call to tell me that there are only two female Chief Constables in the whole of the British police force as we go into the new millennium. They are the highest ranking women, but the truth is that women like this are partly promoted for propaganda purposes, even though to get those positions they probably had to be twice as good at their jobs as their male counterparts. None of the high ranking officers are publicly gay, transsexual, transgender, androgyne or intersex identified.

If gender history is not to repeat the gender past then we all better wise up now!

4

Sexuality

A lot of people at the end of the 20th and beginning of the 21st century remain confused between sexuality: the activity and preference of sex (what you do and how you prefer to do it) and the performance of gender. It is easier to think of sexuality as being the direction in which an individual wants to direct their sexual desires, forces or libido. A further definition would be to say that a person's sexuality is also a matter of how they see their own sexual activity in relation to who or what they have or want to have sex with.

Hetero only?

To say most people are open about their sexuality and can even wear it publicly as an acclaimed part of their identity would be incorrect, because there are many places in the world where it is not possible to make such declarations.

Gay in private, straight on the street

It can also not be worn as an identity, in a social and moral context, when people of one particular sexuality assume a position of superiority over people who have different sexual preferences. Animosity often happens if assumed religious or moral superiority leads people to believe theirs is the only one true or correct way for others to behave.

Heterosexuality has often been blamed for levelling such criticisms at many other sexualities, but that is not always true, because I have seen gays take the same standpoint too, against heterosexuals, bisexuals and

70

transsexuals. Such prejudices are always born out of ignorance and driven by fear.

No non-perverts allowed!

If you know a person's sexuality then that is one of the indicators as to whether they are available for sexual encounters or even emotional involvement. While it is possible to be sexually involved with people who you are not emotionally involved with and vice versa, individuals are generally seeking both. In saying this though there is a danger that I may sound as if I am advocating that people should only be looking for both sex and emotional involvement, but I am not. Good sex can be had with a person you are not involved with.

Only fucks with strangers...

In some English-speaking cultures, words such as *straight* have been used to depict heterosexuality and words like *bent* to imply that someone is homosexual. The words, when used offensively, can hold the presuppositions that only heterosexuality is normal, but as we move between cultures it is plain to see that is not true. In some places bisexuality is normal and in gay subcultures gay is normal as the dominant statistical average.

Slightly bent but available for straight sex

Owning language and empowering it can dilute the insult in such labels as *bent* or *queer* because the user to whom it applies can gain power by using it descriptively about themselves. This has happened in the gay community and also the trans-community when people have referred to themselves with the same terminology, but a different intonation. Since people other than heterosexuals have identified and recognised their economic purchasing power they have empowered themselves by turning insults into positive statements.

We're here, we're queer and we're going shopping!

I once had a conversation about this with the Australian writer Kate Cummings and she saw the adoption of such phrases as buying into abusive language but I cannot agree with her. What I tried to explain to her was that in Soho, London the trans community had claimed the word *trannie* as a identity that positively described themselves, thereby disempowering any abuser wishing to use language as a weapon against them.

Trannie power...Beware politically sensitive individual reorientating sex, gender and sexuality...please wait for clear signal to advance safely

People can also have an underlying sexuality, which for many reasons, they may not be consciously aware of or may even be hiding. Again, cultural myths have gathered around this kind of scenario, because there are not only latent or secret homosexuals who are living as heterosexuals, but also open homosexuals who secretly have heterosexual encounters. Hidden sexuality can involve anyone who secretly sleeps with anyone outside their own declared public sexuality.

Queer men who sleep with straight women... just occasionally?

Some gay men and women do, at times, sleep with the opposite biological sex, either in a moment of passion, as an experiment, or secretly. It is also common that heterosexuals just as frequently have untalked about sex with members of their own biological sex. This, however, does not mean these people identify as being bisexual, it is just simply a matter of brief sexual encounters.

Learner bisexual still deciding

To say that bisexuals are more well adjusted to sexual

encounters with different sexes would be untrue. While out and proud bisexuals are more likely to be well adjusted, there are just as many in the closet as with any other sexuality. This can be understood sometimes because bisexuals often get it in the head from heterosexuals and homosexuals, according to the political agenda of the day.

Please wait because the public thinks bisexuals are still deciding

Transgenderists have sexualities all of their own, since part of their sexualites involves their own particular trans-identities interacting with their sexual partner's identity. The reality is that transgenderists can be either heterosexual, bisexual, gay, or other. Their sexuality is a happening in the creating because it is created by their shifting body type, which includes hormones and/or surgery; without those, they cannot have a transgender sexuality. Someone who is having sex with a transgenderist person is having sex with neither a man nor a woman, but someone who is transgender identified.

Open Day at the body morphing workshop...sexuality up for grabs

My concept that there is no such thing as a concrete or static sexuality may seem contradictory in a book such as this where I label and define the concepts of sex, gender and sexuality. I do, however, believe that nothing is static, correct, real or permanent; sexuality changes in each and every one of us constantly, and is dynamic, even though we may not be consciously aware of that happening.

Trannie-fucker for a night

Sexual excitement and fulfilment therefore can never be solely tied to self-concepts; such concepts must be inter-linked and defined by other's sexualities (you cannot be gay unless there is another person in the world who is also the same sex as you). On a social level sexuality can best be defined by self-identification, but the taboos and restrictions of what is or is not culturally acceptable always mask many people's freedom to express themselves.

No I did not have sexual relations with that woman
(Bill Clinton 1998)

Of course as I write this I can hear some of the readers say that they are definitely not gay or straight or bisexual and that they have never had any such inclinations. To them I say: enjoy your denial, relish in it and own it, since it is exclusively yours. Many of the rest of us are aware that each and every individual finds, at some time in their lives, human contact itself erotic and exciting.

Erotic energy is focused on sexual objects and restrained by social prohibitions

Sexual excitement, let us remember, is defined by unconscious forces and it is not under the control of the conscious mind. Indeed many people struggle with the constant fight to constrain their sexuality, restricted by the limits of their own belief systems and the beliefs they think they should have.

The teenager who gets out of bed in the morning with an erection or a damp patch beneath their groin has not spent the night consciously sorting their erotic dreams into nicely arranged rows of social, religious or moral acceptability. We are all sexual but how we direct those sexual desires defines our sexuality. For some people their sexuality cannot be found acceptable at a conscious level but remains secret and unspoken about.

Sexuality can be a blessing, but for some it is a curse

It might help the reader to see that I have arrived at this open perspective through my own journey and believe ever evolving sexuality is part of the human development we all experience...In my youth I found only older men attractive...time passed, then, in my later teenage years I found both men and women sexually exciting...but along the way my fancies changed many times...until I reach today's set of attractions and live with my younger lesbian lover.

All change...we are all sexual miracles
in the happening

For each of us there is an individual sexual journey that can give us new social permissibility and personal understanding. Fear is what drives people to deny their own and other people's sexualities. Will they succeed or will they fail? Learning just one kind of sexuality can be overwhelming to some people...more than one could be too much for their pre-programming to cope with.

What if people found out I liked sex with Tom, Dick or
Harriet?

There has been no kind of restrictions to the type of adult I have had sex with during my life and each, in their own way, have been sexually stimulating to me. The dynamics of their sex, gender and sexuality has configured my own sexuality as the sex act took place. Some people I liked having sex with better than others and I am sure they would say the same about me.

Am I so wildly different from you?

The answer, of course, is that we are all extreme or watered down versions of each other. Whatever I have been, done and experienced is not so far from you, but what we have all done sexually has been restricted by our own ingested and formulated limited beliefs. Honesty about our sex lives in society is greatly discouraged by those who are often the guardians of our moral values.

I won't enjoy sex with you...I shan't enjoy sex with

> *you...I can't enjoy sex with you...It is absolutely not permissible...have I come yet?*

The release of sexual libido is indiscriminate but the permissibility of the direction of our sexuality is not only directed by biology but social constructs too.

It is like a filter system that goes through the whole three concepts of sex, gender and sexuality, tailoring our experience in the making with each encounter being different. Not only are no two sexual partners the same but also no two sexual acts can be the same either. So there is never a right or wrong to sexuality because it is an act, history of or anticipation of sex, and not soley social interchange.

> *So if I'm a dominant straight man in jack boots and suspenders having S&M gay sex with a leather queen who used to be a biological woman...what does that make me?*

The most profound learning that I have had about human nature, after having worked for more than 30 years in dealing with people and their sexual desires, is that people take sex far too seriously. The best moments in bed can be had when the whole act of sex goes wrong, one person loses concentration and falls off the bed in fits of laughter. It can, after all, be a wet, messy business that can depend for success on a variety of things, such as the day of the week, or what you had for breakfast.

> *Many people torment themselves with their fear of failure during the sex act*

Sexuality is such a huge subject that none of us can ever know everything about it and we can treat it healthily as a lifetime journey of exploration that can give us a great deal of pleasure. A person's gender performance in society, however, may not necessarily reveal their sexuality, for they may be excellent at giving other people the impression that they have a completely different sexuality.

Politicians, preachers, lawyers, doctors, soldiers and the rest...often lie about their sexuality because they believe they would be penalised if they told the truth.

No the Minister is not gay...he is just busy and under pressure

When engaging in sexual activities some people are not always upfront about their biological sex. Transpeople sometimes engage in sexual encounters, presenting themselves as their opposite biological sex, even though it may be the sex they believe they are inside and the cosmetic sex they are heading towards. The partner may have sex with them without even knowing the truth. Prefemisexuals (see p108) can be good at trick-fucking when they fake vaginal intercourse by using their anus and holding their genitals to one side. Premascusexuals (see p108) may use sex aids to penetrate their partners without those partners being aware that it was not a penis.

Simulated sex is common among transpeople because they may need to appear as their cosmetic sex

It is possible, as seen in chapter two, to be a man without a penis and a woman without a vagina. The mascu-sexual (see p108) identifies as a heterosexual man when he is having sex with a woman and as a gay man when having sex with a man. The reverse is true for the femi-sexual (see p108) in that she identifies as a lesbian when sleeping with a woman and as a heterosexual woman when sleeping with a man.

Sexuality can be determined by the mindset as well as the body

The transgenderist does not claim to be their opposite biological sex even though they are doing fluid gender roles and may have altered some of their body to represent their original opposite biological sex. It therefore follows that they are not doing gay or straight sex either but doing transgenderist sex. Their body is in between male and female, their gender role is opposite to their original biological sex and their partner is having sex with someone who identifies as both male and female.

Sexuality can also arise out of gender performance

The femisexual, however, has a vagina and identifies as a woman so when she is with a man she is heterosexual and with a woman a lesbian. She does not at any time identify as her original biological sex and now cosmetically represents her destination cosmetic sex of female. Due to the limitations of phalloplasty premascusexuals must also come under the same category as mascusexuals

Sexuality can change when the cosmetic sex of the individual changes

Mascusexuals identify as their cosmetic sex of male and can have genitals that represent that sex. Some surgically constructed penises are used for sex and when a woman has sex with a mascusexual she is having a heterosexual encounter.

Congratulations – you are now deep in sex, gender and sexuality cyber-semantics, philosophy and politics

The question as to what the sexuality of the androgyne is can give variable answers because they can be either a gynophile (attracted to women or vaginas) or a phallophile (attracted to men or penises) depending on the identity of the person to whom they are attracted. If a person identifies as both sexes, then that gives rise to a new sexuality based on their own particular identity. The person who is attracted to the androgyne must logically be an androgynophile.

Every sex therapist, psychologist, psychiatrist, endocrinologist, genital reconstructive surgeon and sex, gender and sexuality fluid person can benefit immensely from understanding these extended concepts

Sex with sinandrogynes then would mean that a person is having sex with someone who was identifying as neuter, so the suitor would be termed as a sinandrogynophile. These people's sexuality must again be defined by who they are having sex with, history of sex and/or anticipation of sex, and what the other person's sex, gender and sexuality identification is at that time.

Every human being has a right to a name, description and choices

As we move deeper into sex, gender and sexuality, we can see the absolute absurdity of using that old male-female heterosexual model. Human knowledge needs to extend as nature develops, science evolves, life is experienced, socialisation grows and a vast diversity of sexes, genders and sexualitys emerge.

But what of prohibition?

Guilt and shame are social constructs that are derived from the rules and regulations by which each society chooses to restrict its citizens' behaviour. Every society has its niceties and forbidden fruits that are associated with rewards and punishment. Mainly in patriarchal cultures women's sexuality and freedom of sexual choice is constrained in order to reduce their power and enslave them in the home.

What of equal rights?

Gay people, transpeople and other minority sex, gender and sexualites are robbed, beaten up, sacked from work, thrown out of their homes and suffer many other abuses all over the world while governments turn a blind eye. It is often the countries that put themselves forward as having the best human rights records that may be among the most ardent offenders, such as Britain, the US and France.

In May 1999 the street magazine the *Big Issue* ran an article on being gay and Muslim, in which Sheikh Sharkhawy, a cleric at London's central mosque, was said to be arguing that male homosexuals should be put to death, and lesbians committed to life imprisonment. He was quoted as saying: "Gays are the cancer of society and must be removed to prevent the spread of Aids and pae- dophila."

So why not just live a quiet life as a heterosexual, respectable suburbanite?

A great number of sex, gender and sexualitiy fluid peo- ple find ways to live their lives to the full by taking public office, changing their societies and introducing new philosophies and laws to be more egalitarian. Gay rights movements exist all over the world now and link up with each other through the Internet, forming even bigger polit- ical pressure groups to fight for equal rights. Trans-groups have joined them in fighting for the millions of under-rep- resented and isolated transpeople across the globe.

Surely people in public office would not behave in a prejudicial way?

The truth is that people in bureaucracy are often the most prejudicial sector of any society, as their jobs depend on following rules, whether they be ridiculous and outdat- ed or not. There is also a high level of ignorance in many government workers because they live in a cultural vacu- um with limited understanding about what happens in society at large. These are often solid jobs that can last for life so people have a tendency not to further their educa- tion beyond what they know and with which they feel safe.

But doctors know what they are talking about don't they?

Again the answer must be that to a large extent, the majority of professionals in medicine, psychiatry and psychology have been more than slow to push forward human rights issues. In general the training in these professions includes only the very basics of sexuality and the courses are so impoverished that professionals are unable to deal with the diversity of human sexuality that will face them in their careers.

Is transvestism a sexuality?

No, it is just a desire to dress up and ceases to be transvestism when you move to another culture when the dress code is different. The fetishistic transvestite, on the other hand, can derive sexual excitement for the clothes that they wear during sex, so the answer could be yes, too. However, social transvestites who simply dress up recreationally and do not get involved with sex while dressed are not associating the sexual excitement with that particular kind of dressing. One kind of transvestism over a long period can sometimes lead to the other, but not necessarily so.

But surely transgenderism must be associated with sexuality?

The answer again is that sometimes it may be associated with sexuality but in some cases it is not. Social transgenderism, where someone wishes to change only part of their body, is not necessarily linked to sexuality. For many people who have never met a transgenderist it can be very confusing to distinguish between the varying types of transperson. The issues with each transperson, however, are really quite different but unfortunately even many sexologists are ignorant and need to educate themselves more.

Why study the extremes of sexual behaviour?

Because only by studying the outer limits of our knowledge about sexuality can we understand the commonality of sexual desires even better. A greater understanding of sexuality can only be a good thing in helping ourselves and others to enjoy sex fully and not enter into denial. Ignorance is dangerous, hurtful, malicious, prejudicial and disempowering to minorities' sexualites which lurk, at some level, inside all of us.

We all have sexual fantasies that we would never dare mention to another human being

Every month many people walk into my office asking if they are normal because they are having sexual fantasies that frighten them and they think such thoughts might be unacceptable. They all go red and apologise for coming to me and paying me money to help them sort out their thoughts. Each time I tell them that even though they may have 10,000 sexual fantasies a week, unconsciously and consciously, it does not always mean those will transpire into reality. To pick the best and most applicable exciting fantasy, the brain produces 10,000 and then dumps 9,999.

We have sexual denial in order to regulate our sexual and social behaviour

Since sex is the expression of sexual libido, sometimes we are overcome by our feelings and urges. It is not, however, acceptable within our societies to openly sexually express ourselves so we deny that we are having those fantasies, urges and desires. Sometimes this causes harm to ourselves and others, and the denial gets out of hand as it is turned into repression. We can internalise those desires and the unnatural restraints can make us ill – physically, mentally and even spiritually.

We all have sexual realities which we do not reveal

Some people are more sexual than others and some

have low sex drives with little interest in the subject. Others seek out new stimuli to vary their sex lives constantly throughout their lives. There are also people who avoid sex, and this is not always because of past negative encounters, but because it may take up too much of their time focusing on sex, so they explore life in other ways instead.

For me, sex, both personally and professionally, has been one the greatest adventures of all

It is interesting to debate the sexuality of a client of mine who stayed with a partner who varied their sex and gender. Her lesbian partner started life as a biological female. Their relationship was gay to begin with but her partner underwent sex and gender realignment to become a transman, which meant that my client was then heterosexual by definition. My client, of course, throughout stayed a biological woman with the same gender but the other person's transition caused her to be gay, and then heterosexual.

John Money in *The Destroying Angel* catalogued some of the Puritanism movements that over the past 150 years prohibited American sexuality. Pat Califia in *Sex Changes: The History of Transgenderism* told of her own journey from separatist lesbian to enlightened trans-historian, fortunately with the humility that saved her intellectual neck.

In 1997 Sydney, Australia saw a new wave of gay bashing in the light of a right-wing backlash by politicians such as Pauline Hanson, who also stirred up racial prejudice about Asian immigration and the Aborigines.

The Internet's sexuality newsgroups, going into the 21st century, carry bulletins about attacks on and murders of sex, gender and sexuality minority groups in south America. Since these cultures are often run by unstable, corrupt governments with little accountability upon the world stage it is very difficult for international pressure groups like Amnesty International to uncover the truth and confront these undemocratic regimes. Furthermore, rather than upset tenuous diplomatic relations with foreign powers governments make no protests about many human rights atrocities, and see little profit in dictating morality with what may be a potential trading partner.

In 1991 some British MPs were protesting about the publication and stocking of a book of lesbian photographs by the female photographer Della Grace, who later became the self-identifed FTM intersex Del La Grace Volcano. International newspapers, however, are always carrying scandalous stories of sexual infidelity among politicians and churchmen, who survive and deny accusations of corruption but generally have to resign when involved in revelations about their own sex lives.

In 1999 Del was involved in the publication of *The Drag King Book* with Judith "Jack" Halberstam, which deals with any subject relating to female masculinity (see Judith Halberstam's book of the same title for inspiration), male impersonators, cross-dressing, drag kings, butch women or basically any and all depictions of female-to-male gender performance. It will take a time for the public to realise that much of what happens in this book is not to do with sexuality but comes under gender performance even though in some cases the two cross-connect.

So sexuality is not only a process of making it up as you go along but also a constant reservoir of titillation to the public at large. Your sexuality identification can work for you or against you, according to geographical location and the mood of the day; this I doubt will ever change because the nature of humans is that they are always seeking to redefine their moral codes.

Finally, geneticists have tried to put forward studies that declared that certain gay men and women studied had gay genetic configurations. Unfortunately for them their studies were flawed from the very beginning because it was impossible for them to define what homosexuality was and where it began and ended. The people they studied were open homosexuals but there are many people who may classify themselves as gay but do not make public declaration and will not have such genetic configurations. Does that mean they are not really gay then?

The nature verses nurture argument of whether a person is born with a specific sexuality or socially develops their sexual preferences according to programming is futile within these pages. From a scientific, reductionist point of view it may seem fascinating to the researcher. To sociologists, and campaigners of equal sexuality rights for all free thinking adults, it is an incumbance that only serves to detract from the main focus of sexuality equality.

Negative Cultural Restrictions That Prohibit Self-Fulfilment: The "No" Disease

I am sure we can all remember at some level that one of the very first words we learnt before or after toddling on chubby little legs was "NO". It is of course the duty of a parent or carer to teach that to a child very early in order to prevent us getting into danger. We all internalise that voice as we grow, and without it, there would have been many times when we would have got into deep trouble.

"NO", however has its limitations, but that nagging little voice inside our heads tells us not to touch hot stoves, play loose and fast, sleep with strangers or gamble on outside odds. That part of us has a job to do and that is to repeat "NO...NO and NO", over and over again. Beliefs, values and attitudes surrounding those negative cultural restrictions often lead all of us, at times, to forsake opportunities to have a rip-roaring time expanding our daily experiences beyond our own normalities.

Freud called the "NO" the superego – the part of us that carries our perceptions of the rules of the road which lead us to becoming responsible adults and citizens. Margaret Thatcher's policies called it returning to good old-fashioned family values (strangely they conveniently forgot to remember poverty, starvation, slavery, sexism, racism, bigotry, and lack of education).

Oh sure...sometimes it's better to stay safe...be better safe than sorry...not to get in too deep...take lower risk options...let someone else do it first.

Risk, though, is the very essence of the road to success

and fulfilment of desire. Without risk Einstein would never have published his theory of relativity, Dolly Parton would be flat-chested, Bill Gates would be as poor as a church mouse and Viagra would be something that only the people next door had taken.

So am I advocating throwing your knickers in the air and embarking on a life of unadulterated passion. Well...YES...actually I am, because there are times when it is OK to let go of your inhibitions. It is good to go a little crazy now and then, fully departing from the sobriety of Monday to Friday and 9 am to 5 pm. It doesn't mean the devil is going to put its slippers under your bed or that no one will ever take you seriously again. It doesn't mean you are going to be considered the neighbourhood trollop, or if you are it's time to move.

In everything you do in this life it helps if you remember O'Keefe's number one rule of life: "Have Fun". If it is performing heart surgery (preferably qualified), adding up the national taxes, painting your face so you look like someone else, arresting a bank robber or counting the threaded stones on your worry beads, always remember: "Have fun".

Over-seriousness is the most awful disease there is. It can shorten your life by years, bring on cancer, make you go bald, see penetrative sex as a sin outside marriage. Remember "NO" is a habit you can get help with and should, especially if it has got out of control. Make sure you say "YES", much more often.

So always remember as you read this, wherever you are and whatever you are doing, even when you are burying your granny (please make sure she is dead first), on your knees before the president or having your fifteenth face lift...FIND A WAY TO MAKE IT FUN.

Oh! And remember at some time in our lives haven't we have all been transvestites?...Think about it...

Questionnaire

Discover your knowledge of sex, gender and sexuality variant people within your world

1. Name ten male gay saints

2. Name ten lesbian politicians

3. Name ten transsexual political activists

4. Name ten feminist heroines

5. Name ten transgendered people

6. Name ten androgyne or intersex figures in literature

7. Name ten of the world's most powerful heterosexuals.

It is unlikely that any of us will be able to complete the whole of the questionnaire. What it will show you is how knowledgeable you are about other people's diversity, what areas you can look at in future, and in what areas your present knowledge is strongest.

5

The Science of Truths and Non-Truths

The Nature and Art of Science, Medicine and Social Psychology

In pursuing my studies of sex, gender and sexuality it has been necessary for me to look at several theories of the origins of human behaviour. What I have been struck by is the absolute conviction with which each researcher and theorist honestly adheres to their well presented, defined and structured explanations. This, in turn, causes me to take several steps back and look at the logic of their conclusions and the means by which they were deduced.

What I have found is that according to the principles of each of their disciplines of biology, psychology, neurophysiology, genetics, behaviourism, cognitive connectionism, psychoanalytical theory, and reincarnation they may all be correct. The problem arises though that when we leave the postulates of each discipline, the specifics of those conclusions can no longer be understood within the wider philosophical world.

The question I must therefore now ask myself is: Even if there are absolute truths that emerge from science, medicine and social psychology about sex, gender and sexuality, are they simply lost in translation to other disciplines?

The first answer must, undoubtedly, be yes, for the calculations of a microbiologist cannot in anyway be translated into the interpretations of a social anthropologist explaining why men over six foot wore bright green dresses during an eclipse. What is more relevant is that no matter how many times a neuro-surgeon draws the distribution of neurones in the hippocampus, it will mean very little to a social worker unless that person chooses to study the discipline of neurophysiology.

The second answer to my question is that we all understand some very basic principles of general science and that if an idea is suggested to us then we are capable of seeing the logic behind a hypothesis. However, the difficulty here arises in that our understanding of other people's disciplines is so limited as to not allow us a full assessment of the validity of their argument. Therefore we must rely on their orientation and efficacy of themselves in their science when connecting cause and effect in a way that can reproduce repetitive results.

But the danger is that repetitive results can always be achieved by alternative explanations of the nature of the world and its mechanics, and so we are led to see how tenuous the strings of any philosophy are held aloft. It is all too easy to forget that, to the mass populous, the world seemed flat for a very long time, which was an idea that served them well. The flatness of the world went unchallenged because challenge had no purpose and may have caused disturbances of too many perceived realities, values, and beliefs of those times.

A third answer is one that is less comfortable to those of us of a scientific bent who choose to orientate ourselves primarily within our own disciplines, and structure our philosophies in our own perceived orderly and dependable manner. This is the principle that we all actually create our own realities both subjectively and out of the constituents of the world around us. Although we live in an environment that is fundamentally existential, our applications of science, medicine and social psychology are designed by us to fit our own needs and interpretations of the time, place, and personal interest – of course, I'm making all this up and you, the reader, are making up how you understand it – or not.

In this work, as I look at the widening of definitions and degrees of sex, gender and sexuality, I am inclined to go for the third answer as I continue to be a constructionist, building models of human behaviour that I, and I hope others, can use both to understand ourselves and our interaction with each other in our greater environment. I am aware this puts me in a position that means my model of Human Pan-identity may be no more real than those built by Darwin, Freud, Erick Erickson, Alder, Kinsey, Lang, Masters and Johnson, and Money, but I feel safer in not deluding myself that I alone know the truth. It is more comfortable for me to side with the psychologist and psychedelic guru Timothy Leary in not only creating my own reality but also conceding to the passing and extinction of my ideas. Most of all though, I acknowledge that my ideas may be merely a stepping stone by which others may orientate themselves to pastures new.

So in my presentation of the pan-indentity wheel of life (see chapter six), I insist the reader not only agree but disagree with me in every aspect of its construction and deconstruction so that you may arrive at a greater understanding of your own constructed realities, values, beliefs, attitudes, and philosophies.

Science can only be an explanation and manipulation of the present and in the greater plan of things, chaos is too large to make its whole meaning known to us.

The Attribution of Power to Semantic Components of Language

It is evident through the semantic (science of meaning) study of language, and the sociological observations of power distribution in societies, that the components of a word can deliver to, or deprive a person of freedom and civil rights.

For instance let us compare the words *grandmother* and *grandfather*, each of which have a diversity of unspoken meanings associated with the subjects' sex and gender. Other associated meanings may also be triggered in each of us on hearing a word, calling up memories of our own subjective experiences and personal perspectives. Furthermore, unconscious attraction or prejudices may be stimulated simply by the fact that we, as the user of the word, may be different from the person we are talking about.

We can be aware that the attribution or deprivation of power in the semantic use of words that indicate sex, gender or sexuality is not necessarily safer if we neuter all language and strip it of identity. *Grandparent* is neither better nor worse than *grandmother* or *grandfather*, just different. Also to simply call someone a person and ignore their sex, gender or sexuality identity is not nessarily more politically correct, because it may rob them of aspects of their core identity and civil rights.

According to the language being used, an indication may be present that the subject matter may be female, male, neuter or other. Such diverse interpretations of sex, gender and sexuality meaning may or may not be present in the surface structure of the word or phrase.

In a sentence such as: *A person has checked into room number 6*, the pronoun does not carry with it the kind of information that will indicate the person's sex, gender or sexuality.

However, with a sentence such as: *A lesbian has checked into room number 6*, information about the person's sex, sexuality and gender is fully present.

In the second sentence we also need to consider context, in so far as, if the lesbian had checked into a gay women's hotel then it is unlikely that prejudice would be present in the components of the sentence. But if we use the same sentence when the lesbian had checked into a hotel, in a society and area that scorned freedom of the female sex, gender interpretation and sexuality, then prejudice could be present in the same sentence.

We must also consider the tonality of the user of the sentence because an auditory interpretation can display attraction, indifference or hostility towards the lesbian. What may also be present are subtle body language indications which show that although the sentence is linguistically delivered with one meaning, the user could be displaying hidden agendas about their comfort with the lesbian's identity.

The recipient of the combination of communications must also take responsibility for the way in which the communication is delivered or interpreted. If the lesbian is comfortable with her own identity, whether she is present or not during the sentence delivery, she will influence its effectiveness as a communication. You cannot insult someone, to their face, by calling them a lesbian if that is either a compliment or an indifference to them. The prejudice in a communication is diluted if the person fears no insult.

The complexity of human communication will always permit the user and recipient of it to redistribute the power attributed to its linguistic components. Language is a dynamic living, developing, growing, changing and sometimes dying form of human interaction that cannot stay static because its very essence is that it changes both with the users and the recipients. The richness of the possibilities of descriptions of human experience should not be feared but explored and embraced in continuously standard and non-standard forms. Most importantly minority groups in any society need to constantly redefine themselves and the way they are addressed.

Constructionists vs Deconstructionists

In any movement developed to obtain power for oppressed minorities, the argument of whether to label ourselves or pretend we are all the same rages, often causing division within that movement. The knock-on effect of this is that the majority at large find new labels for themselves, discovering things about their own identities of which they were not previously aware.

Picks and Romans, Catholics and Protestants, heterosexuals and homosexuals were all, at times, without labels and identities since we all seemed to have emerged from the same subdivision of a common group of amoebic cells. Nature being what it is has a compulsion to replicate and at each turn of events slightly altering its descendants from those that formatted the previous cluster of ever communicating molecules, cells, tissues, eyebrows, sub-personalities and state-of-the-world thinking.

There can be no such thing as a mistake in nature because it does not understand such judgmental social constructs. What there is, is variation, which simply means nature is doing things differently which is par for the course.

Constructionists such as myself believe that we need many more descriptive labels for the human experience. Only by using extended identification can we then go on to ensure that human equal rights are established and maintained. Afro-Americans did not have equal rights until they identified themselves as being other than non-whites in their society and demanded the same equality as Caucasians. Until they were able to identify themselves as Afro-Americans and not non-Caucasians, their argument for equal rights was poor.

Let us always remember how tenuous equal rights for subgroups in any society are and remain, since constant change indicates a healthy society that thinks, breathes and grows, socially expressing human achievement. But the human rights of any sub-group in any society, unless closely monitored, will be swallowed up in a single generation, simply by the process of constant change.

The deconstructionists take a different viewpoint; they claim that the labelling itself causes discrimination and allows those with prejudice agendas to use those labels as weapons. While it is true that labels can be used as weapons, is that any reason not to acknowledge the differences of identification?

The deconstructionists do have a point though, because when in the 1970s the women's movement split off into so many splinter factions, it lost some of its momentum and some of the progress in women's liberation was slowed down for a while.

Model Building

In radical movements that are built around creating better human rights for all people, there can often be a call to de-categorise the differences between us. When the cries of

"Let's not differentiate between skin colour, race, creed, religions, linguistics, sexes, genders and sexualitys", go out in an attempt to belay prejudice, the liberation effects created are short-lived.

Seventies feminists lost their appeal to the masses when they began to be perceived as men imitating women. Palestinians lost their protection against Zionists when Palestine ceased to exist. Child protection cannot exist for 13-year-olds when they are considered adults after they reach 12 years of age. The homogenisation of identity, no matter what elements are involved, destroys some rights that previously were specific to those people's separate former identity.

I am not suggesting that the union of identities is solely destructive because it is not – it is sometimes extremely generative, but with that union must also come, to a certain degree, a loss of some civil rights, and a partial existential crisis of being.

Yes, it would in some ways be great for a die-hard socialist like myself, if we could all be treated and respected as the same, but as Karl Marx's legacy proves – reality is often far away from a philosophical idealism. Getting back to the basics of social structuring, it is plain to see that human beings and other animals have an innate desire to sort themselves into groups of identified similarities and non similarities.

We cannot help as creatures but to group together in an infinitesimal amount of different ways, and in order to do that, we need social structures, assimilation, behavioural modelling and intellectual identification. The danger that arises should we not do this is that our own singular special needs are lost in the melting pot of life, and we enter into a denial that there are always certain considerations that each and every individual needs.

The adverse effect that happens, should we become too subjective and obsessive about our own needs, is that we become devoid of consideration for others. This is the kind of accusation that is easy for political prejudice to use against minority sexes, genders and sexualities.

So, since human beings are compulsive social modellers, sorting and separating themselves into differences, I argue that it is the duty of those who are different to take the responsibility to identify themselves as being different and demand their civil and human rights.

It is the duty of the oppressed to demand their rights of the oppressor, not the duty of the oppressor to offer them
(Martin Luther King)

As I see it, we have gone through a dark age when we have denied nature and pretended that there are just two sexes and that is it. At that time anything else was classified as an abomination or sin and stripped of any claim to be part of humanity. Of course in many parts of the world this continues under the banners of righteousness of fundamental fanaticism.

So social model building not only occurs naturally but can be a very positive assertion to broaden flexibility and even educate the mind. The public may not be able to take the abolition of sex, gender or sexuality, but what it can do more easily is tolerate the extension of an existing model that started with the simple recognition of man and woman. By adding many more categories to this basic model we can now help bring the world nearer to the acceptance of identities that are other than the statistical average.

The danger in intellectuals concerned with human equality and liberation from oppression not building models that promote social tolerance is that they leave it open to the fanatical fundamentalists to build models that destroy and oppress human differences, particularly for minority groups.

What the Public Will Allow

I have always felt I have been an observer on the outside looking into society. I could never in any way describe my life as having been mainstream. Nothing I have done has been vaguely average and I think this has profoundly affected the way I think about what society will allow.

Just recently an eminent psychiatrist turned to me at a conference on human sexuality and said: "I don't think the public will allow that". He was referring to the administration of cross-sex hormones to transvestites and transgenderists. I did not understand his comment – surely society will accept anything that is easily and gently introduced. All our social attitudes were once new and strange ideologies that identified the initiators of those philosophies as radicals.

There will always be fundamentalism, which can take many forms, such as religious mania, social purity, ideological superiority and of course moral correctness. These kind of ideas can be propagated by housewife campaigners such as Mary Whitehouse, who objected to sex and swearing on British television in the 1960s to date. Jean Marie Le Pen, the French extreme right politician who would like many of the French naturalised Africans shipped back to their country of origin, is seen by some of his compatriots as sensible and by others as extreme. Mao Tse Tung, one of the initiators of the Chinese revolution, in retrospect, was not only thought of as a hero, but also as a megalomaniac.

Social anthropologists tell us there is no such thing as a static society that is unopen to new ideas and development in understanding. There is a general set of ideas within any social group which are waiting for opportunities to breed and propagate new ideas that are different from the presently accepted social rules and regulations by which their predecessors have lived.

Learning to Conceptualise New Agendas

If you are reading this work and you are a professional in the health field, you may already be aware of the differentials of sex, gender and sexuality being separate aspects of the human experience. This, however, is not necessarily true, because during my studies and in seminars I have taught, I have come across highly qualified and experienced professionals who have never before considered separating out these three aspects. What they have done is label them all under the category of sexuality which, although it may have been theoretically correct many years ago, is now no longer acceptable.

One of the drawbacks of labelling all three under human sexuality is that it tends to distort and confuse the separated issues that a client may bring to the consulting room. People who simply have gender issues may be classified or diagnosed as being a certain sexuality which, on closer examination, they plainly are not.

For the lay person trying to understand the separateness of sex, gender and sexuality it may be even easier than for some professionals because they have not previously been indoctrinated with theoretical models of human behaviour. It is, after all, easier to paint a fine work of art on a clean canvas than it is to paint over another masterpiece.

The Right to Define One's Own Sex, Gender and Sexuality

The world is a very diverse place – from the salt flats of the equator to the snow plains of Alaska. Equally as fascinating are the variations in human biology, psychology, sex, gender, sexuality, sociology and philosophy. We are the products of our own individual bodies, and our bodies and personalities are also the product of our own developmental self-image and interaction with the world. Our differences are tall, small, fat, thin, black, white, healthy, diseased, adventurous, reclusive, male, female, and everything in between.

As Einstein taught us, we are only limited by our own imaginations. Yet within different cultures there exists the social structures that we construct, to either give us the freedom to explore in safety or prohibit us from going beyond our own perceived boundaries.

In retrospect we can wonder if Madame Du Pompadour, Hitler, Winston Churchill, and Margaret Thatcher knew they were all drag, or if they felt secure in their delusionary conformity. Did they really know they were dressing up each and every day of their lives to fulfil the expectations of their audiences?

Sex, gender and sexuality can combine in a myriad of ways that produces as many kinds of human beings as there are people in the world. In the amalgamation of humanity, through the ever smaller melting pot of planet earth, each time we define ourselves we then seek to defy that definition in order to evolve.

To be human is to grow beyond what we presently are, and to confine, repress, restrict, imprison, deny or oppress that process leads to the social, mental and physical diminishing of good health. Unless we do harm to others, in an egalitarian society, we should be allowed to define ourselves as we so choose.

In Africa, physical alteration to the body comes about through stretching the neck by using huge rings. In one tribe they lengthen the earlobes and perforate them with holes up to an inch in size. Permanent tattoos are commonplace throughout many cultures, such as Celtic pagans who tattoo their spiritual identity onto their bodies. Skin piercing, branding and studding not only takes place in indigenous cultures but is now very popular in the West. In Japan cutting off the little finger was a sign of an unpaid debt and putting pearls under the skin is a form of symbolic endurance. Circumcision also takes place sometimes because the individual chooses it as a personal option.

Pregnancy and the creation of a new human being is a matter of freedom of choice, as is the option to end the life of a foetus by abortion. The self-administration of mind-altering drugs is a common occurrence and let us remember too that some teas and coffee fall into that group. Let us also not forget that billions of pounds are made daily by the medical profession in face lifts, rhinoplasty, breast alteration and a plethora of cosmetic enhancements in the name of vanity. The alteration of the body as a way of exploring experience whether physical, mental or spiritual can be found in almost every culture on earth.

For thousands of years human beings have explored

their sex, gender and sexuality continuum. So what was all the fuss about mental stability in the 20th century?

I think we have to seriously look at the roots of psychiatry and psychology in terms of being based in theological monoidealism and sociological and religious indoctrination. In philosophical terms the white, patriarchal, Christian-based cultures have behaved like the proverbial ostrich with their heads in the sand.

However, to accuse only Christianity as being the perpetrator of prejudice, bigotry and the hangman mentality would not be fair. In each and every culture the ethos of consensus is often generated, corrupted and manipulated by those with ulterior motives in the form of political gain or moral supremacy. There is and always will be profit in righteousness, especially when you learn how to franchise it.

As individuals we each have the right to take the course of events that we believe will most benefit us as human beings and enable us to be the best we can in order to contribute to society. Often when this involves the exploration of sex, gender or sexuality the societies in which we live attempt to invoke moral servitude in order to constrain the will of the individual. Precedents are always set for what is perceived as the need to educate people to conform to the so-called concepts of the masses.

Evolving as a species depends on a continuing proliferation of life experiences. There will always be differences, diversity, variation and those who seek to explore beyond statistical averages. If you fool yourself that someone else will fight for your right to do that, you will be a long time waiting.

No matter where, why, how, when, who or what you are, it is your responsibility to debate, discuss, conjecture, persuade, write about and sometimes even fight to maintain the right to define your sex, gender and sexuality as you so choose.

Honesty requires you to fully acknowledge that no one else is going to do it for you, and sex in the closet can cause serious damage to your drag.

6

The Development of the Pan-identity Model

The development of the pan-identity model of sex, gender and sexuality started at the very beginning when the first one-celled lifeform split into two, inciting differences simply by their separateness from each other. Ever since that moment each organism has strived to claim its own space and differentiate itself as an individual, quite unlike any other. This process of separateness and difference is the very essence of the development of any species. Creating differences guards against disease, attack or elimination by the mere fact that some may be resistant to noxious forces.

Multiplicity creates diversity and develops Darwin's theory of natural selection where the strongest survive and proliferate into even more diverse new species. Humans are no different and in our natural environments we continue to become more and more and more diverse. But the earth is a small planet in the overall scale of things and we now seem to have become more of an infestation upon its surface as opposed to a complement to its ecosystem.

Humankind's battle to become ever different is leading to its overpopulation and inbreeding that forces it to breed with the same. I guess this is why, at the turn of the century, we are so desperately trying to travel beyond our own solar system to give us room to diversify into an even greater number of species.

During the process of diversifying we also gather into groups, societies, nations and sects and exhibit quite the opposite behaviour – of trying to stay the same as the ones that went before. The socially constructed rules and expectations that we live by attempt to guard against this change happening too quickly and giving us a feeling of being in control of our ever changing environment.

So nature's polarisation between trying to evolve differently and socially contructed ideas about staying the same creates a pushing and pulling attitude in human beings causing them to be in a constant state of flux over what is normal and what is not. For a scientist, however, normality can never exist, only a momentary observation of what is the statistical average and even that is dependent on how the person is approaching a study.

The pan-identity model of sex, gender and sexuality has always existed in many different forms in thousands of cultures for as long as there has been differences. For the world today, though, it is a struggle of how to keep so many people on such a small planet catalogued, civilised, and peacefully coexisting without conflict. Unfortunately people are mistaken when they think that sameness will be the salvation of our species because it cannot be, and Darwin's natural selection continues.

Evolution and survival can only come about through truly acknowledging, recognising and valuing our differences, which make us all such unique individuals. It is this quality of differences that has evolved naturally in humankind in order to help us become the highest intellectual lifeform we know (which isn't to say we are – it's just what we believe).

It is the overzealous and out-of-control pursuit of sameness in humanity that could be its ultimate enemy and downfall. The search and implementation of absolute sameness, through intolerance and fanaticism has started each and every war we have ever had or ever will have. And only the ultimate acknowledgement that differences are good has ever ended those wars and freed the oppressed from oppression: The Holy Crusades, Moses out of Egypt, The American War of Independence, The French Revolution, First and Second World Wars; women's liberation, rights for children, the fight against the slave trade, racial equality, gay liberation, religious freedom and now trans and intersex identity awareness.

If the reader now thinks I am an antagonist against the over-dominance of one sort of human being over another they would be right. I am not a war-monger; however, I believe those who allow themselves to become the objects of other's discrimination become the weak and then the weaker, until they exist no more.

So, with these thoughts in mind I started some years ago to think beyond the constructed identities that society handed me on a plate. I needed to go beyond the constraints of the accepted normalities and breathe life into the differences that I observed in others. I am not silly enough to think that the pan-identity model of sex, gender and sexuality is complete or beyond its crude inception. For it is neither, but simply an evolution of the previously perceived narrow concepts that, in my childhood, constituted what the public did or did not expect us to grow up to be.

The Treatment of Sex, Gender and Sexuality States by Respectful Pansexual Usage of Sociolinguistics.

I am not only a clinician who works with members of the trans-fluid community but I am also a transsexual myself. I have blossomed as a person and as a professional after having started to undergo treatment for sex and gender confirmation some 30 years ago. My considerations here are not only from a clinical point of view but also a consensus of opinions I have noted during my 30 years of living both in and out of the trans-community.

The socialisation, medicalisation and legalisation of sex, gender, and sexuality in an ever-evolving society requires the development of language to progress, in order to bring in line the semantic use of adjectives and nouns with the true meaning of experience. Language is a fluid, active, live, dynamic, and developing tool that uses all sensory means of communication. Its use can invoke either positive or negative reaction for its deliverer or recipient.

The inappropriate use of words can cause offence. In addition, if a person misuses language, they are not only unable to communicate meaning correctly, but are also miscommunicating meaning. To call a gorilla a monkey is not to do justice to the gorilla, because it does not describe the fullness of that animal's experience; to call a ballerina a bricklayer is not only describing the ballerina incorrectly, but may also be insulting her, since it is robbing her of her status as a ballerina.

In applying the logic of these analogies to the field of sex, gender and sexuality, it is easy to see how an individual can be robbed of the validity of their subjective experience by being referred to inaccurately. Unfortunately, many clinicians working in the fields of sex, gender and sexuality do not take sufficient care to offer their clients the linguistic options of description that can respectfully represent the clients' experiences.

Many transsexuals are deeply offended when called *Female to Male* (F-M) or *Male to Female* (M-F) as they do not see this as a full representation of their experiences. These descriptions can not only be lacking in content, but can also be loaded with the meaning that the transsexual is in some way being dishonest about their proclamation of belonging to another sex or gender than that prescribed at birth.

When examined more closely, the linguistic surface structure of the terms *sex-change*, *M-F* and *F-M* reveals that such terms are misnomers when applied to the transsexual experience. They are falsehoods that do not leave any of the users with the full satisfaction of descriptive language. Their deep-root structure is, in fact, found to be a contradiction in terms. Here I am not speaking of those who find themselves sex- or gender-dysphoric or even those who may be experiencing confusion in connection with their sexuality; I am specifically referring to the true transsexual, who believes they are the opposite biological sex to the one their physical body denotes.

The English dictionary defines sex as a reproductive process and at present we cannot change people's reproductive processes, therefore it is incorrect for us to label transsexuals as *sex-changes*. There is no such thing as a sex-change in the human equation. No clinicians, surgeons or social workers can actually change the sex of their clients, so to lead them to believe we can is nothing short of dishonesty. We cannot change biological males into breeding females, or vice versa, although that may soon be possible.

What people want, when they ask for a sex-change, is for the clinician to help them affirm their believed sex. Using the term *sex-change* when talking about transsexuals, bestows biological expectations upon them that they cannot perform. It disempowers the transsexual because they feel they were never their original biological sex and do not want to have to live up to the biological expectations of breeding when they cannot.

Such bad use of language is harmful to the social, legal, psychological, and physical well-being of those in the transsexual community. In the past, ignorance could be blamed for these misleading terms. However, as we go into the new millennium, sufficient knowledge of the experiences of sex, gender and sexuality can no longer excuse such careless use of descriptive words. For a professional working in the field of sex, gender and sexuality to refer to a client as a *sex-change* is no less than negligence on the part of that professional.

The management of the masses by the few is not exclusive to the medical model or political engineering, it is also part of the systemics of all intellectual disciplines. To the general physician the management of sex factors may come under their general idiom of sexology. To the sexologist the differential, specific, descriptive requirements of language demands a greater use of terminology than that used by the GP, psychologist, psychiatrist, sociologist or gender legislator.

However, clinicians, sociologists and law-makers try to measure the transsexual condition against a bipolar male-and-female model of language that is not applicable to that specific experience.

The use of language is as an important way of treating the non sex/gender-dysphoric, sex/gender-dysphoric and the ex-sex/gender-dysphoric, as is the scalpel, hormones or surgery. How we relate to others verbally through the descriptive pronoun or personal naming is a public declaration of what that person's status is in society at large.

My name is Tracie, therefore my value as a human being equals whatever the user of my name sees, hears, and feels about me. When I say *Tracie* I am placing my own value upon myself. When others say my name, Tracie, they are placing their value upon me. If I am called *she* then I am identified within our society as female but if I am called *he* then my whole value as a human being changes regardless of my culture of origin.

In order to allow the users and recipients of language describing sex, gender and sexuality experiences to feel more comfortable, there needs to be new words which are specific to those experiences, and not borrowed from the heterosexual bipolar model. Furthermore the use of other terms of extended sex, gender and sexuality also needs to be addressed by professionals in these fields.

We are our language, and we become our descriptions, just as new descriptions are sometimes needed to relate to new realisations of experience. The following terms in the pan-identity wheel are an attempt to extend the English language to incorporate the variety of trans, intersex and androgyne experiences.

The Pan-identity Wheel

This wheel represents the diversity of human sex, gender and sexuality under the new definitions. It is not exhaustive and there may be many more – like a rainbow which has seven colours that can be broken into hundreds of distinct subcolours, which in their own right, have an important space.

To those with the kind of diverse identity that I have not included, I apologise in advance and I invite them to expand the wheel as they see fit.

Further insertions may, of course, be needed to be made on behalf of other identifiable groups.

The Pan-identity Wheel

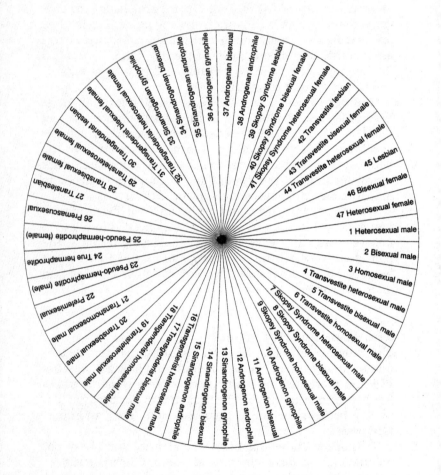

See next page for meaning of terms

MEANING OF TERMS

Pansexual

To take into account the whole span across the sexes, genders, and sexualitys. There could be issues with this word if the interpretation is seen leaning heavily towards sexuality only. Holly Devor came up with the word *transexed*, which in some circumstances, I must agree would be more applicable when referring to a person's biological determination.

Transsexual

One who may begin life as one biological sex, then implements a self-motivated, complete transformation to appear and behave as another sex. They can have an absolute conviction that they belong to the opposite sex and no amount of persuasion can dissuade these beliefs. The transsexual may undergo many medical procedures to bring their body in line with self-image.

Pseudo-hermaphrodite (male)

A male who shows secondary female physical characteristics. Sometimes there can be female organs present. The person may behave in a female manner, but not necessarily so. Surgical and hormonal assistance can be offered to determine sex, if desired. Sexual preferences may swing in any direction.

Pseudo-hermaphrodite (female)

A female who shows secondary male physical (and sometimes mental) characteristics (virilism). Surgical and hormonal assistance can be offered to determine sex, if desired. Sexual preferences may swing in any direction.

The true hermaphrodite

One who is born with organs attributed to both sexes. Surgery is often performed to determine sex, although this may be left until later. The person may be able to reproduce with either sex and have both sets of reproductive organs. Their sexual preferences may swing in any direction.

Intersex
When people are referred to as being among the intersex, it means they are between the extreme male and female spectrum (see chapter two). It does not necessarily mean that they have to be hermaphrodites or pseudo-hermaphrodites, because many of the categories of people in this book could choose to identify themselves as being an intersex group. This is to do with biological sex and has nothing to do with sexuality.

Prefemisexual (transsexual)
A transsexual who is crossing the gender barriers from male to female, but has not yet undergone genital surgery.

Femisexual (transsexual)
A transsexual who has crossed the gender barriers from male to female, having completed genital surgery.

Premascusexual (transsexual)
A transsexual who is crossing the gender barriers from female to male, but has not yet undergone genital surgery.

Mascusexual (transsexual)
A transsexual who has crossed the gender barriers from female to male, having had genital surgery.

There is a case for some people to be self-identified as mascusexual, not having undergone genital surgery because of the lack of advancement in surgical procedures. These people will, however, have had surgery such as mastectomy and hysterectomy.

Complisexual (transsexual) – either mascusexual or femisexual
One who has undergone the transsexual experience, now living in their desired gender role, having had genital surgery.

Primary Mascusexual/Femisexual

One who knows from a very early age that they are identifying as the opposite biological sex and gender to the body they have. These individuals find it impossible to live as their biological sex and begin to live as members of their believed sex and gender from their early years.

Secondary Mascusexual/Femisexual

One who discovers later in life that they are transsexual. These people may have known from an early age that they were not the sex and gender that they outwardly appeared to be, but fought against the issue, often marrying and having children. In other words, they manage to live and survive, although not necessarily happily so, as members of their biological sex

Transman/Transwoman

These are common language terms that have been used to describe those who live across the bipolar gender barrier to their original biological sex. These terms refer to transsexuals and transgenderists.

Transheterosexual (transsexual)

One who has crossed from one biological sex and gender to a realigned destination sex and gender, now having sexual orientation for their opposite sex (a straight trannie – ie a mascusexual who is attracted to females, or a femisexual who is attracted to males).

Transbisexual (transsexual)

One who has crossed from one biological sex and gender to a destination cosmetic sex, now having sexual orientation towards both females and males.

Transhomosexual (transsexual)

One who has crossed from female to male gender by realignment procedures, now having a sexual orientation towards their achieved, cosmetic sex (a homosexual new man ie a mascusexual attracted to males).

Translesbian (transsexual)

A femisexual who, when arriving at the sexually realigned destination, shows sexual orientation towards females.

Transgenderist

A person who identifies as a member of their original biological sex, but through surgery and hormones takes on the characteristics of the opposite biological sex. These people do not wish to belong to their opposite biological sex, and do not undergo genital surgery, since their genitalia are an identification with their original biological sex, which they wish to keep.

This is also used as an umbrella term in the US to cover the whole of the transcommunity.

Transgenderist heterosexual

One who starts as their original biological sex then changes their physical appearance by hormones and/or surgery to live socially as their opposite biological sex whose sexual preference is towards their opposite biological sex.

Transgenderist bisexual

One who starts as their original biological sex then changes their physical appearance by hormones and/or surgery to live socially as their opposite biological sex whose sexual preference is towards males or females.

Transgenderist homosexual

A biological male who changes their physical appearance by hormones and/or surgery to live socially as their opposite biological sex whose sexual preference is towards males.

Transgenderist lesbian

A biological female who changes their physical appearance by hormones and/or surgery to live socially as their opposite biological sex whose sexual preference is towards females.

Androgenon
A person who comes from the male end of the biological spectrum, but who identifies as being both sexes, sometimes describing themselves as the "third sex".

Androgenan
A person who comes from the female end of the biological spectrum, but who identifies as being both sexes, sometimes describing themselves as the "third sex".

Sinandrogenon
A person who comes from the male end of the biological spectrum, but who does not wish to be identified with either of the polarity biological sexes, having negative self-identification of their original biological sex and gender image. They wish to be considered as neuter.

Sinandrogenan
A person who comes from the female end of the biological spectrum, but who does not wish to be identified with either of the polarity biological sexes, having negative self-identification of their original biological sex and gender image. They wish to be considered as neuter.

Androgenon gynophile
One who starts life as a biological male, changes through hormones and/or surgery to become androgynous, whose sexual preference is towards their opposite original biological sex.

Androgenon bisexual
One who starts life as a biological male, changes through hormones and/or surgery to become androgynous, whose sexual preference is towards males or females.

Androgenon androphile
One who starts life as a biological male, changes through hormones and/or surgery to become androgynous, whose sexual preference is towards males.

Androgenan androphile
One who starts life as a biological female, changes through hormones and/or surgery to become androgynous, whose sexual preference is towards their opposite original biological sex.

Androgenan bisexual
One who starts life as a biological female, changes through hormones and/or surgery to become androgynous, whose sexual preference is towards males or females.

Androgenan gynophile
One who starts life as a biological female, changes through hormones and/or surgery to become androgynous, whose sexual preference is towards females.

Sinandrogenon gynophile
One who starts life as a biological male, changes through hormones and/or surgery to become neuter, whose sexual preference is towards their opposite original biological sex.

Sinandrogenon bisexual
One who starts life as a biological male, changes through hormones and/or surgery to become neuter, whose sexual preference is towards males or females.

Sinandrogenon androphile
One who starts life as a biological male, changes through hormones and/or surgery to become neuter, whose sexual preference is towards males.

Sinandrogenan androphile
One who starts life as a biological female, changes through hormones and/or surgery to become neuter, whose sexual preference is towards their opposite original biological sex.

Sinandrogenan bisexual
One who starts life as a biological female, changes through

hormones and/or surgery to become neuter, whose sexual preference is towards males or females.

Sinandrogenan gynophile
One who starts life as a biological female, changes through hormones and/or surgery to become neuter, whose sexual preference is towards females.

Transvestite
One who dresses in clothes associated with their opposite sex, as defined by socially acceptable norms. Of course, such a description relates to male and female only. An erotic transvestite is a person who gets sexually excited by the dressing. A social transvestite, however, simply feels more comfortable dressed in such clothes.

Skopsy Syndrome
Those who strip themselves of some characteristics of their original biological sex. However, they do not identify with their opposite biological sex. This is done for spiritual or religious reasons.

Skopsy Syndrome heterosexual male
One who starts life as a biological male and may undergo castration in order to divest themselves of their maleness, for spiritual reasons only, but still identify as male. Their sexual preference is towards females.

Skopsy Syndrome bisexual male
One who starts life as a biological male and may undergo castration in order to divest themselves of their maleness, for spiritual reasons only, but still identify as male. Their sexual preference is towards males and females.

Skopsy Syndrome homosexual
One who starts life as a biological male and may undergo castration in order to divest themselves of their maleness, for spiritual reasons only, but still identify as male. Their sexual preference is towards males.

Skopsy Syndrome heterosexual female
One who starts life as a biological female and may undergo oopherectomy (removal of the ovaries) in order to divest themselves of their femininity, for spiritual reasons only, but still identify as female. Their sexual preference is towards males.

Skopsy Syndrome bisexual female
One who starts life as a biological female and may undergo oopherectomy (removal of the ovaries) in order to divest themselves of their femininity, for spiritual reasons only, but still identify as female. Their sexual preference is towards males and females.

Skopsy Syndrome lesbian
One who starts life as a biological female and may undergo oopherectomy (removal of the ovaries) in order to divest themselves of their femininity, for spiritual reasons only, but still identify as female. Their sexual preference is towards females.

Celibacy
To be celibate is to refrain from sexual acts, either through choice or because of an inability to indulge for physical, mental, social or spiritual reasons. While in many cases it may be a matter of choice, for others it may be a matter of prohibition through beliefs, mindsets or life circumstance constraints.

Asexual
This is often confused with celibacy, as it can mean to be without sex or sexuality. A human being can never, in biological terms, be asexual, because we all must start with a genetic X constituent and therefore we have female characteristics.

I have not, at the moment, placed celibacy on the pan-identity wheel, but perhaps the insertion of this constituent of identity can rightfully find its place in the future. The pan-identity wheel must always remain a work in progress, for its finalisation defeats the object of the exercise by creating new polarised stereotypes.

Hir

This term has been used in some publications as a pronoun to represent those people who identify as being androgynous, or third gender. This could also be used as a possessive adjective by adding "S" – ie "hir's book".

Sinhir

This term could be used as a pronoun for people who identify as being sinandrogyne. Again the possessive pronoun "sinhir's" could be used.

I recently received an acknowledgement back to speak at an international conference on sex, gender and sexuality. On the bottom was a comment: "Suggestion to simplify terminology". What made me roar with laughter is that this was a group of people who were supposed to be the world leaders in developmental medicine and here they were, seeking to constrain thought.

It is absolutely imperative that language represents society's needs, desires and evolution. For an individual to sound off their opinions that people's experiences should fit into existing language is illogical. Each of us can only subjectively experience our own life patterns, and everyone has a right to expand linguistically in order to fulfil their interaction with other people and the greater environment.

Some people have been critical of attempts to create new terms, but it is not for them to tell others how they must express themselves or be addressed by others. In the next section of personal stories, it becomes obvious that there does need to be a whole new set of extended terminology in the English language, as many of the people I have interviewed have said that there have been no nouns, pronouns or adjectives for their kinds of identity.

My ultimate analogy to parallel the importance of the development of The Self-Identification Pan-identity Model of Human Sex, Gender and Sexuality comes from ancient Greece. The one Mother-Earth goddess of ancient Greece was fragmented and disempowered by the arrival of the patriarchal skygod. Her power was broken down into the six separate godheads of Demeter, Hera, Athena, Aphrodite, Persephone and Artemis.

Now is the time to emulate that strategy by dissolving the male-dominated, straight-jacketed Adam and Eve model of sexuality through the religion of science, by recognising the profusion of human diversity.

Language is a tool in medicine more frequently used than any other

LIFE

AS SEEN THROUGH
THE EYES OF THE SEX, GENDER
AND SEXUALITY DIVERSE

7

Stories and Interviews

I once again thank the people who, within this book, tell us the way it has been for them, educating us about their experiences. I caution the reader about ever thinking in terms of what should or should not be but simply ask them to embrace what is possible.

Christie Elan-Cane

I identify as a Third Gender person because I cannot identify as being male or female. In a society that will only acknowledge the gender roles of male and female I officially, legally and socially do not exist at all. I challenge society's assumptions that we are all part of a bi-polarised gendered system because now I have placed myself I find that gender has become irrelevant. I cannot relate in any way to this male-female gender system and I realise now that I was never a part of it. I had to get the surgery I needed to find my identity in a body that I was comfortable with.

I was given a female identity at birth because my body was physically female but it was never right. I did not want to be a girl although I was never terribly boyish either. Things began to get much worse when I reached puberty because I hated the changes that were happening in my body. I was very traumatised by the way my body changed dramatically almost overnight.

I felt embarrassed and ashamed of the tits that had forced their presence upon me and were now bound to my body. When I suffered a period I felt as though I had been physically violated. I realised very quickly that my feelings of negativity towards my new body were not what was regarded as acceptable or even "normal". I had to hide my feelings and hope that one day I would accept the changes and grow to like my body as it now was, but it never happened.

When I reached my twenties I began to fantasise about changing my body. I wanted to get rid of both tits. I wanted my chest to be flat, like a man's, although I did not consider myself to be a man. I wanted the womb removed. I wanted the periods to stop forever. I hated what was going on inside my body and its bloody physical manifestation. I hated my body but it went much further and deeper. I hated the idea that I was perceived as a woman.

I did not really think of myself as being a woman but I was not a man and I thought there was no alternative. I had to identify outwardly as a woman and I felt very uncomfortable in that gender role. I was repelled with the knowledge that, despite my androgynous appearance, I was still perceived as a woman. I wore large baggy clothes and found it almost impossible to look at myself when naked because I was repelled by my body and I knew that I would never be happy until I had changed it but I did not know how or where to go for help.

It never occurred to me to visit a gender clinic. While I was aware of transsexuals, I could not equate my negative feelings about my own body and gender image with transsexuality. It was outside my life experience. I certainly did not think I might be a suitable case for treatment, had the treatment I needed been available at a gender clinic. Until I was able to get the surgery that transformed my life. The only thing that mattered was getting rid of the offensive body parts. I was not capable of thinking beyond changing my body because I could not move forward while trapped inside a woman's body. I often felt that I had a male psyche because all my friends were male and I could get along with men in most situations whereas I found it very difficult to get along with women.

I felt I had nothing in common with women. I used to wish that I had been born a man and I frequently dressed as a man and I liked to confuse people. I would get a buzz when I walked down the street and I heard whispered voices in my direction: "is that a man or a woman?" But I could never honestly say that I felt I actually was a man. That is the fundamental difference between someone like myself and a female-to-male transsexual. I was not a man born into a woman's body, just wrongly born into a woman's body and gender role.

I was 26 years old before I finally found the courage to do something positive about changing my body. This was the beginning of a long and arduous attempt to find a surgeon who would be willing to perform a double mastectomy. It took three years before I was able to find a surgeon who was willing to help and then it took another two years for me to raise the necessary money to pay for it. During this time there were too many disappointments to mention and there were times I felt suicidal because my situation seemed to be hopeless. I had dark moments where I began to wonder whether I was paying a terrible price for believing I could cheat nature. But I got there in the end and I was finally able to have both tits removed at a private hospital in central London.

It had taken so long that I could not dare to believe it was real until it was over. I had not told a single person what I was doing. None of my friends or acquaintances had any idea where I was. It hurt that I felt I could not talk about something that was so vital to my existence. I was very afraid of getting a negative reaction when I most needed support and so I decided to say nothing, at least until I had had the operation. I had never had any feelings of shame about what I was wanting to do, only regret that my body had worked against me in the first place.

It felt so strange to finally be there at the hospital. I had borrowed most of the money to pay for the surgery with a series of loans which I had no real way of repaying. I was worried about the trouble I knew I would get into but I figured that, in the circumstances, the repossession man could not do very much. Some of the hospital staff treated me as though I was a curiosity but most of them were very nice. The anaesthetist asked me whether I was sure I wanted to proceed with this operation before administering the anaesthetic and I knew that if I did not go through with this now I would regret it for the rest of my life.

I awoke several hours later and I was aware of a nurse standing by the bed. I asked her whether the operation had been done and received the reply that the operation was a success. I was not able to see my body but I did manage to lift my hands to my chest and I could feel through the bandages that I was flat chested. I cannot describe how I felt at that moment, other than it was the happiest moment of my life.

The operation was a success and I made a quick recovery and I felt almost immediately that I had embarked on a journey. Not a physical journey but rather a journey of self-discovery. I could not really understand the motivation that compelled me to change my body and when I thought about it there were more questions raised than answers. The only thing I felt sure about was that I had never felt so positive about myself and that I would never regret the action I had taken, despite the fight I had had with the so-called medical professionals I had encountered along the way who had refused to help me. I had done it anyway and it felt so right. I had proved to myself that I was right all along. I felt that my position was vindicated and it was not long before I started thinking seriously about the next stage of my transformation.

I felt that I had somehow got away with having the mastectomy but I would have to go through the NHS to get a hysterectomy and I dreaded the anticipated battle. I waited nearly two years before I presented myself to a gynaecological clinic and told them I wanted a hysterectomy and asked whether they could help.

In the event I was fortunate and got a sympathetic hearing and I was referred to a consultant within a few weeks. I remember the consultant examined me and then asked me whether I felt myself to be a man or a woman and I was quite startled by this question. I realised I did not know the answer but I wondered whether this was some kind of trick question to test my mental stability, and I am ashamed to say I replied that I felt more like a woman because that was how I had always lived. As it turned out,

121

I was asked the question to determine whether the ovaries were to be removed. I suppose I would have to say anything in order to get this operation but it was good to feel that now I was dealing with people that were on my side.

After I had the hysterectomy I knew that I had reached the place where I wanted to be. I had the physicality I wanted and which felt completely right for me, the feeling that I was on a journey had intensified throughout the intervening two years and I now felt compelled to find an identity I felt comfortable with. I knew I was not a woman and that I had never been a woman. So many things about my life that had confused me in the past were now somehow coming together and falling into place. It was like I had spent my life shrouded in a fog and the veil was being lifted. Now I was no longer trapped in the body of a woman there was no need to pretend anymore that I was a woman. I briefly flirted with the notion of adopting a male persona but the idea was never realistic because I could not have passed full time as a man without unwanted hormone treatment and I did not feel that I was a man.

I did not see why I should have to swap one identity that was wrong and which would ultimately make me unhappy. I had to accept I was neither male nor female. This was something I knew would be beyond the comprehension of most people and that I would be marginalised to the extent that I had no place at all in mainstream society, but I had no choice other than to accept what I knew, after a long and tortuous journey, to be true.

I have now lived as a Third Gender person for nearly seven years and I am used to being treated as a freak. Unable to complete a form that asks my sex and gives the options M/F, not having a title that I can relate to (Mr and Ms being inappropriate as are *he* and *she)* and experiencing difficulty in every social situation except among other transgendered people, I rage and agonise over the limitations that have been placed on my life. It is only now that I have had to place myself outside a gender system I cannot adhere to, that I have come to realise just how outmoded and irrelevant that gender system is.

Bini

Unlike most people I don't remember having rigid structures in my childhood. Having been born and raised in
India for the first five years of my life, I then went on a
world tour of the 60's hippie communes and rock concerts
with my mother, who was well heeled and bohemian. My
father, I believe, was tall, blonde and blue-eyed, like me,
but since I was a child of passion, and he was a married
British civil servant, we have never met. Gran and grand-
dad, however, adored me, calling me their "Raphaelite
Angel" and left a trust that enabled me to live in a way that
meant I could do anything I wanted, anywhere, at anytime.
The only stipulation in the will was that I had to go back
to India for 4 months of every year to teach English and
school with the nuns, which has turned out to be a blessing not a chore.

As a child, people naturally assumed I was a girl
because I was so pretty, covered from head to toe in flower
power clothes, beads, bangles and being a very loving free
spirit. Mother choose never to correct them and always
told me I had to find my own way in the world and that
convention would not be my path as it had not been hers.
She was only half right as it happened because I guess I
am a mixure of the establishment ie of my grandparents'
lifestyles and the free spirit of mother, who when last seen,
was negotiating land rights for Amazonian Indians.

I fell in love with a Bombay politician when I was 16,
and although I know he was besotted with me too, his family did the best they could to make me leave the country
for fear of scandal. I remember that not being able to see
him again hurt so much that I decided not to tie my existence to any one human being ever again.

In coming into my inheritance at 17, I decided I had
become too masculine and underwent castration to allow
myself to be androgynous which was the most comfortable
place for me to be in what the West calls the sex and gender identity. For me it was not a matter of comparatives
because androgyny was where I felt I had always been and
I had no intentions of letting the testosterone of manhood

take that away. I've never missed sex as it has never been a big thing for me since I was brought up surrounded by concepts of love and spirituality. I took female hormones to make me less masculine, but when I grew breasts I had them removed because I have never wanted to be a woman, just me. Facial hair was never a problem because it came for a time in my teens and then was removed by electrolysis after I had been castrated, or rebirthed as I like to think of it. I can pass as either male or female since at 40 I still have long blond hair and dress in an androgynous style.

I've known many hijra and sex changes too, but I never identified with what they were trying to achieve. In fact I have only ever met two other people who identify like me in my entire life. One was a Buddhist monk and the other a fashion designer who lived a double life so as not to harm their career. I suppose there are many out there but I am very much a recluse who does not meet people. In public places it could sometimes prove dangerous for me, since people often become hostile when confronted with something they do not understand.

When I was 25, one of the nuns had an existential crisis of being and decided she did not want to wear the habit anymore but wished to stay on and teach the children. Since my house was next door she came to live with me and we became soul mates. I am very close to her but I love to travel and spend a great deal of my time visiting different countries and writing about art and politics. I have several pseudo names as I am wise enough to know the world wants to try to fit me into boxes, or stereotype any talents I have to fit their concepts of what should be male and female.

The people who have least trouble with the androgynous way I present myself are the children I teach at home. All they have ever known since they were small is the way I present myself and it does not occur to them to question beyond initial curiosity. When they grow up, because India is such a diverse place, they try to bring their children to be taught in my classes too.

My choice to live my life androgynously as I do, representing both male and female, I suppose had a certain element of compulsion when I look back. It was, however, a choice and had I chosen to be male or a transsexual female then people, I think, generally would have thought it quite normal in some ways. If I lived my life again, and I think I might, I would make the same decisions and have the same path because I am happy, free and most of all fortunately can pass as both sexes in a world that is concerned with my gender more than it ought to be.

David (Western Australia)

I was born a male and named as such. After a couple of weeks of not feeding properly some tests were done and it was found that I had congenital adrenal hyperplasia (Addison's Disease). At about one and a half years I was taken to Princess Margaret Hospital for "investigative surgery". I don't know what inspired them to look inside – I assume my penis wasn't normal. About seven months later they cut it off.

As far as I can guess, doctors presumed my penis was an abnormality, when it could equally have been construed it was very abnormal for a bloke to have a uterus and no vagina. Anyway, they decided for my parents and me I was going to be raised as a girl.

The difficulty of having to behave like a girl through school wasn't a very enjoyable experience, and I won't dwell on it; suffice to say, if a normal two-year-old boy lost his penis in an accident it'd be inconceivable to expect him to put on a dress and behave like a girl for the rest of his life – which is what I feel I was expected to do.

At about 14 I was sent to a girls' boarding school, which in most circumstances would be a bloke's dream come true, but having to constantly resist the temptation made it a bit of a nightmare really. One of the most embarrassing moments was when I was reading aloud in class and my voice broke. Having to do swimming classes when it was quite obvious I didn't have a girl's body wasn't a lot less humiliating.

At some stage in the next year or so I was put in hospital where I believe I was to be made more like a female. A doctor I hadn't met before came in to tell me what they planned to do. That was when I said I didn't want that. He left the room without saying anything, and the endocrinologist came down a bit later and said he was going to refer me to a psychiatrist. That was the ultimate insult. Having first been denied by doctors my physical sexuality, it seemed my mental state was also going to be determined.

During my stay at the Hospital's D block (D for demented, I was sure) I was told by a nurse she was taking me for a test somewhere. Upon asking what sort of test, she said an EEG and I'd have to ask the doctor (psychiatrist) if I wanted to know what for (doctors were still expecting me to ask them what the hell was going on). Anyway, at the electroencephalograph place, after having all the wires stuck to my head, I was told to relax and look at some damn picture on the wall. I didn't know what any of this was about, so I looked anywhere but at the picture and hoped the whole lot of them would drop dead and leave me alone.

About a year later I had surgery, which I suppose can only be described as a hysterectomy. The endocrinologist referred me to a plastic surgeon. When I was about 18 he and a urologist constructed from my forearm a replacement for what I lost at two. After the operation the surgeon told me there was a baby in PMH with the same problem I'd been born with – they were going to cut his off too. From my experience I thought that'd be the wrong thing to do.

I expect doctors, like most other people, don't make mistakes intentionally. Cutting off the part of the anatomy which distinguishes a boy from a girl seems a very confident decision to make, especially if there's no outward indication the child's a girl. Since my initial operation, no doctor involved has contacted me to explain why they thought it was necessary, or find out if it was the right thing to do to me – which it wasn't.

I expect it's all been fairly difficult for my parents, brothers, relatives and everyone I've known, to come to terms with my past, and they probably had, and have still, as many doubts and unanswered questions as I did.

Alexia

From what I remember, starting out as a transsexual in the early 1970s did not prove to be that much of a problem. For those fortunate enough to "light the fuse" as teenagers it was not exactly uncharted territory.

A decade earlier April Ashley, a famous British transsexual who had already established herself as a household name, may well have been the cause célèbre behind the music industry's androgynous hijack. Yet despite good efforts from Queen, Bowie and Marc Bolan they were far too pedestrian to capture my imagination.

Spoiled for choice, the New York Dolls were much more inspiring. Great big panda-eyed six footers in crippling stilettos and Kabuki make-up, all on drugs, naturally. I could also relate to their lyrics, for example: "Meanwhile, back in the jungle" which said it all for growing up in the village from hell.

That gave naff a whole new meaning; in fact I still get excited when I hear of a demolition plan to make way for a new motorway. Sadly, only the good ones get bulldozers. While my parents took being pillars of the community to some far-off horizon, my sister married a vicar.

The only saving grace was my grandmother's hypochondria – that was bags of fun and meant that the house was free on Sundays while they took off with all the unnecessary medicines. I thought I looked fabulous cycling down the High Street in a maxi skirt and purple eye shadow but the parishioners didn't. It had the same effect on them as the full moon on a pack of wolves.

My mind was made up anyway. It was obvious, sod this lot, jack in the school tie and move to London to live as a woman. It is amazing how clear everything is when you're 16 and within a year I was a transsexual prostitute hooked on barbiturates and living in Earl's Court. Well, I guess that was obvious too.

The best way to overcome temptation is to yield to it and this wasn't the time or the place to be a killjoy. It encapsulated everything I had ever dreamed of: freedom of choice, meeting other transsexuals and the means to try all the illegal substances. Fortunately the prescriptive ones triumphed, in the form of breasts.

When I was 19 I had those augmented by a Harley Street surgeon, highly recommended and an absolute magician. He must have been, because a year later Esther Rantzen, a chat show host, exposed him as a dentist. I thought there was something odd when he offered me a large whisky after the op, not helped by the fact that his shaky hands couldn't even hold the bottle.

In those days my friends were far too glamorous to worry about fate. "You pays your money and you takes your chances." Besides, wangling scripts out of a Harley Street quack was almost a way of life. Imagine trying to relate the tit job story to a room full of "sisters" where there wasn't a steady hand among them.

With the 1980s came the most powerful drug of all – love. Pig one and pig two. Pig one was a bank robber who could have charmed the knickers off a nun. The trouble was that he kept getting caught so I still had to turn tricks in between his prison sentences.

The sex was very intense. He liked doing it with a vengeance, usually after one of our many fights. We had this fantastic idea that following his next pull-off, I would have my sex-change operation and we would go to live in Australia. Dream on! I finished up in a Soho clip joint and he got 14 years.

It was there that I met pig two, a moment of weakness, on my behalf. I should have heard the alarm bells ringing when he ended up legless on the Château MacDuff. Very surprising as the place didn't even have a drinks licence. I think it originally left the shelf as Galloway's cough syrup.

Had I known then that I was about to spend the next 10 years of my life with this person I would have drunk it myself. It takes a lot more than an addictive personality to live as a housewife in Germany. Whatever they tell you, swapping thigh length boots for sensible court shoes and pencil skirts invariably takes its toll.

Actually that was the least of my worries. He developed a cocaine habit and became a serious gambler. Fine by me. However, kicking it was a different story, especially when the God-squad syndrome set in. If he did it to frighten me it worked, I was up and out of there as fast as a rat up a drainpipe. Eventually he went back to live with his wife so I suppose every silver lining has a cloud.

Back in London I was amazed by how much everything had changed. The telephone boxes had become like wallpapered sex libraries. In one I had to take down an advertisement just to let some light in. Had to get myself fluent too in all the trans-new-speak. I had always thought that I was a pre-op transsexual but apparently that's an anachronism.

"Alexia, thy name is Transgender" they now tell me. It's not as if it reaches out and grabs me. Categorically speaking it's "every woman for himself". It leaves me none the wiser; I mean – what is the difference between a Siamese sex change and a Thai post-op?

Personally, whenever I face the mirror and drop the towel I feel completely normal. By some strange twist of dentistry I see perfect 38C cup breasts and matching genitalia. Stuck for a label, I'd say that I am an unfinished symphony. Who knows, I might have another nose job?

Maria

I am a transsexual "new woman". My age is a post carboniferous (since I gave up smoking) – 47 although my youngest daughter's description of me is of being from the dinosaur's Jurassic era. I was married for 17 very unhappy years hoping that my innermost feelings would subside but they never did, so in 1991 at the age of 41, after a year of counselling and prevarication I embarked on the change of lifestyle that has led me to where I am today.

I commenced hormone therapy on my birthday and then moved out of my home in Middlesex and away from my children to live in Eastbourne. I remained in regular contact with my eldest daughter to whom I'd explained my status after a row with my partner, during which she had raised the spectre of exposure of my condition in the local neighbourhood.

My son was told about me by a family friend and he came to meet me in Eastbourne; it didn't seem to phase him at all. I used to spend more money on phoning the children than on food and their mother was never in when I called. They were suffering terribly as for seven months I stayed on the sidelines, an unwilling second-hand witness to their systematic abuse, until I could stomach no more. On discovering my eldest had been ejected from home for the second time I returned to take over responsibility for her care. All three expressed a wish to live with me but only the older two were able to join me by their own volition when we were forced into emergency accommodation.

I had to undertake a court action to try to obtain a Residency Order for my youngest. It was very hard to beat the inherent bias of the Court Welfare Services but I planned it like a military operation and when it eventually arrived the report was reasonably favourable.

I had a large advantage insofar as the children hated my former spouse's boyfriend. The school performance of my youngest went straight downhill when I left, levelled off for a while and plumbed to new depths on my ex-partner's new boyfriend's involvement. Her mother went back on every contact arrangement she made and blamed me for all her problems. She was forced to give me temporary care of my daughter over the post-Christmas holiday period in 1992/93 and allowed me to have her full time at the end of January.

I won when she gave me voluntary custody on the advice of her counsel before the hearing. It seems that the boyfriend had taken offence at the court welfare's report and he was reluctant in the extreme to commit himself to appearing in court, particularly as he had not the slightest interest in anyone else's children other than as a possible future sexual conquest. My transsexuality hasn't been an affliction on my children nor any drawback to their development. If anything it has made them more understanding and tolerant of others. And I'm sure it will be the same for the lovely grandchildren I have, and I see that bringing great joy into my life.

Frankie

My mother and father split up when I was five years old but even before this my father was seldom at home as he worked away. He had a mistress whom he had been seeing since before I was born. He later married this woman. She was to become his third wife. I have two older sisters, one older brother and one younger half brother. My older brother is 16 years my senior and left home when I was still very young, so from an early age I lived only around females. My mother was not a particularly nurturing parent and my sisters understandably took their cue from her. Love was never really mentioned among our family nor were we affectionate with each other, honest or open about the way we felt. We lived in an atmosphere of suppressed emotions. As a child these remote females were the only real role models I had.

I remember that at about the age of six I went and collected some of my mother's and sister's clothes from their rooms and put them into my own chest of drawers. A couple of days later they just vanished. I'm not sure why I did this but I do remember having a lot of strange feelings and dreams. I began having dreams and daydreams in which I was a fully grown woman. In some of these dreams I had a small child. I now believe that this child was also me. I was physically affectionate to this child and encouraged him to be feminine and to wear female things.

I began secretly wearing my sister's and mother's underwear and afterwards carefully replacing it where I had found it. Nobody knew what I was doing and I certainly didn't talk to anyone about it but somehow, in the repressed atmosphere of the house, I got the idea that what I was doing was wrong. I soon became quite paranoid and obsessive about it. These feelings must have been leaking into other areas of my life because I remember when I was seven and eight I was having this weird delusion in which I believed that my whole life was being filmed. I used to sit on the loo and replay this film in my head.

We had already moved house three times by the time I had begun cross-dressing and what friends I did have I was now separated from. I felt lonely and disconnected from people so I a spent a lot of time in the world of my imagination. My secret femininity further compounded these feelings of isolation. I constructed a fantasy world where things went the way I wanted them to. It was a world where I was special and appreciated, a world where I impressed people and I was loved. I felt like a ghost, half in this world and half in the world of my imagination. In my progress among the practicalities of everyday life and in my interaction with other people I did not live up to the expectations I had created in my daydreams.

I was constantly disappointed in myself. I also became rebellious and resentful towards people and towards the world in general, which I found to be painfully mundane in comparison to the world of my imagination and to the way that I felt when I secretly cross-dressed. If ever I was told what to do I felt as if my very nature was being attacked; I took it as a reproach to the way that I was. To escape from the pain of these feelings I would become stubborn and angry or I retreated back into my fantasies, often taking vengeful thoughts with me.

I was frustrated by my apparent lack of effectiveness. Other children seemed to have a lust for life that I did not possess. I didn't feel close to anyone. I didn't feel that I even knew anyone or that anyone knew me. I felt like an alien that had just dropped from another planet, unsure of how to behave and unable to relate. I spent a lot of time mooning around in the garden. I would poke about in ants and wasps nests, I was always turning over stones or pieces of dead wood to see what creepy crawlies I could find. I was something of a nature boy and a dreamer.

When I was about nine I found a magazine called *The Lesbians' Review* among my older brother's things. It was while looking at this that I experienced my first sexual feelings. This magazine, combined with my transvestism and my feelings of femininity assisted my sexuality in fixing itself to all things feminine.

We moved house again, this time to a much smaller place. I lived there with my mother and sister, who is three years older than me and I continued to secretly wear their clothes. From the age of about 11, it became an auto- erotic ritual and I suppose something like an addiction. Cross-dressing began to give me intense sexual feelings and a powerful adrenaline buzz brought on by my absolute dread of being caught. These two feelings combined put me into what I can only describe as a heightened state of awareness and excitement. My senses seem to sharpen into an acute alertness as I listened for a key in the door, footsteps on the path or my mother's car door banging. I can now see that my fears around getting caught greatly contributed to the intensity of the experience. It worked a bit like this:

A powerful tension existed between my sexual arousal and my fear of being discovered. At a certain point, while masturbating, these two feelings would begin to feed off each other, causing the excitement to climb higher and higher in breathtaking leaps until I was virtually vibrating between them and in a state of euphoria. Orgasm was often extremely intense, almost ecstatic. However, when my arousal subsided along with the convulsions this tension would quite suddenly snap. It seems that without the arousal to keep the, what was by now extremely inflated, fear in check I was left in a very vulnerable state. Terror would explode in on me, causing me to panic. I would remove and replace the clothes as fast I could, all the while totally convinced that, even though I may have been cross-dressed for an hour or more, any second I was about to get caught.

It was as if I believed that getting caught would quite literally cause me to die of humiliation. At this point I would often become aware that my body was emitting a very particular scent. I don't know if this odour is a hormonal thing or something to do with all the adrenaline flying around in my system or what. To this day I often emit this peculiar odour when crossdressed; maybe it's testosterone abandoning ship in disgust, I don't know but I am curious to know if there are any other trannies out there who have experienced the same thing. After this I would take a bath, feeling deeply ashamed, confused and full of self-loathing.

When I had calmed down I would experience a kind of depression similar to the feelings associated with coming down off stimulant-type drugs. In later years these feelings would often lead me straight to the pub where, after having a few drinks, I would begin to feel all right again and able to look people in the eye. This is the negative cycle that I became locked into with my transvestism for many years.

I became involved in the drug culture from an early age. It began with sniffing petrol fumes when I was about 12 and progressed through cannabis, alcohol, amphetamines, LSD, magic mushrooms, Ecstasy and ketamine to heroin, crack cocaine, methadone and various other prescription drugs. I would often cross-dress when I was coming down off hallucinogens. I remember that I once dressed up as a gypsy fortune teller and sat around waiting for my mother to come home, totally convinced that I would be able to predict her future. She was detained and never came home that day.

I was quietly rebellious at school and often skived off to dress up at home while my mother was at work. I was expelled from school when I was 15. When I was 16 I got a job and bought some feminine clothes of my own. At this time I was seeing a girl from the office where I was working. One night we made love with me wearing her clothes. It was a spontaneous thing, it only happened the once. She didn't know about my transvestism and I was too afraid to tell her.

By the time I was 18 there was just me and my mother left in the house. One night I came home really drunk and upset. I had still not told anyone about my cross-dressing and the burden of carrying around this secret was becoming too much for me to handle so I decided to tell my mother. Unfortunately this did not go well. My being drunk did not help but this was the only way I could get the courage to talk about it. Her reaction was quite negative and it was obvious that she really did not want to know. I was devastated and felt really ashamed and rejected. We were not to talk about it again for another 10 years. Soon after this she asked me to leave home, she says, because of my drug taking.

I have been playing the guitar since the age of 14 and had been involved with a couple of bands so when I left my mother's house I linked up with some musician friends and rented a large house with them. I also got a new job as a truck driver and spent much of the next seven years travelling and working abroad. It was during this time that I found out that I was not strictly heterosexual. I met a transgendered woman in a bar in Hamburg. By the time I'd found out that she was not a biological woman I had also found out that I didn't mind. This new twist to my sexuality confused me for some time afterwards until I came to accept it but I did not tell anyone about it, I was too ashamed. I continued to cross-dress in private when I was home.

Every now and then I would get so full of self-loathing that I would throw all my trannie things away. I still believed that what I was doing was wrong and that if I tried hard enough I could change myself. I just ended up buying more, wasting a lot of money and losing loads of nice things. On one occasion I burnt all my clothes, make-up etc on a bonfire in the garden when no one was around. I was jumping about in quite a state shouting "Out...Out" as if my transvestism were some kind of demon that could be exorcised.

Up to this point I had told just a couple of girlfriends but had never talked about it in any depth. They had both received this information with a strange expression, quickly said that they weren't bothered then never referred to it again. I didn't push the point – it was all too scary for me.

When I was 25 I was made redundant and went off travelling in India. One of the many weird and wonderful things that I saw there was a troop of travelling trannie musicians. I asked an old man about them. He said "they are not man, not woman, they are receiving a penalty kick from God!" It made me laugh at the time but now I wonder whether this man wasn't actually saying something positive about them. I had automatically taken this to mean that God had awarded a penalty against them. In fact he may just as well have been saying that they had been given an easy shot at goal. I loved India but it was there that I first encountered opium.

On my return to England I moved to London. For the first two years I lived in Kings Cross with a girlfriend from my home town in Dorset. I was suppressing my transvestism again. I was drinking quite heavily and taking lots of drugs. I was also working hard, driving in the daytime and waiting on tables in the evenings. When this relationship ended I began squatting. During the next six years I must have moved house about 15 times.

I began to talk more openly about my cross-dressing and visited a few makeover establishments around town. I was 29 when I first went out dressed, I felt comfortable and confident. Nobody could believe that this was my first time out. After this I went to the Way Out Club, Ron Storm's, Partners Wine Bar and the Da Pucht Club a few times but mostly I would go out drinking in Camden Town and to various squat raves that were happening at the time. I had a couple of bisexual experiences with other transvestites and was beginning to accept myself and realised that I was never going to change this side of myself and therefore I may as well enjoy it but really I was still very insecure about it.

I was playing bass in a band at this time and would occasionally perform dressed up. I had a girlfriend at this time who seemed to enjoy my transvestism and she was very encouraging but with hindsight I can see that I was still resisting my true nature. I was feeling self-destructive and I started messing around with heroin when I was about 30.

I finished with this partner and took up with someone else. I lived with my new partner in a semi-derelict house in Hackney and we hit the drugs in a big way. We were soon both addicted to heroin and were bingeing heavily on crack cocaine, often injecting both of them together. We became more like partners in crime than lovers. My habit drove me to theft, fraud, drug dealing, prostitution and begging on the street. My whole life became about three things: acquiring the money for drugs, buying and selling drugs and taking drugs. Sad but true! The drugs suppressed everything that was positive in my life, including my transvestism.

In August 1997 I had some luck. I got a council flat in Stoke Newington and a social worker. I continued to use drugs until November that year when I got a place in detox' and from there into a residential rehab' in Islington where I am now. The first three weeks were the worst but since then I have been feeling better almost every day. The programme here consists of daily group therapy, one-to-one counselling, integral healing, shiatsu and acupuncture as well as lessons in computing, photography and video, relapse awareness and fitness.

I did not intend to out myself as a trannie but I soon realised that I would have to in order to be true to myself and my peers and the group. The other residents have been mostly male, many of them ex-convicts. None of them had really encountered transvestism before.

I planned my revelation very carefully in order to be prepared for any negative reaction. Initially I faced a lot of prejudice and open hostility, which was hurtful and sometimes difficult to endure but I felt strong and dealt with each situation as it arose. I soon realised that this was an invaluable and possibly unique opportunity in my life to really explore my feelings, confront my fears and maybe even build some self-esteem out of years of self-loathing. After all, it is a rare thing to be in a place where people's fears and prejudices are actually confronted and the resulting issues dealt with. The most difficult thing has been talking to the group about the auto-erotic side of my cross-dressing. I now regularly cross-dress both in the hostel and at the skills centre where we spend most of our day. My peers are now much more comfortable around me, as am I around them. We have even been out as a community to an Narcotics Anonymous rave with me dressed. There were no problems and we had a lot of fun.

Meeting my mother and sister dressed was another major milestone for me. They came a hundred miles to visit me at the hostel and were really sweet and supportive. It means so much to me to have their acceptance even though we are not a close family. I can't tell you what a relief that is.

My experience here has made me realise that gaining acceptance as a trannie is an ongoing process. It is a journey without destination, the important thing being the manner in which I travel. People's fears and prejudices are a bit like the proverbial onion, remove one layer and another appears. It requires a lot of sensitivity, understanding and respect if they are to be overcome. It is as difficult for other people to unlearn their negative patterns of behaviour as it is for me to unlearn mine. Anger can be useful too but must be employed with responsibility and intelligence. Be an actor not a reactor, as they are fond of saying here.

As a transvestite I now believe that I am part of a valid and ancient tradition designed by nature. It is up to me to calculate my risks and have the courage to merge with my destiny. It is up to me to play my part in carrying this tradition into an uncertain future.

Chris

Starting life abroad, as a small and shy boy, I remember vividly getting ready for my first day at school. It probably sounds a bit trivial but it was my socks that upset me! I had been so used to wearing white socks and was deeply shocked when I discovered that the school uniform for boys included rough grey socks that looked more like brillo pads than things to put on your feet. I suppose it was like I was suddenly being introduced to the world of boys

– a land I did not know. I belonged to a species that was alien to me.

I loved spending time with girls. When I was in high school we had this association we called the "People people" which was made up of what we felt were visionaries. We found, behind the school, an area of high bushes that we made a tunnel in. This became a secret little hideaway where we would write poetry and have discussions about life. Admittedly we also sometimes smoked a little marijuana, a habit I have since dispensed with.

I did not realise at the time but these were sometimes the girls that had a bit of a reputation. I know that two of them (we were all about 16 or so) used to pretend to be prostitutes and pick up men, and then run away having pocketed the profits. We were a real mix of people, but the main thing was that they were all girls. This did not seem strange to me at the time. I later realised that some boys thought I was quite cool because I spent so much time with these racy girls.

But in all this I always had a big problem with true romance. The problem is that I did not know how to go about it, or even that it existed. It was only after some time that I became aware of this thing called sex. You know how people are colour blind? Well I think I was "sex-blind". If I did fall in love it was always from afar. I was always falling in love with unreachable goddesses. I would write endless dreamy poems and have great conversations about life and other profundities.

But I was a boy and I was supposed to make some kind of romantic overture. I'm sure a part of my brain was not connected, and I would just freeze. Even if a more confident girl made herself known to me, I would still find it impossible to make a move. I remember a girl taking me for a walk in a very secluded area near a beach as I rabbited on about life and the meaning of the universe...

Actually my first sexual encounter was with a man. I had been hitchhiking, as one did in the 70s, home after my performance in an opera. The guys in the car suggested I go along to a barbecue. I agreed and went along. It was only later on that I suddenly became aware that I was getting some attention. Without knowing what was happening, I knew all the rules. I knew how to get attention and I sub-consciously loved it. I still did not understand that this might have something to do with sex.

On the way home we discovered that they were suddenly low on petrol. It meant that I would have to sleep over at the home of the driver of the car. I can't remember his name, but I'll call him Pete. Pete had been doing this attentive thing throughout the evening and some other layer of my brain understood it all. I did not think to question his integrity. So I spent the evening at his place. Although it was not full sex, it was enough to disturb me deeply. I did not mind him, and could feel comfortable with all that. It was me that was all wrong. For many years later I would imagine being a woman with him.

When I came to England as a fresh-faced 20-year-old I was in a bit of a state. I had become obsessive about cross-dressing and eventually found my way to Charing Cross Hospital and the Gender Identity Clinic. I remember getting my first hormones, and taking the first pill. I immediately felt all good inside. Silly, I know, but it's how I felt. Little did I know how much more there was to it...

I had a rather stormy time with my girlfriend at the time, and she eventually left me lying in a bit of a heap in my tiny flat in South London. It was a long time before I started getting any confidence, and that passage between genders is a very tricky one. I was never terribly confident as I was not really like the "proper" transsexuals I had met. They seemed much more feminine, and much more outgoing. Sometimes I thought that maybe I was just a fraud. I suppose it is all too easy to underestimate how big a thing it is to create a whole new life, and that it's not just like "slipping into something more comfortable".

Whenever I read about people "changing gender" they always seem to have a big dip in their career. In my case it seemed to work the other way round. My career really took off when I started living as a woman, and I did really well. I was in a band a year or two later when I met my first official boyfriend. He was a lovely and gentle man. He was very tall (which suited me), kind and funny and most of all, he loved me. It was the first time for me to be in a relationship with a man. He was completely straight of course, and I would see his parents every Sunday for lunch, and go out with his circle of friends too. I stayed with him for some years, till about six months after the operation...

After that I seemed to gravitate to other women and just seemed to feel more comfortable like that. The first time was as I was sitting in a pub in Soho after work. I just got talking to this beautiful young American musician who was working part time in the pub. I did not think of anything romantic and we just spent a lot of time talking. Nevertheless, the next morning I woke up upstairs in the pub. It was my first introduction to the gay women's scene, and I found it a bit daunting at first as she was quite the "Belle of the ball" at all these amazing clubs, and I am a little shy even these days.

Well I was still going through so many changes and we eventually parted company. After a few more "adventures", I met an Oriental young woman. My life changed a lot when I met her. She did not seem to see gender in the way most people see it. Perhaps my experiences have given me very sensitive antennae. I feel immediately where someone is coming from, in terms of gender. I have met very few people like this.

Our relationship flourished and we lived together. I had never been with someone who cared for my life, going far deeper than just emotion. Perhaps it sounds a little melodramatic, but I really felt that I had not met someone who cared for me before, and that in some strange way she had saved my life. I feel so moved that she came along when she did. But time was running out...her visa was about to expire. So eventually there I was at the airport waving her goodbye. Our relationship entered a new, and rather disembodied, phase. We had long, expensive silences on the phone, and then I would have to phone back just to make sure.

For two years we agonised about how to be in the same

country. I was aware that although I was living as a woman, the law regarded me as male. I thought perhaps I could use this to my advantage, and get married. In the end it proved far too complicated. Eventually, getting sick of it all, I just thought "Oh hell I'll just go back and live as a man and then we could get married." So we did. So there I was, after living as a woman for 7 years, back as a bloke. It took much more courage than starting to live as a woman. Perhaps because it was not something I had much enthusiasm for.

Nevertheless...I had had a lurking suspicion that I really should try to live as a man. I felt that even though it was abhorrent to me, I should really really try and live in my original gender. I never wanted to live as a man, but I felt I would try my best.

Going back to living as a man was not easy, especially in my work, but I always have had good friends and lots of support. I went on to taking testosterone and lived as a man for about 6 years. It's weird really...the male hormones did not really do much to me till the last year or so. Then it suddenly seemed that my sex drive was skyrocketing, I was getting panicky, and worst of all, I was getting hairy. I was getting hair in places I had never had hair. My resolve strengthened. I remember saying to the psychotherapist: "I don't know much about gender but I know about hair. If I am hairy I would rather die!" She was surprised to find such strong feelings in such a seemingly vague person.

Over six months or so I gradually got more clear. I did not want to fall into the trap of thinking too far ahead of myself. I was no spring chicken now and had to be careful. Here I was in a good job, with good relations within our extended family. I wanted to avoid taking any steps that I was not fully ready for. All I was sure of was my body. Over a period of some months I found a wonderful endocrinologist. I have never felt so respected by a doctor. He found that I had suffered some bone loss, and certainly needed to be on some hormones. When he had to do an examination, even his touch was a healing touch. On the basis of my life and relationship with my partner, he was happy to allow me to back onto oestrogen.

And so here I am, like the beginning of this little story, thinking how far I have come. I realised that my greatest asset is my journey. I do not know very clearly where this is all leading. I may live as a woman. I may not. I may find that living as a woman allows me to be more masculine. Who knows? I certainly have no illusions about changing my gender role in society. The last few months have been very turbulent and at times I have no idea what my future holds, which is scary...

The whole world seems to have changed around me. It's like I've just been given a new set of arms and legs, and I don't know how to work them. I seem to make a lot of mistakes, albeit in between meeting so many amazing new people. It all feels rather delicate, as if I've come out of some kind of shell. At times all these changes feel a little disembodying. Sometimes I feel I am just here for a little while, passing through, travelling on. I am a creative person, who lives through images and loves images, and I yearn for intense moments that I can capture in my work. These moments make me feel truly alive.

The main thing is I do not want to censor myself, or fit myself into some kind of "gender box". I am, like anyone else, a mix of different experiences, wishes and dreams. I believe in the eternity of life and here in this life I am a human being. All I want to be is the greatest and truest human being I can. Like everyone I just want to fulfill my potential, and have goodhearted pure friends.

Mark (USA)

My childhood was very much of the Fred and Wilma variety (we even watched the Flintstones!). My parents were very happily married as were my grandparents and virtually every other couple I knew of. From the beginning, however, I identified with the girls rather than the boys. I was in the "good" reading group in the first grade, which was almost all girls as I recall. Some might say that this was because most six-year-old boys are farsighted enough that they have trouble learning to read from books while girls can do it and I was so near sighted that I read the print easily. Or it might be explained that I came from a literate family and was encouraged at home to read at an early age. At the same time I didn't like sports much (again with my eyes I was not well co-ordinated.)

The first time I noticed my difference myself was when I was about seven, and my mother left me with a friend of hers that had both a daughter and a son and I chose to play with the girl. We got all her dolls down off the shelf. As time went by, I played more and more with the girls (at lunch there were always two separate groups, one was the boys and the other girls and me.) My 5th grade teacher (I was 10) got very alarmed at this and marched out into the schoolyard during lunch and bodily removed me from the girls' group and put me with the boys and from then on I ate with two boys who weren't too athletic. I think she talked to my mother about it but my mother didn't tell me. She and my father were already getting worried and told me I was not to read books other than my schoolwork.

My father (who was a very sweet man, passive but totally hetero) tried to teach me how to catch a ball but it was hopeless. They thought that my "problem" might be due to some hormones my mother had taken when she was pregnant with me (she had miscarried a child before my birth and was starting to have the same troubles again when she was carrying me so she took the medicine and I didn't abort. Those drugs have since become illegal here).

I can remember also that I was starting to get very interested in make-up and hairstyles then and jealous of girls that they could wear them and we couldn't. As an adolescent, my classmates thought I was strange in Junior High (age 12-14) but I was generally left alone and had no friends. However, when I transferred to Senior High (age 15-17) all hell broke loose. This school was in a much more conservative neighbourhood and I was harassed mercilessly for the three years I was there.

My parents and the school principal knew about it but did nothing, believing that if I were pressured enough I would stop being "like that." What they didn't know was that I had sexual feelings for women as well as men or the boys I knew. I tried to date some of the girls in the school but they wouldn't be seen talking to me, much less go out with me. I could tell much more about this period but it is too painful to go there now.

During this time I was vaguely aware about homosexuals as there started to be articles in the press (especially a long article in *Life* magazine.) I was deathly afraid that I was "that way." I loved Judy Garland's singing and became very alarmed when I realised she had a big gay following. I was full of self-hatred and thought a lot about killing myself but was afraid I would bungle the attempt. Fortunately, as I was finishing High School, I got a job in a theatre and started to make friends who accepted me as I was. I dated a few girls and had a few attempts at having sex with men which didn't go well (I would not plunge wholeheartedly into the gay scene until I was 25, as a way of escaping from a disastrous relationship with a difficult woman).

I was not interested in transvestism *per se* but liked to paint my face with women's make-up (I loved the colours of red lipstick and blue eyeshadows) and when hippies started having long hair, I let mine grow too but I also had a beard for several years. I thought it was unfair that society let women copy men's styles (such as wearing short hair and pants) but it wasn't allowed for men to emulate women. Eventually when I started acting more (on stage) I came to regard make-up as a nuisance. I had short hair for a long time (about 12 years) but now have it long again. It is my gay friends who are most alarmed by the long hair and my colourful clothes. I love brilliant colours and need to have them around me which bothers my stylish friends since the styles now are so colourless.

My androgyny has been quite a problem in the workplace. Here in California there are now laws protecting gays from being fired or harassed but my hair, colourful clothes and general manner has been a problem in the workplace. Ten years ago I worked in a small office for a very "out" gay man who also felt a real moral obligation to read *GQ* and other magazines like that and follow the styles to the letter. I had short hair then but still he was threatened by my manner and kept telling me to tone it down as it embarassed him when we went somewhere together to work.

Later, when I was teaching school, it was the same thing again. I still had short hair and I wore severe black suits (some of which I would get at Marks and Spencer when in London). I even took lessons to make my speech more masculine but to no avail. Homosexuality *per se* was nothing new to the Latino students I was teaching. (I speak Spanish fluently and could understand what these boys were saying to each other. Often it was very sexual).

One Mexican friend of mine told me that if a heterosexual Mexican man has enough money he'll get a female prostitute. If he has less money, he gets a fairly convincing transvestite (there are streets here in town where they all hang out.) If he can't afford even that he does it with another man but gets drunk or pretends to be so drunk that he didn't know what he was doing. The thing that is worse than death is to be effeminate and not have a moustache. One Latino guy called me up on behalf of his friend who was looking for sex. He said in Spanish: "We're not drag queens" (he said the word "drag queen" in English since there isn't a spanish word for it), "We have moustaches!"

I was once cast as a drag queen in a play and had to wear a lot of make-up and thought it was a big bother. Other than that I have never been in full drag, not that I think it is wrong, I just am not interested. Nor did I ever consider a transsexual operation because I like being a man. But I want to be my kind of a man and there aren't many like me. A long time ago I was in a restaurant and Christine Jorgensen was there and I looked over at her table. She looked very nice and I was very proud of her for doing what she did because it was the right thing for her. At the same time I was glad that it wasn't necessary for me. I think women's bodies are wonderful and wish I could get carnal knowledge of more of them, but that was always difficult and lately I have stayed with men.

A lot of gay men are uncomfortable with me but many more don't care one way or another. I wanted to get married and father children and tried very hard until I was 40 to find some woman who would accept me but I never did. I know a number of guys who are completely homosexual and have managed to get married and have kids because they seemed hetero even if they weren't in fact. Sometimes their wives didn't know or pretended they didn't know but went along with it anyway because the guy had money or was prominent in some way and thus a good catch.

I thought I was reaching an understanding with one woman when one day she said: "Why do you keep looking at my breasts?" I said I thought they were beautiful. She said she thought I was gay. I said I was bisexual. She seemed very disappointed and that was the end of that relationship.

Julia

I have taught English in two state-run south London secondary schools since I began teaching seven years ago. Throughout, I have faced various expressions of homophobia from my pupils. My current school, an all girls inner-city secondary school with 85 per cent of the pupils from ethnic minorities – primarily girls whose families have come from the Caribbean and West Africa – is, however, where I have encountered homophobia from pupils most constantly.

There, are, I think, several reasons for this. Having moved from a mixed-sex school, I believe that an all-girls environment can intensify the teenage female desire to form homogenous groups. Teenage girls tend to gang up with each other and in an all-girls school they don't have the boys to challenge or dilute their conformity. Instead, there's the teacher as a target. Initially, I was shocked and disappointed at the cruelty and homogeny of the 15-16-year-old graduating age group of girls I was teaching. They seemed to be reaching out for a homogenised identity which at its worst is intolerant and sheltered, while simultaneously lacking in curiosity, independence and ambition.

Another factor that's led to the high level of homophobia directed towards me at my current school has to do with the extreme misogyny that so many of the girls accept as part of being a woman. And although it is a stereotype and a generalisation, I feel it is true that it is particularly the British Afro-Caribbean and Asian descent where the misogyny is strongly verbalised. I know that all my pupils bring with them some culturally-inherited misogyny, but it is unfortunate that many of my ethnic minority students are intent on reinforcing it publicly. It is also sad that they do not see that tolerance should and can extend beyond issues of race to sexism. Women are all too often blamed, whether it is in life or literature. For instance, my first year teaching *Macbeth* at my current school left me at a loss. Lady Macbeth is a real villain in the girls' eyes. It's entirely her fault that Macbeth kills Kind Duncan and they are glad when she dies.

I cannot honestly say that I am surprised that my pupils are so homophobic, but I am surprised and depressed that they are so obviously misogynist. Their "cut-out" of a woman is so limited and reductive that people like me cannot be considered women. I can only hope that some of them will grow up and out of such debilitating views.

Of course, having homophobia directed at me isn't the result of some grand coming-out ritual that I undertook upon my arrival. My status as a lesbian is not something I've spelled out to my pupils. It didn't take long for my graduating class to come to a tacit understanding of my sexuality and I am comfortable with that. If I have helped students guess my sexuality it has been because I do not conjure up fictional boyfriends or lie about my marital status, and because I cannot help but look like a bit of a dyke – I look androgynous, have short hair and wear trousers.

Given the homophobia my pupils already express, I would be undermining myself if I came out. I feel my lesbianism would become more important than the fact that

I'm the teacher. I don't come out to my students because I need both to protect myself and maintain my authority.

The way in which my pupils manifest their homophobia comes in two varieties. It is either direct or demonstrated in their responses to literature. The easiest jibe is to call me "Sir", instead of "Miss". I usually have to let this go. Another favourite is to rub their upper lip poking fun at my facial hair. As I am sensitive about facial hair to begin with, this game of theirs is difficult to deal with. That said, the only way to deal with it while it's happening is not to allow myself to respond. There is a fairly constant stream of giggles and murmuring under the breath which I am used to now.

The area where I can and do challenge my pupils on their homophobia is when we are studying literature. Sometimes what they say is simply ridiculous. For instance, once I was teaching the Blake poem *London* and there is a line: "And blights with plagues the marriage hearse". Upon hearing it one pupil shrieked: "Was Blake a poof?" I really was taken aback because it's quite a leap to go from an image of marriage as death to the assumption that the poet was gay.

The Arthur Miller play *A view from the Bridge* is another text that gets them going. I choose it in part because it offers a comparison between stereotypically macho men and a man who, although straight, is effeminate. In it, Rudolph is a dress-making, opera-singing blonde Italian and my pupils are shouting "Queer", despite the fact Rudolph is in love with a woman.

As an English teacher I feel I am in a privileged position with regards to Section 28, the ludicrous law against promoting any kind of homosexuality to minors. Love, sex, and death cannot help but crop up, as do pieces of writing that deal with moral and ethical dilemmas. Because of this I haven't felt the chill hand of section 28 on my shoulder reminding me not to "promote" homosexuality. I feel free to discuss homosexuality and how it relates to a text – no one could accuse me that such a discussion is promotion. It's PSE (Person and Social Education) teachers I really feel sorry for – they can barely mention the word "condom", let alone talk about homosexuality in a grown-up manner.

It is the restrictions like section 28 and the alarming homophobia and misogyny that pupils bring into school that makes being a gay or lesbian teacher difficult. As time goes on, I find that I am devising ways to deal with every new version of homophobia I encounter in the classroom, but I cannot honestly say the pupils are becoming more tolerant. It does wear me down at times.

Of course, there are moments when the issues of homosexuality are raised by pupils and it isn't a weapon. A few years ago, I was teaching some of Anne Sexton's fairytale transformation poems. One pupil – a surly, but able girl – brought the *Collected Anne Sexton* into class. She pointed out a poem that I had not selected, but that was her favourite. It was *Rapunzel* and the first line is: "A woman who loves another woman is forever young". This pupil wanted to embarrass me, but she also wanted to tell me something about herself. She has since come out.

Alan

Now in my late thirties, I have taken on the role of "house husband" for the majority of our 11 years together. Coming from a traditional farming background, where stereotypes are often entrenched, it may at first seem unusual to be living a reversed role life within the confines of the rural environment in which I was born and brought up. However, as with most social situations, once people understand that our lives are sincere, honest and happy, then our "unusual" domestic arrangements are accepted without comment, even by the most entrenched observers.

The reason that our domestic roles have taken on their current pattern has been due to the way we have worked together over the years. There has been no major theoretical discussion on the matter, our natural interaction has led to the current situation with the minimum of debate. It always strikes me as ironic that the radical student element we lived with years ago have opted for the yoke of convention as soon as it was offered – civil service jobs, mortgages and traditional gender roles.

Our personal situation grew from communal student living where the cooking was done by those most enthused about food and the cleaning and other chores by those that became most upset about the state of the house. When any one individual became overwhelmed by the workload, he or she would demand a review of the situation. Since leaving the confines of student life, we have tried to apply the best principles of this practice to our mutual benefit.

Under these circumstances it can be seen that we have developed a flexible arrangement for family life. We have one son aged seven, and are about to have number two child in a matter of weeks. This will involve a reassessment of our income, and will lead to me having to increase my portion of the family finance (it should be understood that as well as managing the domestic affairs – shopping, cooking, cleaning and parenting, I have a number of part-time commitments, as do the great majority of modern "homemakers").

It has long been an ambition of mine and my partner to be working part time, leaving both of us with quality family and personal time, while still maintaining sufficient income for domestic needs. I feel highly privileged to have taken the majority role in the raising of our son to school age and look forward to sharing that experience the next time about. It is somewhat academic to attempt to assess the effect this role reversal has had on us socially, sexually or financially, as we have only lived how we live; all I can say is it has worked for us to date: we are solvent, socially accepted and happy.

Anna

I am 36 years old and married with two children, aged 10 and 13. I have been living with my partner John for 15 years, and married to him for the past five years. I became the major breadwinner in the family when our second child was eight months old and fulfilled this role for six years. This situation developed quite gradually.

151

John and I began our relationship in the early 1980s when the country was deep in recession and unemployment levels were extremely high. Consequently, being out of work and in receipt of benefit was not unusual, in fact common among our peer group. So, for the first couple of years of our relationship money didn't really seem that important. Neither of us was qualified in any way and job opportunities were few and far between.

We were fortunate to be able to rent a cottage on the estate land where I was born. The cottage was very small but it was a "peppercorn" rent and very secure. We didn't plan to start a family but I became pregnant in 1984 and our daughter Juliet was born in March 1985. We were still in receipt of benefit but somehow we always managed to get by.

John is a musician and has been playing in bands regularly since he was 15 years old. This is nearly always cash work and this money, together with the odd casual work that he managed to get, helped to sustain us. Over the next couple of years he tried various jobs and training schemes but never seemed able to stick at anything for very long. This was partly due to the fact that he is a musician and therefore often out until the early hours and found it very difficult to get up in the mornings.

As our daughter became a toddler I began to try to contribute to our finances. I started a small business with a girlfriend and opened a little shop. This was not a huge success and ended when we both became pregnant. After the birth of our second child, Miles, things became quite strained in our relationship. We were living a very hand-to-mouth existence. By this time I was in control of our finances, John was heavily into cannabis and the likelihood of him getting regular employment seemed very remote. Things became very bad and at my request he moved out and stayed with friends, but with the promise that things would change after six weeks, he moved back in.

I think that at this point I decided that if this relationship was going to work then I would have to go out and get some regular work and by default John would have to stay at home and look after the children. I heard that some friends were looking for someone to run their shop and I got the job. At first it was on a part-time basis but the hours soon increased.

We never really discussed the implications of this new situation but as the years went by and especially now, with the benefit of hindsight, I think that it changed our relationship dramatically. I felt, at times, pleased, to escape the drudges of domesticity and at other times resentful at having the responsibility of being the bread-winner thrust upon me. Mostly I think that I felt guilty, and consequently never quite at ease with any of the roles I was trying to fulfil. I felt as if I was spreading myself too thinly, failing as a mother and as an employee.

When I arrived home in the evenings feeling tired, the children demanded all my attention and because I have quite high standards, the house never seemed cleaned to my satisfaction, therefore I spent a lot of time, when I wasn't working, catching up on the housework. I felt as though John's input was only ever the bare minimum and that our lives were not progressing. My wages and the benefit "top up" and the cash that John earned just about kept our heads above water, but there was never anything left over for any treats.

I had massive resentment towards John, who after spending all day with the children, often went out in the evenings to rehearse, or play with a band. This resentment crystallised into a total lack of sympathy and reluctance to try to understand any of the things he was going through. He did actually become very depressed during this time. This depression often manifested itself as an aggressive anger directed towards me and sometimes towards the children which further hardened my attitude towards him.

So we continued in what was often a ceaseless pattern of resentment, guilt and feelings of inadequacy. I think that I managed to keep a lid on these feelings most of the time in the interests of family harmony and because I was too busy just surviving!

Our friends were very supportive and so were our families to a degree. Because we are both from working-class backgrounds it did not seem strange to our parents that I, as a wife, should be going out to work but they did find it difficult to come to terms with the fact that John was the principle carer of our children. This, they still regard as an exclusively female domain.

Things became easier once both of the children started full-time at school and these days, our roles are split much more evenly. We both do everything with very few exceptions.

Interviews

Zach Nataf, founder and organiser of the UK's Transgender Film Festival, October 1998.

Tracie (T). When did the film festival come about and how?
Zach (Z). Spring 1997. Actually it was the year before that. I was working at the London Film Makers Co-op'. At that time they were building the Lux cinema where the festival is held now. They were restructuring and I was made redundant but the fact that it was a launch year for the cinema seemed the perfect opportunity to launch the festival, something I had been thinking about for a year or two. Having seen so much transgender work being showcased at lesbian and gay film festivals in London, New York and San Francisco I knew that historically there was enough work for a number of seasons of films and that with more being made there would probably be enough material for an annual festival if we could get something like that off the ground.

I didn't have anyone to work with initially, then I started working with people I had met either in the FTM network or at Transgender Pride. It's a really big job, you know – grant applications, looking for work to show, trying to get sponsors on board. I did get some positive response; as someone who had worked in the independent film sector I already had a few contacts and I basically began to follow them up. It got quite hairy as a month before the festival was due to happen I lost the people I was then working with and there was still a lot of work to do.

Finally I got Annette, my partner, on board who was a film-maker herself and someone who'd interviewed a lot of transpeople. Unlike the people I'd been working with before, Annette was already working in the independent film sector and I think had a much clearer idea about just how much work a film festival would be, so finally I had the help I needed. We practically did it just the two of us that first year.

T. What was the reaction to the first festival?

Z. Well the first year was an incredible buzz; everyone was really excited about it because it was the first time that in all our diversity, I think, that people had come together to celebrate to discuss, to debate. People came from the US and Europe – it felt like a real international event. We took over the Lux cinema for five days last year and that was very exciting. Even the press were interested, because it was the first event of its kind certainly in the UK. There had been seasons of trans-films but this was the first international festival so, the press responded well to that. The funders – well they thought it was a great idea but they gave us hardly any money.

I think we have a good track record now in terms of value for money because nobody gets paid but that can't continue – people have to get paid some kind of fee next year. I think the show is very professionally done. Most of the crisis management that goes on I think we manage to keep from the audience who I hope just see the professional face of it although we are all still learning as we do the job and there were more of us to share the work this year. Generally the response was very good. The funders, when they saw what we did were absolutely amazed that we could do a festival of that scale with no money. We need more money really. We need bigger sponsors to get involved and that is something we are starting to work on now. You need at least a year's run up in order to get the bigger sponsors on board.

T. What about grants?

Z. Well London Film and Video Development Agency have had faith in us. They have had a new chief exec' who has also had faith. Channel 4 are very interested; they didn't fund us this year although they inadvertently did by allowing us to show one of the films that they have a licence for, but for which there's no distributor in Europe. Anyway they seem keen to carry on contributing so I think that we'll have them on board next year just as long as we can get to them in time – that is before their budget is spent.

We've had trouble getting money from the Arts Council because their budgets are spent two years in advance and when we need to get the application in we are right in the middle of the festival so that has made things difficult. The lottery, we didn't get that this year on a technicality. It would have been £6,000, which would have gone down very well. Also one of the councils did fund us but are saying that they didn't. I can't say who as I don't want to get into trouble. We've already had some legal dealings with them.

We have had donations from the community, which has been very important, some from individuals, some from Press for Change some from the Gender and Sexuality Alliance, so the community seems to be 100 per cent behind us and not just in terms of turning up.

T. How do you see the festival continuing?

Z. The most important thing is that I would like to see the festival continue as an annual event and for it to grow. This year we had more of a cross-over audience, which I don't think is a bad thing – lesbian and gay, and general non-trans audiences. I would like to see it tour so that other transpeople who cannot come down can get to see the work in their own regions in Britain and also internationally.

That people get paid, that we have an office, you know those basic kind of things so that we have a higher profile in terms of attracting sponsorship. It may grow in terms of the number of days, it may grow in terms of the number of venues and we may become involved in encouraging work to be produced because once a festival exists people will begin to produce work for that festival.

T. And if it gets charitable status?

Z. The Alchemy Trust which is sort of the umbrella organisation, will be applying for charitable status so the film festival will be just one event. Some of the offshoots from the festival that we have done this year, like the live perfomances, the photography exhibition that raise funds for safe sex for the community, will all come under the umbrella of the Alchemy Trust and other things like publishing eventually so that we will be able to attract funds in different ways as an educational charity.

T. So if you had any advice for anyone from another country wishing to do something similar what would that be?

Z. I think it needs to come out of the community itself. A vision of the community as far as possible. There is the San Francisco Tranny Fest that happened three or four days after our festival last year and so that's the first one to happen in North America, I think, which is interesting because again it's about funding. It sounded like it was a great event, really exciting – we have an exchange with them. There's one in Canada as well and again that's a half-day event but they will only show work made by transpeople, which I think is brilliant, but as a result it's only a half-day festival so I'm hoping that will grow as well and that there will be more work, of course, coming from the community.

Susan Stryker, Social Science Research Council Post-Doctoral Fellow in Human Sexuality Studies, Affiliated Scholar, Standford University History Department, USA, October 1998.

T. What was the thesis of your PhD about and how does it bear on your present work?

S. I earned my PhD in US History at the University of California at Berkeley in 1992, and wrote my dissertation

157

on the origins of Mormonism. That seems like a topic quite removed from my current research interest in transgender phenomena, but some common concerns underpin both projects.

My dissertation poses the following question: In 1825 there was no such thing as a Mormon. In 1845 there was a Mormon cultural identity, Mormon church, Mormon scripture, uniquely Mormon forms of kinship; there was a poltical movement and a massive migration across the continent. How did that identity-based socio-cultural formation arise? I took the insights from my doctoral work and applied them to the study of different communities, ones organised around sexual and gender identities rather than religious ones. But I've been interested in identity, community, and culture thoughout both phases of my work.

T. How exactly would you describe your post-doctoral work?

S. I'm looking at the formation of transgender communities in the San Francisco Bay Area in the US.

T. Over what period does your work extend?

S. Pretty much the whole 20th century. There are two convenient points for stopping and starting the work. I begin in 1905, with some letters written to Magnus Hirschfeld by a transgendered German expatriate living in San Francisco. They constitute one of the 17 case studies that Hirschfeld used in his important early work on transvestites, and thus represent the beginning of sexological attention to transgender issues specifically. I end with the passage in 1995 of the San Francisco transgender anti-discrimination ordinance, which represents a high-point in the political accomplishments of the transgender community whose roots here stretch back to the turn of the century, if not before.

T. How do you think not having a well recorded history affected the rights of sex, gender and sexuality fluid people?

S. To paraphrase Desmond Tutu, the surest way to destroy a people is to convince them that they have no history. I would say, though, that it is not so much that we have a badly recorded history, so much as that we have a badly disseminated one. We don't remember our own history, and have only recently begun to write it. But I find pieces of it under every rock I turn over.

T. How will things change when transpeople do have an official catalogued history by recognised historians such as yourself, that is not mixed in with gay people's history – or are they inseparable?

S. Well, I'm better at talking about the past than the future, but certainly one of my goals in writing history is to help shift the terms of contemporary discussions of transgender issues. I find current discussions too caught up in moral questions – should transsexuals have the right to change their legal sex? Are FTMs traitors to feminism? etc – and too easily dismissed as simply the latest trendy, politically correct flavour of the month.

What I hope my historical writing can do is show how regardless of what you think of transgendered people, there are a lot of us and we have been socially and politically active for a long time. We are a presence in both history and contemporary society. Greater awareness of this simple fact cannot help but change how we wage our battles for civil rights and human dignity. We will seem more substantial, both to ourselves and to others, and will not be as easily dismissed.

As for the relationship between the gay/lesbian community and the transgender community, I think that, in San Francisco at least, they are inseparable. They have such large areas of overlap that to leave out the intersection of the two would be to do real damage to our understanding of the subject. Of course, due to their position of relative dominance, gay and lesbian scholars who ignore transgender issues tend to do just that – their blind spot, I feel, seriously hampers their work, and their understanding of their own past.

T. By what means has your data been collected?

S. I'm, of course, familiar with the medical and psychological literature on transgenderism, but I'm really trying to steer clear of having that framework inform my work too much. While attention to these discourses is important for how they shape transgendered lives, what I am most interested in is how transgendered people themselves have understood what they were doing, and how they have situated themselves in the world.

So I conduct interviews with older transgender people, devour autobiographies and other instances of transgender self-representation, and immerse myself in transgender community publications. There's more of this stuff around than you might think.

However, I'm not content to stop there. I'm most interested in the intersection of individual lives with the broader social fabric. Therefore, a lot of my work is in sources that are not directly related to transgender concerns.

I'm looking at urban renewal and struggles to define the built space of neighbourhoods where there were high concentrations of transgendered people; trying to understand the relationship between the police and the vice trade; investigating community organising among the poor; reading the daily papers for their coverage of sex and gender issues; looking at avant-garde art and radical political movements that celebrated gender transgression; placing what I know in the context of feminist and homosexual history; paying attention to AIDS and how the epidemic has shaped transgender social services.

By focusing on a specific geographical location such as San Francisco, I can open up a very wide-ranging exploration of how transgendered people fit into the society in which they live.

T. Do you think having a San Francisco trans-history researched by a transperson will be different from if it had been researched by a non transperson? Why/why not?

S. Yes, I think it is different, simply because I have a different kind of entry into the community. People I interview are often willing to speak more openly with me than they would with a non-transgendered person. I ask different questions, both in interviews and of the written material I examine, because I have a different stake in writing, and different emphases in my interpretation. Positionality is always important.

But that's not to say that non-transgendered people can't do good work in the field – a non-translesbian historian at the University of Cincinnati is doing the best historical work on transsexualism that I know of. She's a wonderfully generous colleague who has been very supportive of my work. I think non-transgendered people who are willing to put their own position of embodied difference on a par with transgendered experience, rather than thinking that they are the normals who have something authoritative to say about us freaks, have some very valuable contributions to make to the study of transgender phenomena.

Happily, I keep coming across more and more of those people – which seems to suggest that the message of the transgender political movement is beginning to be heard rather widely, and taken to heart.

T. When is your book out?
S. That depends on which one you are talking about. I have a book under contract to Oxford University Press, whose working title is *Ecstatic Passages: A Postmodern Transsexual Memoir*. It should be out late in 1999 or early in 2000. However, that book does not deal extensively with the historical material I'm currently researching. I'm actually working on a documentary film based on that work, though later I plan to write a monograph.

Also, I have other, less demanding book projects in the pipeline. These include the edited journals of gay FTM activist Louis Sullivan (which have been languishing on my desk for more than five years, but I think a publisher is finally in sight), as well as a selection of my short published works and a transgender studies anthology, based largely on the special issue of *GLQ* that I edited earlier this year. So I'm a busy girl these days!

Matthew Carlos, co-editor of US-based magazine Transgender Tapestry, October 1998.

T. What kind of people are your readers? How many are there? Where are they?

M. The readership includes crossdressers, male-to-female and female-to-male transsexuals, youth and intersex – basically all categories and sub-categories of transgender people with the majority historically being crossdressers coming on board, then there were more transsexuals and recently a lot of transgendered people – transgender being a sub-category meaning those who do not opt for sex reassignment surgery, but do take hormones.

T. What about circulation?

M. The circulation has been between 8,000-10,000 copies, the majority going to members of the International Foundation for Gender Education, but also quite a few available on newstands internationally. In the next 12 months we are looking at increasing circulation from 10,000 to perhaps 20,000.

T. When did you take over as co-editor and what changes are you making?

M. I became co-editor just after the summer 1998 issue went to press which would be late May. As for changes, I'd like *Tapestry* to become accessible in its content and also as accessible on newstands as the US magazine *Out*, with hopefully as great a circulation, although that could take some time. *Out* is the premier magazine for gays and lesbians in the US and the audience we are trying to appeal to is not just the transgendered community but mainstream queer community as well as mainstream America.

I'd like a person who is interested in art to see the cover of our winter issue and say: "Isn't that a wonderful piece of sculpture – I wonder who did it?" and then start reading it and say OK this person happens to be transgender, or say someone likes the music of Marilyn Manson and wants to buy the issue because this musician is in it and the person is transgender or transsexual.

T. Are there any obstacles you see in the way, particularly in the US for transgender, intersex and transfluid education?

M. I would say the growing religious right. They are combating liberal education on homosexuality pretty vigorously at the moment, taking the stance that if you are homosexual and you are practising your sexual orientation you will be going to hell. This is going to pose difficulties when trying to educate about transgender issues.

Also in middle America, the central states, there's this desire to have what's being called traditional family values, which basically means more or less rigid categories of perception about the world which are really mythological: the ultra masculine male, the ultra feminine female, the 2.5 children – one male, one female. It's going to take, I think, maybe 20 years before transgender becomes acceptable in the mainstream.

T. How is the magazine funded?

M. The magazine is funded through subscriptions and newstands as well as through the IFGE which publishes the magazine.

T. What do you see as the future of the magazine?

M. We need to begin to embrace and form workable cooperative relationships with the intersex community, the transgender community and transsexuals, which would mean broadening out from our primarily crossdressing readership. We need to involve contributors from around the world and include articles on global topics, or the magazine won't be able to increase its circulation and will remain what here in the US we call a zine.

The crossdressing community seems quite small and closeted whereas the out, more vocal community is the transgendered. And they are going to start their own publications, I think, and they are also going to begin forming a voice, a united voice, and *Tapestry* being somewhat established already can provide the medium for that voice to be carried to the rest of our community and the American culture and the rest of the world. If we don't do that, if we don't reach out and co-operate with TG people then they're going to meet their own needs themselves.

We are also thinking of starting a new professional journal, the working title of which is currently *Gender*. It will be a sort of academic, professional, medical kind of journal. Right now we have Sheila Kirk who is interested in helping us fund it. There seems to be one publication in the US that deals with gender and it has a very feminist slant rather than a transgender perspective.

The other thing that we are going to do is publish parts of the magazine on the website and some of those articles will be translated into other languages such as Japanese, French, German and Dutch. And we will begin to accept articles in those four languages, farming out translations so that we can publish an English version in our magazine, having the original language version on our website. We hope that this would be free, as we don't want to charge for it. Hopefully this would develop into foreign language versions of *Transgender Tapestry*, a full magazine of around 107 pages. We'd also like to go bi-monthly sometime within the next eight months to two years. But that is dependent on funding.

Theresa Mills, vice-chair of Amnesty International UK, Gay, Lesbian, Bisexual and Transgender Network, November 1998.

T. Is the AIUKGLBT network a special sub-section of Amnesty International?
T.M. Yes, but it's a network.
T. And is there an Australian or American version?
T.M. There is definitely an American one and it's slowly getting around the world. I'm not sure of the actual numbers at the moment but of the GLB networks that there are in other sections, they are all slowly taking on the T issues.
T. When was this T put on in the UK?
T.M. The gay and lesbian section of this network was formed in 1991 and it was decided in 1996 that bisexuals and transgendered people should be included. At that time there was a membership of about 300. The membership at the moment stands at about 900.
T. What are the aims of the GLBTN?
T.M. To bring about awareness of these various issues and

to be able to focus attention on these issues more intensely than the general Amnesty International itself. To liaise with other like groups globally and if we come across any breaches in human rights then we hand these cases on to the researchers of AI in those countries.

If the researchers can see that there is a case to answer we will carry out the campaign on behalf of what would then be classified as prisoners of conscience. I'd like to make one thing clear. We are not a political organisation – we have no political affiliations at all. It's one of the things that helps us to keep our integrity.

T. So you are a neutral human rights campaigning organisation?

T.M. Precisely.

T. There was recently a major case where a transsexual was granted political asylum because of the violence and problems that they had suffered in their own country. When AI makes representation, is it to change the circumstances within that country or is pressure applied in order to rescue people?

T.M. Our first priority, I think you'll find, will be the people themselves. If we consider that person to be harassed for their beliefs, they are then classified as prisoners of conscience and then we can act to extricate them from that situation if at all possible. We also make representations to the political leaders, the military or government and also to their embassies in this country.

T. So, on behalf of GLBTN, are there many countries where you are currently making representations?

T.M. The latest one is in Malaysia, an action that has just come through. This is over convictions for sodomy after an unfair trial. This a gay issue. A former deputy prime minister and his brother were accused of unlawful acts and of course there is a very political undertone in the way that they are being treated.

Research has been carried out but it's an area where AI has to be extremely careful. That means carrying out verification of reports and intensive research. That's why it often takes some time before we can take action. We have to be 110 per cent sure that we have the facts and that they are correct. And that brings us credibility because when Amnesty does act, foreign powers do tend to listen because they know we have done our research. We do have that respect internationally.

T. What about cases that at the moment involve the transgendered community?

T.M. There's nothing ongoing at the moment, although we have had reports through from Lithuania which we've looked at but after doing some preliminary research we discovered that this person, although being victimised, was receiving no more unfair treatment than a transsexual might incur in this country.

As it turned out she had contacted other organisations – TransEssex and Gendy's Network, and it seems that TransEssex have taken the lead over this one and have got in touch with people over there and it's my understanding, unofficially, that she is currently in this country. Whether this is for a visit or permanently, I'm not sure. But it's one of those cases where for us to research thoroughly would have taken an awfully long time whereas it was possible for another organisation to help her out.

T. What are your plans for the future of AIUKGLBTN?

T.M. Well obviously we wish to continue to expand and bring about more awareness of transgender issues as well as continuing our work with gays and lesbians. We are getting involved with more representations in this country and we are also beginning to establish links with other countries as well. We have always had these links with the gay and lesbian side but we are now beginning to get these links with the transgender organisations.

The other thing we have going on at the moment is lesbian disabilities. Although there are already quite a few organisations around the world dealing with this issue, we have, at the moment, a particular committee member who is very keen to bring this issue forward. She has been a great help in raising awareness of trans issues and we are hoping she will be able to do the same thing with what we call Lesdis.

And again we hope to liaise with more transgender groups locally. We are hoping to produce a film by the millennium as a direct response from the Gendy's Network presentation that we did. To be quite honest with you that was the first time I'd seen that video, *Raised in Silence*, and although I thought it was very good, it concentrates mainly on gay issues and I feel that we need a much broader spread to cover GLB and T. So this idea seems to have exploded. We've already got £1,500 in funding and that's before even our first sub-committee meeting on the subject.

We have an award winning playwright on the committee and we have been in touch with directors and a certain well-known producer who, if we can get to help us, would be an excellent asset as far as getting sponsorship is concerned. We haven't even started campaigning for sponsorship yet but it's all looking very good. The original idea for the film is for it to be released globally, because we already have the network in place to do that, in several languages. It is aided by the fact that here in London we have the international secretariat and lots of incredibly talented people who can actually help us with the various languages.

In March 1999 Amnesty International (UK) GBLT held a conference in London for delegates from all over the world. The meeting was a forum for the exchanging of ideas and sharing of experiences in order to assist transglobal networking and establish a more effective role for the movement.

PAPERS &
ARTICLES

8

Papers and Articles

Dis-Embodiment: A Virtual Identity
By Dr Stephen Whittle, PhD, MA, LLB, BA
The School of Law
The Manchester Metropolitan University
March 1999

Transsexual and transgendered people have always spent large parts of their lives managing a "virtual identity". Using Goffman's concept of virtual social identity as opposed to "actual social identity", the transpeople, whether they are pre-transition (ie in those times before they start living in the gender role to which they wish to be ascribed) or post-transition, spend large amounts of the time they are involved in social intercourse pretending or pastiching a person whom everyone else assumes or demands in effect.

Whether pretending to be a person of the gender designated to them at birth, or performing gender as if a non-trans/gendered/sexual person of their new gender role, there are in the real world very few opportunities in which their actual identity as a transgenderist can be fully disclosed. If nothing else, to do so would often put their livelihood at risk.

Daily, transpeople are involved in portraying a holographic version of the self which cultivates the others' consensual hallucination. So the cyberworld of virtual reality, virtual space and virtual beings is not a new and strange world to the transgenderist, but it is a world in which they have in-built expertise and of which they already have a range of experiences, albeit that these were gained outside of cyberspace.

Ironically the cyberworld in which others have to learn how to manage their virtuality, is a world in which, in particular, the transsexual's actual identity can thrive. The result of this thriving has been the creation of a virtual publication bank, a series of online newsgroups, both on the Internet and through private listings operated via e-mail and, most importantly a huge activist base which does not require any of the real body to exist in real space, other than those aspects of the body required to participate in cyberspace.

This Embodiment: A Real Identity in a New Land

By now, everyone who uses a computer as a means of long distance communication, will know the old joke that somewhere a dog sits at a computer surfing the Net, and yet nobody knows it is a dog. The potential offered by computers for humans to escape the body in the same way as the dog does is seen by many as one of the greatest advantages of computer technology. That escape from the body is not just of interest to those who study the Net, it has in recent years become a cultural obsession transformed by Judith Butler and others into the study of gender performativity, and the linking of the materiality of the body with utopian analyses of the gendered world's future.

What though is most noticeable about the few analyses that exist both about gender and about computers is that they have never come from the dog (or not in as much as he has admitted his authorship). However, as far as the transgendered users of the Net are concerned, the dog has, in recent years, found its bark.

Further, one of the frequently condemned features of a transgendered life is that it abounds in stereotypes which reinforce oppressive gender roles. As Janice Raymond put it in her introduction to the 1994 edition of *The Transsexual Empire: The Making of the She-male*:

"transgenderism reduces gender resistance to wardrobes, hormones, surgery and posturing – anything but real sexual equality. A real sexual politics says yes to a view and reality of transgender that transforms, instead of conforming to, gender" (Raymond, in Ekins and King, 1996, p 223).

If this is indeed the case, then the transgendered movement would indeed have little to offer the rest of us. It would have merely become a self-help network in which people are taught how to reinforce the values of a white, heterosexist patriarchy.

Such a view singularly fails because if the pundits are right and there are far more transsexual women, than vice versa, they are, in fact, struggling to become the oppressed, and to leave behind a position of privilege.

The reality of the oppressed experience is, in fact, all too real for the majority of the transgendered community. It is that oppressed experience that the community ultimately wishes to address. Firstly, though, for there to be a change in emphasis as to the nature of the important issues in their real lives there was a need to open the doors to those who were previously unable to have a voice in the politics surrounding transgenderism (or as it was then transsexualism) because of their social position, both within and outside of the community. And it was in this task that cyberspace offered the opportunity to address the community's hierarchical structure and its supposed values.

Very few members of the community would argue against the fact that there was in the real world a hierarchy within the community itself, that was very much based around issues concerned with "passing". Passing – some notion of feminine or masculine realness – would provide for many, a physically safe, although restricted, way of living in the real world. But the truth of the matter was that even the most passable transsexual woman could find themselves vulnerable, as witnessed by Caroline Cossey (Tula) when her privacy disappeared after the tabloid rag the *News of the World* published an exposé of her transsexual status in September 1982.

The hierarchy that existed based on passing, within the community, was such that those who were the most non-transsexual looking were awarded status and privilege, while those who were most obviously transsexual or transgendered were often the butt of private jokes and exclusionary behaviour. By default, they were also to be the frontline of any political or social movement that existed. By not passing they daily face the street issues which often result in emotional, financial and even physical scars. However, the privileged few would get to dictate the terms as to what were important and significant issues. If you pass then the issues are bound to be based around things such as: further privacy rights – the right to have birth certificates reissued, and further relationship rights – the right to marry in one's new gender role.

Leslie Feinberg, who in particular has asserted that the community can no longer afford to use this assimilationist approach to activism, states it as one consequence of early minority rights activism, and in such a small movement it is far too limiting:

"When a young movement forms, it gets a great deal of pressure to put forward only its best-dressed and most articulate – which is usually a code word for white...These 'representatives' are seduced into thinking the best way to win is to not rock the boat and ask for only minimal demands. A more potent strategy relies upon unified numbers...We need everyone and cannot afford to throw anyone overboard. After all, we could never get rid of enough people to please our enemies and make ourselves 'acceptable'" (Leshko, 1996).

The plain fact is that the majority of transsexual women cannot and will never pass, and so assimilationist politics are wholly inadequate. For these women, their issues are not necessarily going to be those of the privileged few who could seek integration. For them such rights are meaningless in the context of their lives – if you cannot pass, beyond the most casual of inspections, then any reissued birth certificate will certainly not prevent your discovery as a transsexual woman, and you are very unlikely to find a relationship which is so conventional that marriage matters. It would only be by opening the forum to these people that a unified group could form which could address fully the legal issues that really mattered.

Cyberspace initially affords a place in which the body is fully malleable, indeed even disposable. The body is not seen or felt in passing. Thus it has been a locale in which transsexual women have been able to discuss over whether looks are important without looks getting in the way. However, as argued by Argyle and Sheilds:

"Technology mediates presence...Bodies cannot be escaped, for we express this part of ourselves as we experience together. Although some attempt to conceal the status of their bodies, it is betrayed unless we resort to presenting another kind of body in our communications" (in Sheilds, 1996, p 58).

This failure to escape without taking on a further presentation is what is essentially advantageous in redrawing community relationships in the transgendered community. The presentation of the body is signified through the pure signifier of the self – the name (of the word). Baudrillard states the idea of the Virtual as:

"the radical effectuation, the unconditional realization of the world, the transformation of all our acts, of all historical events, of all material substance and energy into pure information" (Baudrillard, 1995, p 101).

The ongoing presentation of pure information without the body, has redrawn the battle lines for many transgendered women.

The issues of concern have changed, and instead of birth certificates and marriage, they are about the right to personal physical safety, about the right to keep a job regardless of a transgendered status and resultant lifestyle, about the right to be treated equally before the law and the right to medical (including reassignment) treatment.

For transsexual men the pre-eminent issues were to be different. For most men passing was never an issue – any transsexual man can take testosterone, grow a beard, have his voice break, and pass anywhere, anytime, with great success. The issue was "does the penis make the man?" The hierarchy within the male transsexual world was based around surgical status. But phalloplasty is a notoriously difficult surgical procedure, with few success-ful results. Furthermore the good results were only obtained at a very high price; several years of frequent hospital visits as an in-client and an awful lot of money. Yet many men felt driven to complete their passing by undertaking these procedures.

If it is extremely difficult to be a woman with a penis, imagine how much more difficult to be a man with a vagi-na. Without the phallus, no matter how well they passed when clothed, they would always have to disclose in inti-mate relationships, never participate in men's sports where showers and baths were the norm, or even where it was just customary to go and pee up against a wall or bush. In a male world where "cunt" and "pussy" are the ultimate insult, the phallus became the object of desire, the definitive and supreme sign of passing. Green and Wilchins (1996) argue that the potential for passing has cost transsexual men a great deal, not just in terms of their failure to become involved in political activism, but also:

"in hospital rooms across the country, trans-identified men continue to happily sacrifice their bellies, forearms, thighs, and whatever tissue and tendons are left, in pur-suit of the Magic Phallus, and there are more than a few of them on crutches for life as a result of such operations. Many more bear hideous scars on large sections of their bodies in exchange for a tube of skin that hangs ineffectu-ally, forever dangling, a mocking reminder that they can-not 'get it up'" (p 1).

One problem with phalloplasty, and in particular those which had poor results (which I suspect are the majority, a fact confirmed by many surgeons who perform this surgery) is that many men were left severely disabled, unable to work and ashamed to socialise. Wearing incon-tinence diapers is not conducive to a good self-image.

Cyberspace provided a space in which the (invariably housebound) victims of such surgical procedures could talk freely about their experiences, without presenting their failed body image, and others who had not yet undergone the procedures could assess whether they wanted to take such great risks in an attempt to fully pass. This opened a discussion around what makes a real man, and the body was able to be dismissed as a socially controlling mechanism that dictated power roles but which in this situation was shown to be an inadequate mechanism.

Many transsexual men started to view the body differently and as a faltering sight of passing. In order to pass the manipulation, they had to go beyond the real into the hallucinatory. Frequently in online discussions we see the "dick" referred to, but it is a virtual dick:

"When I do IT, I feel as if I have a dick – does anyone else feel this 'phantom' dick'?" (L Bear)

"I think we all feel that – it isn't just sex, but often my dick makes its presence felt." (Max)

This combination of manipulating the body image and the potential privacy of a public display of the personal, along with the nature of controlled extensive publication, alongside the new spatial dynamics of and within cyberspace has contributed, over the last five years, to an immense change in transsexual/transgender politics.

Cyberspace presents a safe area where body image and presentation are not among the initial aspects of personal judgement and social hierarchy within the transgendered community, so extending the range of potential community members and voices.

References

Baudrillard, J, *The Virtual Illusion: Or the Automatic Writing Of the World, Theory, Culture and Society*, Nov 1995, Vol 12 No 4, p 96-107.

Ekins, R, King, D, *Blending Genders: Social Aspects of Cross-dressing and Sex-changing*, Routledge, London, 1996.

Goffman, E, *Stigma: Notes on the Management of Spoiled Identity*, Penguin, London, 1990.

Green, J, Wilchins RA, *New Men on the Horizon*, FTM Newsletter Iss 33, January 1996.

Leshko, I, *Determine, Define, Modify Gender*, WWW: Planet

Q, 1996.

Sheilds, R (Ed), *Cultures of Internet, Virtual Spaces, Real Histories, Living Bodies*, Sage, London, 1996.

A Gender Clinic Nurse/Counsellor's Reflections of Being Involved in Research around Investigation of Clients' Needs

This author of this paper must remain anonymous for legal reasons

My personal and professional interest in gender identity began with an undergraduate dissertation which examined how the psycho-social and cultural processes influencing the carer's perceptions of the needs of gender dysphoric people. Initially in 1995 I worked in a liaison capacity, but post-graduate research illustrated the potential of my future role.

Gender stereotypes

The role I occupied had been given the title "Nurse" at its inception as a professional label was required for employment purposes. My research illustrated that this labelling process affected the way in which I was perceived by medical professionals. (This is not typical of a nurse's role in the abilities and skills a nurse uses). For my part I began to become unsure what a typical role was. I did, however, wonder if this response was indicative of medicine's perceptions of what nurses did or did not do. Whatever the cause...the result was that this labelling process suggested a degree of gender stereotyping in a pure form.

This was supported by my own observations in the work role. I, as a biological woman, would be required to sit in on psychiatric assessments of new clients as well as those in transition. I noted that the individual would be criticised by the person running the clinic for their behaviour or their dress. Gender dysphoric biological males presenting as females were consistently told: "You do not look very feminine!" While I, on the other hand, would be wearing jeans and boots and sporting a very short hairstyle. Although I was culturally looking and dressing quite boyish, nothing was ever said to me, therefore I felt the comments were, in actual fact, simply personal constructs of the interviewing clinician.

It was my experience that both male-to-female and female-to-male transsexuals were both initially treated as women. Clients were assessed in the clinician's subjective terms like "how pretty they looked", and butch dykes were considered to be good material.

The limitation of the medical/social focus
The stock medical response to people presenting with Gender Dysphoria seemed to be: "All we can do is to make you feel more comfortable by approximating your body to how you feel inside." This cannot stand alone and means nothing to these people. The need for reality testing and supported self-diagnosis seemed more imperative. The knock-on effect of lack of psychological preparation for surgery and realistic post-operative care were and continue to be poor prognosis and recovery. If a client has only limited knowledge they may well believe the medical profession can recreate a whole new person, perhaps with ovaries, fallopian tubes or with the ability to conceive or father a child. Some of them didn't even know what they were getting or what their new genitals would look like.

Support only existed on an academic level for me but there was none for the clients. I believe that this was due to a combination of factors; principally the emphasis was on curing a medical condition.

Playing two roles
During the pilot study I was involved in, it was suggested that the respondents gave their consent openly to tell me their stories and because of a rapport between myself and them, they trusted me. Although I was aware that I had two roles, the clients saw one person in me. Simply telling their stories, often for the first time, opened deeply buried emotional wounds. I received repeated phone calls

requesting support and I began to feel very unhappy at having to tell clients that the interviews had been simply a means of collecting data.

My role within the clinic began to be viewed as "someone you could ring who understood your problems". Consent had been given by the clients, not simply because of a rapport, but because in the clients' eyes I had developed a therapeutic alliance with them, and they trusted me.

The study had a profound effect on their perception of the role I occupied within the clinic. Now, in retrospect, and with the benefit of counselling training, I have identified ways in which the study was unethical. It placed clients at risk. It had potentially and practically breached the *Nuremberg Code of Ethics for Research* (1947) which talks of voluntary consent, without the intervention of force and fraud, deceit, duress, over-reaching or other ulterior forms of constraint or coercion.

An extract from my reflective journal illustrates: "I feel like bait set up to catch prey". These issues left me feeling that my integrity was so compromised that I was unable to proceed with the idea of any further research. This was compounded by a myriad of problems, principally a lack of resources and support to develop my post. The continued emphasis on curing a medical condition meant that the supportive, caring elements were not developed and did not exist.

Challenging traditional views by attempting to develop a client-centred service

My experience of being involved in the research pilot taught me the complexity of the issues that surround such research and how limiting the medico-social lens had been. I was increasingly aware of the need for adequate practical and emotional support for clients and their families who attended the Gender Identity Clinic. Clients were often placed in a position where they had to prove their sanity and were often overly intimidated to discuss human issues.

I sent a copy of the co-authored paper to a local mental health group. I received an interested response asking for more information on how I aimed to address the needs of clients and their families. The insights that had evolved through the hands-on experience of acting as clinician, researcher and participant were combined with the knowledge base of an American transsexual psychologist in the field who I shall call Dr X.

An unexpected twist

During this period I wrote to a GP whose client had serious difficulties with Hormone Replacement Therapy (HRT) medication. I suggested that rather than allowing her emotional state to deteriorate further, why didn't he explore other options such as the private sector? This client had met Dr X at a recent conference where she had shared medical and emotional problems with the clinic and they spoke at length.

The next thing a psychiatrist who was the previous leader of the clinic began to behave very oddly towards these developments. He had even intercepted and replied to a letter from this client's GP, which had been addressed to me. I was stalked by him and as his behaviour became worse I eventually rang a therapist friend to ask her what suggestions she had in this situation. On her prompting, I took annual leave until the psychiatrist retired and was out of the picture, but made sure everyone knew I was doing this because of his behaviour.

In the interim the psychiatrist had been sending letters to Dr X, knowing she was a transsexual, demanding her signature saying that she would never set foot in the clinic again or talk to any transsexuals in the area ever again. His retirement party was like an episode from Monty Python (and one of the best parties I have attended for a long time!).

All in the mental health trust were geared to intimidate. There was a fact finding meeting number one, fact finding meeting number two, fact finding meeting three...just like Hollywood sequels. It was eventually decided that there was no case which I was required to answer (this coincided with me being published and using the term "sexual harassment"...surprise, surprise!).

The project I had set up with Dr X had received the report from the local mental health group to whom I had submitted my findings. They agreed that a facility, independent of the National Health Service (NHS), was necessary to direct psychotherapy and counselling to clients and the families in addition to raising awareness of the need for this level of support. The aim was to establish a complementary facility to the NHS clinic.

Sadly the new project was seen as a direct threat to the clinic's authority and as they put it: "working against the business interests of the trust"; that is the NHS trust who provided the gender identity service, and which was legally and morally responsible for the clients who came, trusting to them for help (support indeed!).

Subsequently a number of resources of information, including inside information, suggested that there have been others behaving far worse than the psychiatrist attempting to have Dr X blacklisted from the area.

On my return to work I was met with a witch hunt. This was an orchestrated attempt to undermine the gender identity service from within, principally on the grounds of "evangelical psychiatry". What is most disturbing about this attack is that it appears to have been initiated by the head of the school of psychiatry within the school of medicine at the local university.

The difficulty appeared to lie in supporting the view that treatment approached from a holistic base challenged the traditional views of the medical members of the team. As a consequence their behaviour seemed to demonstrate that they felt their professional standing was being threatened.

They responded by retreating into their cultural belief systems and constructing arguments through socio-medical theories. For example saying that "these people" ie transsexuals, are forced into the professional stigma of being seen as mentally ill, therefore the only facilities given by the profession through the trust is a psychiatrist and a room in the psychiatric wing. By contrast a holistic perspective tended to view clients to be potentially mentally healthy.

The positive outcome

A new psychiatrist has taken over as the clinic's director. Although he did inherit numerous problems, namely that the Gender Identity Clinic appeared to have been set up as a hobby clinic by someone who needed something to fill his time, and that there was no infrastructure whatsoever. The old psychiatrist's interference prior to his retirement caused a lot of bad feelings, fear and mistrust because of some basic promises of support which never materialised. Things are progressing in a positive direction now and there is hope for the future that the Gender Identity Clinic will change and adapt to modern approaches to gender identity.

New York City Gender Identity Project, Lesbian and Gay Community Services Centre of New York City: A Model Community-Based Programme

By Rosalyne Blumenstein, Director, GIP, Carrie Davis, Counsellor GIP, Lynn Walker, Peer Counsellor GIP, & Barbara E Warren, PsyD., Director, Mental Health and Social Services, LGCSC

In the tradition of the Lesbian and Gay Community Services Centre's commitment to fostering empowerment for lesbian, gay and bisexual individuals, the Centre's Gender Identity Project (GIP) offers transgender-identified people an opportunity to discover who they are, and to build communities, in an atmosphere of self-acceptance.

The GIP's community-based approach works to help people of transgender experience become freer to celebrate their identities and experiences. The GIP is committed to increasing the visibility of transpeople within the greater queer community and to helping transpeople grow and evolve by challenging the system while respecting difference and diversity.

For many transgender people, societal stigma and the tendency of mental health professionals to still pathologise the trans-experience, results in secrecy, shame, depression and fear. This leads to increased isolation. It can also lead to compulsive behaviour, exploitation, rage, guilt, addiction and even suicide. Many of these difficulties result from the mistaken belief that transgender and transsexual experiences and identities are a sickness we can somehow cure.

HIV and AIDS prevention and intervention are significant issues for people of transgender and transsexual experience. Often HIV/AIDS educational materials are not sensitive or relevant to transgender people. This can increase risk for HIV. Ten per cent of GIP participants are living with HIV/AIDS. The HIV status of 30 per cent of the GIP's participants who are at risk for HIV remain untested out of their fear of discrimination and prejudice at testing sites or among care providers.

In recent years, more people have recognised that transgender and transsexual people need to accept themselves and adapt their lives to their inner feelings. In order to better accomplish this, transgender people have created community support networks and organisations to end isolation, to heal from internalised shame, to decrease risk for HIV/AIDS and substance abuse, and to enable working together to combat prejudice and discrimination. It is with these goals in mind that the GIP was created and continues to flourish today.

History

The GIP was conceived in 1989, when Dr Barbara Warren, then the director of the Centre's Project Connect Alcohol and Drug programme, met with several transpeople to discuss their concerns. Barbara responded and began to work with trans-activists Riki Anne Wilchins and Kathy Ottersten to provide a setting where people of transsexual experience might be able to gather together and work on issues specific to them. The GIP was inaugurated with a core volunteer staff including men and women of trans-sexual experience, Yvonne Ritter, Rachel Pollack, Riki Wilchins, Toni Gilligan, Christian O'Neal and Kathy Ottersten.

Today, the GIP has a staff consisting of a director, Rosalyne Blumenstein, a counsellor, Carrie Davis, and eight stipended peer counsellors and HIV outreach workers. The GIP provides over 40 individual counselling sessions and 20 group sessions each month, as well as a range of community educational, cultural activities and community service activities and programmes.

The GIP acts as a national clearinghouse for trans issues, information and concerns and stands as a model of the first transgender project initiated and fully supported within a Community Centre focused on the needs of the greater queer community. The GIP receives funding from a variety of both private and public funding sources.

Health
Over the years, the GIP has expanded its mission beyond core issues of safe space and support, to address the major issue of health within the trans-community.

In 1994, Barbara Warren and three peer counsellors began to work with the Community Health Project (CHP), New York City's gay and lesbian health clinic, to address the issue of affordable and appropriate medical assistance for trans-identified individuals. In May 1995, the Transgender Health Education (THE) was formed to provide the first enlightened and trans-focused healthcare clinic open specifically to the trans-community. Today THE has been subsumed within the greater mission of the new Callen-Lorde Clinic (formerly CHP), which offers trans-specific primary health care as part of its basic mission statement and standards of care.

In April 1995, the GIP, the Greater New York Gender Alliance and International Federation for Gender Education co-sponsored the First Annual Transgender and Transsexual Health Empowerment Conference. The Fourth Conference was held 25 October and was co-sponsored by the Audre-Lorde Project, a community centre devoted to LGBT people of colour, in Brooklyn, New York. Its theme was *Transworld: A Conference for the Empowerment and Health of Transgender, Transsexual, Two Spirit People of Colour.*

Community

The GIP openly represents the greater transgender and gender variant communities, proudly encompassing the diversity of gender expression. GIP participants include individuals who identify utilising hundreds of different descriptors of gender including:

drag queen, drag king, crossdresser, crossgender, femme queen, butch queen, bigender, transsexual, of transsexual experience, FTM, MTF, MTM, FTF, pre-op, post-op, non-op, new woman, new man, phallic woman, transgenderist, butch, masculine, feminine, questioning, intersex, etc.

In addition the GIP clients and staff reflect the vast sexual, economic and ethnic diversity of the communities we serve including trans-identified individuals that encounter multiple oppressions and may identify as straight, gay, lesbian, bi, omni/pansexual, two-spirit, white, black, Latin, Asian, people of colour, teachers, labourers, professionals, activists, doctors, students, sex workers, homeless, disabled, etc.

Importantly, 50 per cent of the GIP's clients identify as people of colour.

Ongoing Efforts:

Peer Counselling

The GIP offers free and confidential one-on-one peer counselling for people concerned with gender identity issues, who need information, resources, referrals and would like to have someone to talk to. Within this environment we offer transgender and transsexual people a chance to talk with people like themselves who have worked through similar problems and life transitions.

Support Groups

The GIP continues to manage and support a variety of peer and professionally facilitated support groups addressing a range of needs in the transgender and gender variant community. All groups are confidential and free of charge. Recent groups include:

Women of Transsexual Experience Re-Unite
Transgender and Masculine, Butch or Questioning
Men of Transsexual Experience
Transgender/Gender Identity Exploration Group
The Spirituality of the Transgender Experience
Transgender Information and Support
Fe-MALE, Gender Questioning? Masculine or Butch
New Women of Transgender Experience
Forums and Community Education

Through outreach efforts, the GIP staff works to inform and educate professional counsellors, the lesbian, gay, and bisexual communities, the civil bureaucracy and the general public on gender identity issues. This is accomplished through on and offsite presentations, educational support group sessions, workshops and sensitivity/diversity trainings for substance abuse counselling programme and HIV-prevention and AIDS services agencies throughout the NY metropolitan area. In addition, the GIP regularly sponsors open community forums including celebrations, readings, conferences, and educational trainings. Some recent forums and trainings have included:

Eighth Annual State Wide AIDS Institute Policy Conference
Town Meeting on Trans-Safety and Violence
They Lived it 'OUT' – a night to remember people of trans-experience who have died
GIP/GMHC HIV/AIDS Transgender Legal Forum
Queer Pride Day
National Lesbian and Gay Creating Change Conference
– Film: *Gender Variance Perception – Yours/Mine/Ours*
Sexuality Series 101, 201, 301
Third Annual New England Transgender Health Conference – Safer Sex Outreach

HIV/AIDS Prevention and Intervention Services

GIP outreach workers directly distribute safer sex kits and other materials, street counselling information and referrals to the transgender population who often can only be reached on the street or within the many trans-focused clubs in New York City. To reach the greatest possible number of trans-identified individuals, the GIP works with an ad-hoc coalition of street outreach organisations. The GIP has also created an instructional and informative film – *Safe-T Lessons*, for trans-specific HIV prevention.

Alcohol, Tobacco and Drug Abuse Counselling

Working with the Centre's substance abuse services programme Project Connect, the GIP offers counselling and other services for alcohol/drug use and abuse, co-dependency, adult children of alcoholics, and other addictive-compulsive life challenges.

New Programmes to Meet Emerging Needs

On a regular basis the GIP has been and continues to be called upon to become involved with a variety of issues of major importance to the trans-community that have risen to the forefront. Currently the GIP is part of a coalition of groups titled the Transgender Policy Council, confronting the physical and emotional struggle of trans-identified individuals within the harsh confines of New York City's homeless housing system. This summer (1999) the GIP will co-facilitate the first intersex support group on the East Coast of the United States.

The Lesbian and Gay Community Services Centre

Since the historic 1969 Stonewall riots, our community has grown and changed dramatically. We have built an infrastructure where none existed before – institutions that serve those in crisis: the young, the elderly, people living with HIV and AIDS, survivors of anti-gay or anti-lesbian violence, people struggling with substance abuse, and gay people and their friends and families overwhelmed by the devastating toll of the AIDS epidemic.

187

Our community is infused with an activist spirit that other progressive communities envy, and, as a result, we continue to build many political and legal organisations and cultural institutions. Our community continues to endure a barrage of attacks from the religious right that prays and organises for our annihilation and exploits our lives as political scapegoats for its gain, while we mourn the unyielding, terrifying decimation of our community from AIDS. There is still deadly silence surrounding the epidemic of gay and lesbian substance abuse and other health issues, and there is abundant evidence of increasing anti-gay violence. The Centre provides a secure place to come together and plan, advocate, ACT UP, share our knowledge and our expertise, and shape our future.

The Centre itself produces many health-related, civic, and cultural programmes. They include:

Youth Enrichment Services (YES), an activities-based programme for lesbian and gay youth

CentreBridge, the Centre's AIDS bereavement programme

Centre Global Action Project (GAP), our international gay and lesbian rights programme

The Pat Parker/Vito Russo Centre Library, New York City's largest gay and lesbian lending library

The National Museum and Archive of Lesbian and Gay History

Promote the Vote, the largest lesbian and gay voter registration and mobilisation project in America, created in 1992.

In addition, one of the Centre's prime functions is to provide affordable meeting space for gay and lesbian organisations, many of which would otherwise have no place to go. The lack of affordable, safe space in this city has pushed several organisations to the brink of extinction. Stepping forward more than once, the Centre has kept doors open and ensured the delivery of much needed services and programmes. In 1985 the Centre became temporary home to the Harvey Milk High School, a programme of the Hetrick-Martin Institute. The Lesbian

Switchboard became a permanent tenant after it was evicted from its former home, and Dignity, a Catholic gay and lesbian religious organisation, sought refuge when it was expelled from Catholic churches.

The availability of meeting space has been a major organising tool for our community. Since we opened our doors, the number of lesbian and gay organisations in New York City has multiplied many times. Groups that were born at the Centre and have expanded throughout America have included the AIDS Coalition to Unleash Power (ACT UP), Queer Nation, Lesbian Avengers and the Gay and Lesbian Alliance Against Defamation (GLAAD).

Centre Mediation Service

Mediation is a useful, inexpensive way for people to resolve disputes on their own outside the legal system. Mediators help facilitate a settlement, they don't impose one. Our 20 professionally trained volunteer mediators ready to handle cases such as child visitation, property distribution between separating couples, termination or conditions of employment, dissolution of a business, room-mate boundaries, community agency board disagreements, and more.

Psychiatry Super-imposed: Gender and Sexuality Meet Modern Medicine

By Steve Clarke, RN (M), Clinical Supervisor and Manager of Acute General Care, Worthing Priority Care.

I have worked as a community psychiatric nurse in Ireland for a while. The role was focused on treatment at home for those in some form of need. Often part of this work involved assessment of clients who were distressed and vulnerable; sometimes they did not want to be assessed. In such cases we went in with police present and removed people from their homes for assessment at the local mental health unit.

Assessment criteria I used then were largely DSM 3 (R) led, though Ireland is still considering adopting ICD 10. I would do things VERY differently nowadays and would

189

vere away from psychiatric diagnosis and assessment criteria. Instead I would use the work of Hilda Peplau, and others to assess needs and not label with a diagnosis.

Psychiatry consists of the study of personal conduct. So said Szasz in his seminal book *The Myth of Mental Illness*. In it, he systematically deconstructs psychiatry, examining its history and foundations in Charcot and Freud. Szasz comes to the conclusion that psychiatry misinterprets people's use of signs and behaviours to communicate needs and wants. Indeed, these signs are determined to be neurological disorders. If no pathological basis for this diagnosis can be found, the disorder is categorised as functional, or a disorder of function.

In this context it seems that psychiatry attaches the label "sick" to those who exhibit signs or behaviour that it cannot understand. This all too often applies to lesbians and gay men. Psychiatry's interface with lesbians is particularly poor, and not surprisingly so, considering it is a male-dominated profession. It often sees behaviours that it cannot understand and labels them as "psychopathology".

The following is not an actual single case, but an amalgamation of several that I have encountered over the years.

A woman who was 35 years old was admitted to a psychiatric unit following an attempt on her life. She identified herself as a lesbian and had a couple of short-term relationships, none of which had lasted longer than a few months. The events leading up to the crisis were complicated by chronic pain from a skeletal injury and the use of alcohol and painkillers to cope with this. Along with significant loss of status in the recent past, this picture makes for one extremely traumatised individual. Somebody who needed to be carried for a little while and, hopefully in the context of a therapeutic relationship, could make sense of all the pain around her.

What psychiatry offers is often less than this and is sometimes counter-therapeutic. First come the pills: antidepressants to help elevate the mood, sleeping tablets to help slow the mind down, anxiolytics (or tranquillisers) to help deal with the feelings of panic and fear. As opposed to forming a relationship with this client that showed some understanding of her situation, psychiatry has told her that the way she feels is "sick" and needs to be treated. She is now dependent on it for medication and an imbalance in the relationship now evident.

Many years ago psychiatry shed the diagnosis of sexual deviation that it used to treat lesbians and gay men. This leads us to believe that psychiatry no longer treats lesbians and gay men for deviancy. In this case study, it could be seen that it did. Psychiatry has given itself a catch-all diagnosis that enables it to treat signs and behaviours that it does not understand – the "personality disorder" diagnosis.

This diagnosis, still largely seen as genetic in causation, is given to a collection of personality traits that lead to behaviours that lie outside the "norms" of society. Psychiatry has still to find a suitable medication to treat this disorder and hence it has labelled a large minority of its clients as untreatable, often ignoring therapeutic interventions that can and do work.

Not only do psychiatrists react to this diagnosis, but most other professionals do also, hence further damaging the potential for developing a therapeutic relationship. The stigma of this diagnosis will follow a client throughout their use of psychiatric services. It will be seized upon by different people as grounds to reject people for therapeutic work. This diagnosis was soon given to this woman.

She continued to use the conventional services and had several relapses where she became violent and threatened her own life and the lives of those working with her. It took the formation of a therapeutic relationship, arguably the first that had been formulated, for her to admit that she was distraught with the fact that she was a lesbian. The signs, in retrospect, clearly pointed to the fact that this client did not want to be herself. She chose to be violent towards herself, as a means of self-punishment for being something that she had been told for many years was wrong. Towards those who tantalisingly offered help and then did not give it, she threatened violence.

This continued to be the case, and only when she was given the right to be angry and the roots of the anger were explored did she start to trust. By gradually sifting through the trust issues, she eventually looked at where she, as a lesbian, fits within society and how she could be supported in this decision. Over a period of months she gradually returned to her home from an in-patient setting, and has returned to gainful employment. She slowly stopped taking most of her medication and has never looked back.

People's use of signs and behaviour as basic forms of communication has been in use since the dawn of humankind. Psychiatry has had a lot of catching up to do. As a relatively new science it has examined the cultural norms of mainly western heterosexual cultures and drawn conclusions from this. These conclusions, it seems, are then transposed onto other, non-western, non-heterosexual cultures where norms and values are very different, often leading to misdiagnosis and mistreatment.

As other cultures become more visible and accepted by greater society as norms themselves, psychiatry too must adapt to accept difference in behaviour and signs and learn that often all that is needed is understanding.

Bibliography

Szasz, Thomas S, *The Myth of Mental Illness*, Paladin Co, London, 1961

Peplau, Hildagard, *Interpersonal Theory in Nursing*, GP Putnam & Sons, NY 1952

The World's First International Foundation for Androgynous Studies

By Delphine McFarlane, Director Guild Student Services, The University of Western Australia

A number of senior academics, including the Deans of Medicine and Education at the University of Western Australia and I are involved in a major enterprise. We are asking for expressions of interest at this stage, in the following related ventures:

1. The world's first International Foundation for Androgynous Studies

2. The world's first visual and creative arts exhibition to be entitled *The Hidden Gender*.

An executive committee and an advisory committee has agreed on the aims, objectives and constitution of the world's first International Foundation for Androgynous Studies, based in Western Australia. We have three outstanding patrons for the Foundation, namely Jeff McMullen of Channel Nine's *60 MINUTES* here in Australia, Geoff Somers, MBE and Polar Medal, the British and Commonwealth team member of the historic 1990 International Trans Antarctica Expedition and Sister Veronica Brady, well-known humanitarian and author. The distinguished Australian contemporary artist Robert Juniper has offered his patronage to *The Hidden Gender* exhibition as well as his interest in being a participating exhibitor.

The foundation has been established as an incorporated body to advance the health, well-being, basic rights, social equality and self-determination of those who are physically and/or psychologically androgynous.

To achieve this purpose it will promote medical, social and educational research into the particular needs of androgynous persons; provide a media resource base for information for those who seek it; actively disseminate information about gender issues in general and androgyny in particular, both through scientific research, the arts and the Internet; encourage the active participation of visual and performance artists, film-makers, writers, poets, philosophers, and musicians in exhibitions which will draw attention to the humanity of androgynous persons; create a register of those who choose to leave their names with the foundation, thereby facilitating networking among androgynous persons and others; seek to introduce legislation for the protection of human rights in regards to diversity, education and socio-medical needs;

recognise the existence of androgynous persons through official documents, such as passports, birth certificates etc; influence educational curricula and the media to encourage tolerance and inclusivity rather than fear and exclusion of the unknown.

Property and income of the foundation shall be applied solely towards the promotion of the objects or purposes of the foundation and no part of that property or income may be paid or otherwise distributed, directly or indirectly, to members of the foundation except in good faith in the promotion of those objects or purposes.

This base has been established to inquire further into matters of gender, attempting to redress too rigid a dichotomy between male and female and re-examine accepted criteria for gender status. It covers a wide range of social and medical interests, including those of transsexuals and intersex persons, gays and lesbians, and sporting figures. It covers aspects of endocrinology, urology, paediatrics, surgery, psychiatry, clinical psychology, genetics, law, politics, history and education.

There have been many cases of what is clinically known as Gender Dysphoria where people are unable to decide whether they are more male or female. When they elect for surgery they are often unhappy with the superficiality of the physical transformation. There have been cases of hermaphrodites who have been denied birth certificates and voting rights because of their indeterminate gender and certainly cases of people who have lost their jobs when their condition is revealed.

The whole issue of social identity through gender is a major educational concern, and the foundation will respond to those educational, legal, ethical and historical concerns which further the rights of androgynous people to be treated in a holistic and humanitarian way. The foundation supports and encourages research, dissemination of information, networking and support for and about androgynous people.

The Hidden Gender art exhibition will provide an exemplary way to promote the International Foundation of

Androgynous Studies in a non-threatening and imaginative manner. Further, an exhibition of this magnitude will serve as a wonderful vehicle for all those involved to deal with a subject of immense potential and concern to medicine, the arts, sciences and the social dynamics of the human race.

It would not conduct research, but it would focus public attention on the concept of gender, with a similar view to dissolving the normal assumption of a binary male/female distinction. It is envisaged that a selected number of highly creative and committed visual and performance artists, writers, poets, philosophers, film-makers, and musicians from all genders be given the opportunity to exhibit their works in this show. Invited artists might work solo or together with a team of their own manageable choice, in keeping with the concept and available space. They are encouraged to use traditional and/or modern technological modes of expression in their own interpretation of the issues pertaining to epicene people worldwide.

We intend to have the first exhibition in Perth, Western Australia at a major venue in late 2000 and/or 2001. Should sufficient sponsorship be available, then we hope this unique exhibition could travel nationally and internationally. Such an exhibition could have far reaching implications for human sex, gender and sexuality issues and human rights, as well as create further interest in and understanding of a very little known area of the human condition.

We are writing to people whom we believe have demonstrated a high degree of integrity and humanitarian ideals, and would like to see such an exhibition become a reality, and those who may be interested in contributing to the international visual and creative arts exhibition. Because of the foundation's incorporation as an educational and charitable body, all donations are tax deductible. The response has been most encouraging and we are receiving letters of support from all over the world.

There has already been substantial interest in both the

exhibition and the foundation, even from national and international media, so we would be delighted to receive responses concerning these initiatives. Every letter which expresses support for the above concepts will assist the eventual formation of the exhibition and further the aspirations of the newly formed foundation. We would be most grateful for any assistance for the total concept for we believe it will benefit many people across the world and in this country. We do hope that you will be proud to support the above in writing, and where possible ask others to lend their help to the overall idea by indicating their support in print too. (See p342 for address)

Please discuss these ideas freely with family, friends and acquaintances, whether you fully support the concepts or not. Negative and positive, extraordinary and ordinary, a diversity of opinions and beliefs all contribute to a rich human society.

If That's Your Idea of Non-discrimination
By Christine Burns, Vice President of UK
trans-pressure group Press for Change

On 1 May 1999 a truly historic event took place for transpeople living in the British Isles. The day that Parliament enacted laws to protect transpeople from discrimination in employment.

As one of the core issues which Press for Change has campaigned to achieve for more than seven years, you might think that I and my colleagues would have been ecstatic on that day. You might think we'd have been popping the champagne corks and churning out press releases warmly supporting the government's historic initiative.

I wish we could have done. Sadly that wasn't the case though. In fact, the weekend after the existence of the *Sex Discrimination (Gender Reassignment) Regulations* was first made public, I felt obliged to publish an apology to the people who Press for Change represents, awarding ourselves just seven out of 10 for achievement. Barely a fortnight before that, I had sat in front of the Under Secretary of State for Equal Opportunities, Margaret Hodge MP, and argued long and hard for the legislation never to be tabled at all.

Right up to the afternoon before the legislation was laid before the clerks of the House of Commons I was still frantically arguing the same line to the Minister's officials. But to no avail. The Minister was, it seems, determined we should be "protected", whether we liked it or not.

I wouldn't blame you, of course, if you thought it rather bizarre that an organisation which campaigns for the equality of transpeople should be arguing to the very last minute with an Equal Opportunities Minister for a piece of anti-discrimination legislation to be stopped. It was certainly ironic to be in that position. Yet what we were arguing about was a piece of legislation which gave nothing to British transpeople which they didn't already have, but which has two whole pages of clauses dedicated to taking parts of that protection away.

Two whole pages where civil service lawyers had painstakingly set out to define circumstances in which it was acceptable to discriminate against transpeople uniquely in comparison to other citizens of either sex. A third sex, in fact. Not male...Not female...Not employable.

To appreciate these events, however, you have to go back three whole years to the judgement of the European Court of Justice in the now famous case, *P vs S and Cornwall County Council*.

You can read about the employment discrimination which greeted P on the Press for Change website. Suffice to say here that P, a transsexual woman, was blatantly discriminated after she announced her intention to transition from male to female at work, and as a result took the facts of the case to her local Employment Tribunal. The tribunal decided that it required clarification on the application of the European Community's Equal Treatment Directive, and the European Court of Justice delivered its judgement, in April 1996, that discrimination on grounds related to Gender Reassignment constituted sex discrimination within the scope of the Directive.

197

Shortly after that, a follow-up domestic employment case confirmed that the judgement applied to commercial organisations as well as "Emanations of the State", and from that point it became clear that British courts no longer had any confusion or doubt as to how to interpret the evidence of cases brought against employers by trans-people. No legislation was needed to achieve this. It's the way that the law works.

Politicians are perhaps understandably wary of this sort of "DIY Government" though. Indeed recently Margaret Hodge wrote in a letter to fellow Labour MP, Dr Lynne Jones: "I take the view that it is better for elected representatives in Parliament to determine legislation than for this to be settled by the courts".

Now, if that's not a "demarkation dispute" then show me one! Her Majesty's government was determined to act though, and wrote to Press for Change, in October 1997, to state as much. Margaret Hodge's immediate superior, The Rt Hon Andrew Smith MP, wrote to say: "We expect to begin consultations shortly and to look to organisations such as Press for Change for advice on the workplace problems experienced by transsexuals and those undergoing gender reassignment." In turn, we wrote back straight away with details of a committee of our own experts in the subject (almost all trans lawyers), and waited for meetings to be arranged.

We waited...And we waited...And we waited...

Almost four months later, on 2 February 1998 the silence was finally broken when an eight-page "Consultation Paper" plopped through PFC's letterbox, with a deadline of 13 March for comments.

It was a document quite breathtaking for the breadth and depth of the ignorance which it demonstrated and the discrimination which it seriously advocated. The paper suggested the possibility of restrictions on working with children (up to the age of 18), questioned the point in time at which protection should begin (or in other words suggested a period when protection shouldn't apply), posited rules on which lavatory facilities an employee should use, and outlined a series of temporary or permanent restrictions on certain types of employment which have survived largely intact in the final legislation.

As a blueprint for ignorant and unfounded discrimination against a part of society, the document stands as a masterpiece and can be studied, like all the others in this tale, on the Press for Change website, where it is reproduced in full.

PFC's response at the time was swift and decisive. In the space of just six weeks more than 300 transpeople, their families, friends, and employers were moved to write to the Minister and express what they thought of the proposals and (more importantly) to explain why they were unnecessary and repressive.

The Department for Education and Employment was certainly taken aback by the quantity and comprehensiveness of the response. Many organisations joined Press for Change in submitting detailed critiques of the reasoning in the proposals and, less than a fortnight after the closing date for responses, representatives of the Parliamentary Forum on Transsexual Issues met with the Minister, Andrew Smith MP, and elicited the nearest thing that you'll ever get to a ministerial admission that he and his advisors had got it badly wrong.

A discreet rewrite was proposed, and the Parliamentary Forum on Transsexual Issues was invited to submit recommendations to form the body of it. Those recommendations are now, in fact, published as our own Code of Practice, *Transsexual People in the Workplace*.

Still, however, there was no active dialogue from the DfEE. Then, just before Christmas 1998, we learned that Andrew Smith's junior ministerial colleague, Margaret Hodge, was eager to steer the process through to completion. "Greatly improved" legislation was being drafted, the Parliamentary Forum's submissions had allegedly been heeded and were being embodied into a set of guidelines to accompany it. The end was in sight. Or so we were told, because nobody wanted to divulge the details with us still. Chair of the Parliamentary Forum, Lynne Jones MP, had been shown a confidential copy, but she was sworn to secrecy by the Minister herself.

The new year brought other news though. It seemed that everyone else was being offered an opportunity to see and comment on the DfEE's handiwork. We found examples where this had occurred and lobbied furiously for an explanation. The result...at last...was that in the closing weeks of February we finally got to see the legislation, subject to strict confidentiality undertakings of our own.

We didn't need to confer much to judge what we saw though, and to confirm our belief that UK transpeople were far better off without legislation than with something riddled with exceptions...a bigot's charter.

To be fair, there were improvements. The government had abandoned its obsession with toilet rules and showed some signs of belatedly understanding that transpeople were not a danger to children...if still convinced that they are a danger to what it loosely terms "vulnerable people". Comparing the February 1998 consultation paper with the 1999 legislation, however, it is quickly evident that most of the other proposals had survived intact...with an addition hastily grafted on to deal with the fact that transpeople suddenly looked like being allowed to join the police force.

In February 1999 a Leeds Employment Tribunal had ruled that the statistically minor possibility of a conflict between a transwoman's legal sex (male) and parts of the Police and Criminal Evidence Act was not a valid reason to bar her from employment. Yet, barely a fortnight later, the Minister and her officials faced us across a table and refused, point blank, to remove a clause in the regulations which specifically promoted such discrimination.

Eighteen months after the process began, therefore, the response of the UK government to the European Court of Justice has been to legitimise discrimination which Employment Tribunals and higher courts were happy to rule out. Put simply, the government which said that it wanted to consult and to outlaw discrimination against

UK transpeople has placed itself in the position of leading offender. Thanks to Equal Opportunities Minister Margaret Hodge MP, 5000 UK citizens woke up on the morning of 1 May 1999 with less protection against employment discrimination than they had enjoyed since it was first earned for them in the European Court three years previously.

And the following week the Home Secretary, Jack Straw, announced, in a Commons written answer, the formation of a "working group" staffed from 12 government departments, tasked to spend the next 12 months investigating the problems experienced by transsexual people in general, and ways of addressing them.

Maybe we would feel better if it wasn't apparent that the DfEE's determination to steamroller their own legislation into force was driven by the political need for Jack Straw to make his own announcement before a fictional transwoman got married in a television soap watched by 18 million people.

We'd certainly feel better if the announcement had been preceded or accompanied by an invitation to take part in the process. No such invitation was received though and, at the time of writing this, it's still not clear just how much of a contribution transpeople will have in deciding matters which uniquely affect the quality of their lives.

Time will tell if the Home Secretary's laudable aims are matched by a truly informed search for solutions which work for real people. Barely a year after the first atrocious attempt at the same thing by the DfEE, it's clear that "consultation" is a word not matched by deeds in this government's book.

We'll lobby for all we're worth of course. At the same time we'll be using the courts to try and overturn the blatantly discriminatory provisions in the DfEE's legislation too. On the way we'll have more ignorant presumptions and folklore to counter among people who we pay to know better...people who are supposed to be there to serve us.

What is it they say though? Once bitten, twice shy?

June Brides

By Katrina Fox

First published in *Diva*,

The UK's national lesbian magazine, June 1999

Five years ago club bouncer Beverley Donald and her girl-friend Ronnie travelled to Holland to get married. They went the whole way – vicar, church, confetti and even a gay man in drag who was the bridesmaid. "All my sisters had got married and had a big wedding, and I wanted to as well," says Bev. Of course their marriage was not legal-ly recognised by any country in the world. But that didn't matter – it was the ceremony, the public declaration of their love that was important.

The question of whether we should campaign for the right to marry is an old chestnut that has bugged the les-bian and gay community for a long time. Understandably, as we hear about more countries passing laws granting registration of same-sex partnerships, which allow lesbian and gay couples a melée of automatic legal rights, we feel frustrated that the UK is so far behind.

But do we really want to get married? It seems we do. In *Diva's* sex survey last year, more than half of respondents said they would get married if they could. The Revd Johnathan Blake has been performing blessings and cer-emonies for same-sex couples for five years. The number of his lesbian clients is into the hundreds, he says, and his clientele is 70 per cent lesbians, compared with 30 per cent gay men.

So does this mean there been a change in lesbian/fem-inist thinking on marriage? Owner of Silver Moon women's bookshop Sue Butterworth thinks so. "Lesbians are more open to marriage now. In my youth I was against it, as it was used as a controlling device against women, but it is not the institution it used to be." Angela Mason, executive director of gay pressure group Stonewall, agrees. In the 1970s she was in a campaign called Why be a Wife? "When I was younger, marriage meant discrimination against women; now that's virtually gone," she says.

But some dykes remain vehemently anti-marriage. Writer Spike Katz says: "Marriage is an institution. It is supported, often quite materially, by all those nasty homophobic institutions such as the Church and the State." Fellow writer Cherry Smith is also against marriage, but does recognise the contradictions: "It always struck me as absurd that couples would go to a man of God to get married then to a man of law to get divorced. Yet there is something thrillingly perverse in saying 'will you marry me?' to the woman you love and appropriating those institutions."

Linda Nelson, 47 and Jane Bevan, 35 were "married" by Johnathan Blake in a local hotel. Around 34 of their friends and relatives attended. They chose the passages for the service and exchanged rings. They are not at all concerned about the political implications of same-sex marriage. "We're not activists," says Linda. "Some gay women are anti-everything; they've got a chip on their shoulder. I guess we're just too normal for that." Ouch.

It seems it's the ceremony itself that is important to lesbians – the bearing of witnesses to a couple's love for each other. Yes, they'd like the legal rights and benefits afforded to straight married couples, but are generally apathetic in campaigning for the right to legal marriage.

By contrast, in the US there is a huge gay movement committed to fighting for the freedom to marry. Evan Wolfson, director of campaigning group Lambda Legal Defense Fund and Education, explains why. "To say we shouldn't want to get married is like saying women shouldn't go to law school because the law is a patriarchal system," he says. Fair enough. But then he adds: "There is no single step we could take to end discrimination against gay people than the right to marry."

Wolfson's argument is based on the fact that most marriage benefits are not replicable in US law and those that are, are expensive. In other words, if gay people want their legal rights, the right to marry is the path. But this doesn't help those people (gay and straight) who don't want to get married. Perhaps the fight for the right to marry in the

US is stronger because of the resistance to it – more than half of US states have passed laws outlawing marriage for same-sex couples.

With the UK showing no signs of recognising same-sex relationships, you'd think we would follow the US's line. But gay pressure groups in the UK are looking more to our European counterparts for guidance. Outrage and Stonewall take the view that it is better to fight for equal rights for same-sex partners, which can include, but not have marriage as a priority. Stonewall is currently conducting a survey into what kind of partnership recognition gay people want. "It looks as though marriage is not what people want," says Mason. "They want to be treated equally and there are lots of ways of achieving this – it's not necessary to concentrate on status."

It looks as though we've got our work cut out for us, though. Most European countries with partnership registration have a mutual agreement to recognise partnership contracts in each other's countries. As far as the UK government is concerned, it is a case of the left hand not knowing what the right is doing. When contacted by *Diva*, the Lord Chancellor's office said reassuringly: "Officials in the UK are working with their counterparts in the European Union on how to deal with these issues." Yet a spokesman for the Home Office insisted: "Same-sex marriages, or 'registered partnerships' would require primary legislation to amend the Matrimonial Causes Act and the Marriage Act. The government has no plans to introduce such legislation." Best not hold our breaths, then.

The benefits of marriage are not to be sniffed at – tax breaks, pension rights, property rights, inheritance rights and so on. Registered partnerships give many of these provisions, but still do not allow full equality for same-sex couples, such as the right to marry in a church or adopt children.

Vibeke Nissen, a 52-year-old Danish psychologist and her girlfriend Inge-Lise Paulsen, 53, registered their partnership for purely practical reasons. They believe few gay people in Denmark are happy with the registration arrangements. "We would have liked something created especially for gays and lesbians, instead of a second-rate marriage," says Paulsen. "A major problem for same-sex couples with children is that you get the duties but no rights. You have to support your partner's child but you have no right to the child."

Marriage and registered partnerships also bring with them the thorny issue of divorce. Some gay activists say the only people to benefit from gay marriages are the divorce lawyers, who make copious amounts of money from heterosexual divorces. The emotional effects of a divorce can also be devastating. Marianne, a Norwegian lesbian from Oslo, registered her partnership in 1996, got a separation in March 1998 and is waiting to receive her final divorce papers from the registry office. She still carries much grief about the break-up. "The worst part of the divorce was that I felt really bad that I couldn't live as the person my wife needed. Plus our communication broke down so totally that we are not talking about the same story, or the same divorce, or even the same relationship."

The fact that it takes around a year in Norway to get a divorce (sometimes two, if one person does not want the divorce), can be a strain for some people, as it does not allow them to make a fresh start so quickly. Marianne is considering starting up a support group for lesbian divorcees. Her divorce has not put her off registering another partnership, but she is far more wary. "I've been there, done that, got the T-shirt and next time I won't dive straight into it as the first time. It will be less of an 'if straight people marry we can too' decision and more of a 'do we want to and why?'".

Although there are ways gay people can protect themselves and their partners in UK law, they can often be expensive and complicated. But by providing special rights to married couples only, governments are forcing people to buy into the institution. Instead of gay people becoming a part of that, why not campaign for simple, cheap ways of protecting ourselves and our loved ones in law? Fighting for the right to marry is one thing, but campaigning for our legal rights should surely be separate. No one, gay or straight, should be forced into the institution of marriage merely to be treated equally. Registered partnerships are an option, but we must ensure they provide full equal rights.

Those who want to "marry" or have a public ceremony have the option of going to people such as Johnathan Blake and choosing their own words and service, instead of being beholden to a rigid traditional one based on a heterosexual model. After all, let's face it – the straights haven't exactly got a great track record as far as marriage goes. The number of marriages is continuing to drop year on year, and many end in divorce. Do we really want to go down that path?

What you can do to safeguard your interests in UK law

1. PROPERTY AND ESTATE

Take out a Trust Deed.
This needs to be executed by both parties to say the property is held for the legal owner and her partner on a share basis. This can be 50-50 or 99-1. Even if you have only a 1 per cent share in the property, you can draw up conditions such as the right to remain in the property, or to force sale if you split up.

Establish equitable interest
If your partner owns a property and you have made any improvement to it, or made a capital contribution towards the purchase, or put money into the property after purchase, you have legal redress by having an equitable interest in the property, according to Haema Sundram, solicitor at Judith Burton & Co, London.

But, you must contribute directly to the mortgage, warns Ruth Ross of Simon Woods & Co, London. "If you only pay money to your partner, the onus is on you to prove that it went on mortgage payments."

Make a will

A will is one of the best forms of protection you can give your partner for inheritance rights, says Sundram. Contrary to popular belief, it is extremely difficult to over-turn a will. "It can only be over-turned if a family member challenges it on the basis that it is suspicious, or the person who made it was not of sound mind." The only other way a will can be challenged, is under the Inheritance (Family and Dependants) Act in which a person has to show they were maintained by the deceased immediately before death. If children are involved, they can, however, make a claim at any time. "To dispute a will on the basis that the partner is of the same sex will not wash nowa-days," assures Sundram.

2. ILLNESS

Take out a living will

A doctor has responsibility for the treatment of a patient. You won't find a doctor that will not consult the next of kin, says Ross. The doctor will assess the situation and if the dying person has executed an enduring power of attor-ney (living will) which gives the partner rights over a per-son's property and the right to make medical decisions for them, then these have been known to prove the impor-tance of a partner to a dying person and may influence the doctor's decision. But, warns Ross: "It is not a legal docu-ment, merely an expression of wishes – beware of its limi-tations."

3. CHILDREN

Take out a joint residence order

You can make an application for a joint residence order which attributes parental responsibility to someone as well as the birth parents. The court will decide whether to grant it, although Ross says they are generally more sympathetic nowadays. The birth father has a right to object to this, although it is not relevant where artificial insemination and sperm banks are concerned.

A court is unlikely to grant an order at the start of a relationship, though, says Ross. "You have to prove you are the parent, not that you intend to be. An application will be unsuccessful if made when one party is pregnant or if a child has just been born." Sundram adds that it is more likely to succeed if a couple have been together for some time.

These orders are useful to show your involvement and commitment if you later want to make an application for child contact. The drawback is that it's an expensive process, says Ross, and many couples don't bother with it because it is highly unlikely that they will be granted legal aid.

Same-sex partnership recognition around the world
EUROPE

Denmark – Registered partnership – all rights of marriage except no right to adopt children, have a church wedding, no right to artificial insemination and one of the partners must be Danish. Partnership is not legally recognised outside Denmark except for Scandinavian countries with similar legislation.

Hungary – Co-habitation law which applies to opposite-sex and same-sex couples. _____

Iceland – Registered partnership. Same-sex couples can adopt children who are biologically related to one of the partners.

The Netherlands – Registered partnership, similar to Danish law. However, there are two bills currently going through the Dutch Cabinet – an adoption bill and a marriage bill for same-sex couples. Likely to become law some time in 2001.

Norway – Registered partnership based on the Danish law.

Sweden – Registered partnership based on the Danish law.

Catalonia – Spanish region – domestic partnership.

Upcoming legislation:

Finland – Drafting proposals for registered partnership legislation.

Germany – Drafting proposals for registered partnership legislation.

France – Drafting proposals for a form of legal marriage for same-sex couples.

Portugal – Drafting proposals for registered partnership legislation.

Switzerland – Expected to propose draft proposals for registered partnership legislation.

OTHER

US – In the state of Hawaii, the supreme court ruled that banning same-sex marriages was unconstitutional. But the people of Hawaii voted to alter their constitution to define marriage as a union of a man and a woman and to restrict marriage to opposite-sex couples only. The case is currently on appeal and waiting a final decision on whether the legislature can refuse same-sex marriage.

More than half of US states have passed anti-marriage bills.

Canada – Has picked away at marriage rights one by one under their human rights ordinance, the Charter of Rights and have won several lawsuits on issues such as pensions, taxes and child custody awards.

Australia – Different states recognise same-sex partnerships for purposes of benefits such as pensions and inheritance. In New South Wales the De Facto Relationships Amendment Bill which would recognise same-sex cohabiting couples in the definition of "de facto" is being debated in the NSW Upper House.

PAPERS BY
DR TRACIE O'KEEFE
DCH

This section contains a collection of papers published nationally and internationally over the past three years, as well as a selection of new work being published for the first time

9

Papers by Dr Tracie O'Keefe

Gender and Sex Identity Disorder vs Sex, Gender and Sexuality Exploration

The XVI Harry Benjamin International Gender Dysphoria
Association Symposium
London, August 1999

The course of medical and psychological intervention of psycho-social-sexual conditions labelled gender identity disorders changes constantly in accordance with social perspectives and ever developing models of clinical practice. Both clients and clinicians mesmerise themselves into a numerically recognised diagnosis that can be cross-referenced several times in varied forms of academic literature. At times this can be useful as one professional in the field communicates to another through a coded encryption that contains a large amount of detailed information. On other occasions a client can nominalise the accepted identity disorder or rebuke a distasteful diagnosis in accordance with their own sense of comfort and opinion of that clinical interview.

The gender community attempts to depathologise the condition of Sex and Gender Dysphoria, so that it does not go back into the Diagnostic & Statistical Manual of Mental Disorders (DSM) or International Classification of Disease (ICD) as it was previously. Neither is it thought of as a mental disorder. But the very action of removing all pathology can disempower the sex and gender identity disorder itself by rendering it ineligible for funding from social health systems. This dichotomy of the client group choosing the freedom of self-determination over a perceived authoritarian, uncontrollable medical determination is a hot debate that causes friction between the gender movements and clinicians who provide care as we go into the 21st century.

There can be a point at which a diagnosis can become a burden to the sex, gender and sexuality client, which at times may go unnoticed by a well-intentioned clinician, whose only desire is to help that individual. For some who seek help to eliminate those varying forms of dysphoria, a diagnosis may be a salvation in itself by way of being a refuge from confusion, uncertainty, and which can produce security through feelings of belonging to a particular group of people who have found solutions to their problems.

Within the past few years there has been much shouting from the rooftops by many of the gender community that they have no pathology, but are simply exploring their own selves. From a politically emancipating point of view for a socially oppressed minority this is a fine cry to make. However, great danger lies in wait for the unsuspecting sex, gender and sexuality revolutionary when they proclaim themselves as not having an illness. As the English psychiatrist James Barrett said to me in 1997: "People who claim they do not have a pathology and then make demands for funds to cure their Sex and Gender Dysphoria are in big trouble. You can't demand funds to cure something you have not got."

Those who suffer from a gender identity disorder have a journey to travel that leads them to change the way they present themselves in society. They will portray a social image that will represent a cultural interpretation of a gender that will be female, male, in-between or neither. This interpretation of gender may be other than was associated with their prevalent original biological sex. They may also need extensive counselling in order for them to feel happy with the way they present themselves and in coping with the way in which others react to the image they present.

People who are sex dysphoric have a different set of criteria because their dysmorphobia consists of their emotional incongruencies between dominant biological sex and their mental projection of an ideal self. For those who cannot dispel these incongruencies through psychotherapy there is a need for them to alter their bodies to anatomically represent a physiological interpretation that is other than their original biological sex.

Sexuality Dysphoria, which is the condition of someone who is unhappy with what is happening in their sex life, is now commonly accepted and funding given without bureaucratic aggravation. Many clients seeking help with Sex, Gender and Sexuality Dysphoria find their disposition may be composed of a combination of all three elements. Whatever the combination of dysphorias that a person may suffer – and every person must be treated as an individual – that person will possibly need to have their treatment funded if they cannot afford to go the private route to resolve their situation.

For those who choose the private route and have the commercial means to pick and choose the kind of treatment they have, and when and where that takes place, there is licence to call their journey one of sex, gender and sexuality exploration. They are not beholden to the kind of bureaucracy that demands pathology to be defined in order to supply funds for its eradication.

The client who has any of the combinations of Sex, Gender and Sexuality Dysphoria and does not have sufficient private finances to select the treatment they need or desire is in an unenviable position of having to be pathologised. As I write this I hear the clarion call arising for those who say it should not be that way and society should fund people to pursue their dreams of happiness.

Unfortunately, in all reality, that is unlikely to happen as the demands now being placed on differing countries' funded medical resources are compounded by the day as medicine advances and a wider range of expensive treatments become available. Not only do more sophisticated expensive new treatments become available but also differing client groups often demand that their own form of medical needs outweigh the needs of the sex, gender and sexuality dysphoric.

As a clinician I must confess that I have to conjugate my descriptions according to the individual that I am talking to. With a client, I am happy to say that they can explore their sex, gender and sexuality and that I do not diagnose them because that is something I am unable to do. I do not live inside their body, see out of their eyes, hear out their ears or smell and taste what they do; therefore, I declare it would be arrogant of me to try and offer them a diagnosis of something which is, after all, truly a self-diagnostic series of conditions.

When I am dealing with other professionals I have to turn about face and put on another hat, describing clients as having Sex, Gender and Sexuality Dysphoria. This is never a difficult metamorphosis for me to make as I split the semantics of resolution between those who desire or need to change, the fundholders and those who possess the power to help the dysphoric person realign their sense of self.

Many people who walk into my consulting room are severely disturbed and confused about their sense of self and they do not have a clear idea of proposed exploration. In fact it is quite rare to have someone arrive who has truly made the exploratory journey in their minds before they present themselves for gender and sex realignment. For many, dysphoria is real, not simply a matter of authoritative diagnostics, and in order to help those people find their ways they deserve an acknowledgement of their distress. To be denied their discomfort and label is to forsake human suffering in order to pursue a stridently divine political agenda, which is insensitive and cruel.

Clients in distress, their relatives and friends do not want to know that a dysphoric person should be addressing their political needs over personal fulfilment. They want help, a cure, resolution and they need to know that professional help is at hand to dispel the malady from which a sex, gender or sexuality dysphoric person suffers. Such people are not so interested in cause and effect – only if there is a reasonable chance of resolution.

To those who would do away with any kind of pathologising of Sex, Gender or Sexuality Dysphoria I say:

> *Hands off the mechanism that enables the payment of treatment for those who need community medicine funds in order to be able to go on to lead a comfortable and fulfilling life*

For those who wish to evaluate these conditions to be equivalent with pregnancy I say:

> *Having a baby carries a low risk of killing anyone; however, for so many sex, gender and sexuality dysphoric people, medical and psychological intervention is life-saving treatment*

For the clinicians I urge you to listen to the gender community's message:

> *We will never again allow you to put us in a position where these conditions may be classified as mental illness*

And to the gender community at large I offer more wise words from James Barrett:

> *Be oh so careful what you wish for because you may very well get it*

As well as being a clinician who helps sex, gender, and sexuality dysphoric people I also had the condition of Sex Dysphoria myself. In absolute poverty I relied on others to fight to get the funds for me to have treatment which saved my life. Many years later from a position of resolution I can have the luxury to say that I have enjoyed sex, gender and sexuality exploration, but in all honesty, I would neither then or now qualify for community-funded treatment based on such a metaphorical scenario as exploration.

People who are unable to afford private medicine and are desperate to resolve their dysphoria are more likely to turn to crime in order to pay for their care. Poverty forces minority groups to eventually develop a large number of people who operate outside the law in order to survive. The pressure of trying to attain their treatment drives many to substance abuse and they may very well end up buying poor quality hormone and surgical treatment from charlatans, quacks and fraudsters. Furthermore, people with such conditions, who are unable to get treatment within a reasonable amount of time, are under profound stress and are more likely to be in low-paid jobs, unemployed, or so dysfunctional that they are unable to work at all.

To understand people's dysphorias more clearly clinicians need to expand their concepts from simple gender identity disorder to a growing ethos of gender, sex and sexuality exploration and resolution. Equipped with this knowledge, both clinicians and the gender community can then work more closely hand-in-hand to address the clients' needs and communications succinctly.

It must be remembered that the bureaucrats who hold the allocation of funding for treating clients are unlikely to understand the nuances of interdisciplinary terminology, political correctness or niceties. Their job is to produce the most likely outcome from a series of statistical and legitimised probabilities.

It is imperative that this acrimonious, discursive debate is now settled and an agreed resolution is reached between clinicians and consumers in order that treatment for the sex and gender dysphoric people can go forward expeditiously to fully benefit those client groups. In order for that to happen academics in the field will have to grow larger ears and eyes, and the sex and gender community will need to help that growth to take place.

The leaders in the field of sex, gender and sexuality medicine and the new multiple sex, gender and sexuality political freedom community must work together. This will produce a united front in order to make a case for funding to be provided for those who cannot afford private treatment. It is with pride I tell you that in many cases this is happening and I hope the spirit of co-operation and interactive medicine will flourish and prosper as everyone gains their accolades for maximum collaboration.

The Ethical Administration of Hormone Replacement Therapy in the Field of Sex/Gender Identity Dysphoria

Published in *Reflections International*, June 1997

The discourse of this paper is centred around the correctness of timing in the administration of body-altering hormones to those people with Sex or Gender Identity Dysphoria or those who are expressing their less polarised gender roles. Here the SGID is a diagnosis arrived at by the client with the assistance of a clinician from the psychological disciplines. This syndrome is derived from the individual's perception of their physical body being out of line with their mental and spiritual self-image. It can be deemed that it is a subjective experience and a form of dysmorphobia.

Since the true aetiology of this disorder is not only unclear scientifically, but also in great dispute according to the perspectives of the diagnosing clinician, a common formula of cause and effect cannot be identified. At the time of writing of this paper the debate about the specific aetiology carries on internationally, with many factions not only disagreeing with but also opposing each other's opinions. The nature or nurture question is not a consideration here.

When Dr Harry Benjamin started to treat the prefemisexual, Christina Jorgensen, in the 1940s, he did not ask her whether she had completed a time living as a woman before he agreed to prescribe her hormones. If she had been living as a woman, she would have been considered to be a transvestite, because the official interpretation of the male person living as a female is just that. At some of the major SGID clinics throughout the world many of the residing clinicians stipulate that their clients must have lived in their desired role for a period of time before they agree to administer hormones.

There is no research information to show that those

transsexuals who live in role before being administered hormones fair any better than those who do not. An argument may indeed be put forward that the reverse can be true. Plainly the administration of hormones prior to the social, legal and employment change of identity can, in certain cases, make the transition easier when the time to change roles arrives. Among those who agree with me on this point are consultant psychiatrist Dr Russell Reid, the Canadian psychologist Randi Ettner PhD, the endocrinologist Dr Fred Ettner, and the chair of the Gendy's Network, Alice Purnell, who is also a counselling psychologist.

Some clinicians at major SGID clinics, who are forcing clients to live in role before they are ready, are placing an unnecessary psychological strain on those people. Counter-transference of the clinician's expectations of stereotypical sex and gender roles causes the real-life-test to be in default because it is seen by the client as blackmail and not as a free choice.

It is true that many transsexuals present themselves to clinicians when living in their desired gender roles to request hormone treatment. However, this may not necessarily be the right, correct and proper course of progression for each and every client. It is well known that many transsexuals who present themselves for treatment have learnt what is known as "the script": they have learnt what to say from other transsexuals and they go along and follow a pre-rehearsed performance piece for the clinician.

I have come across many cases where this has happened and the clinician has prescribed hormones and surgery without ever considering the real issues that may be affecting the individual's decision. When this happens some clients regret transition after surgery.

I personally know of the suicides of several of the clients of one major ·clinician in the field who made unrealistic, overly demanding and cruel requests of his clients. Many clients who will live happily as complisexuals may be physically unconvincing in their appearance before the administration of hormones, which take them towards their destination sex and gender. Treatment can have dramatic effects on the appearance of a client and they need to be in control of their own situation with the help of the clinician involved and not under the threats of that clinician.

In fact, the control of the situation should be given over as much as possible to the client because if this does not happen then an over-dependency on the medical system often arises. On this point the therapist, Marjorie Anne Napewastewiñ-Schützer, agrees with me. Also, in Holland the gender team, led by Professor Louis Gooren, at the Amsterdam Royal Free Hospital, have a more flexible approach similar to the one I am suggesting.

In our culture there is an anomaly between males and females. For a female to live with the appearance and cultural dress code of a male in the Western world does not carry a great deal of scorn from the public, in comparison with what appears to be a man in a dress. Therefore the physiological and cultural differentials can be biased in favour of premascusexuals getting preferential treatment over prefemisexuals. In the administration of hormones to the gender dysphoric all clinicians must examine their own personal, subjective stereotyping of sex and gender identification.

There is the further consideration of the freedom to choose. The individual has the right to decide the fate of their own body. For the clinician the first consideration must be what is good for the client, but let us remember here that SGID is not a classifiable psycho-pathology. Forty years ago homosexuality suffered from the same kind of social and clinical discrimination that SGID presently does.

The rise of the transgender movement is now changing the role of medicine in the treatment of SGID. In all the caring professions the clinician's function is moving towards helping the client and not just deciding their fate in an authoritarian manner.

Sarah Allwood-Muir was the British transsexual surgeon who in 1997 changed her role well after she had commenced hormone treatment. She said it was the best way for her to make the change professionally, since she was a prominent medical practitioner. The American eye surgeon, Renee Richards, in the 1970s did the same thing.

To force a client in an SGID situation to wait until they are living in role before allowing them the medication they need is no less than cruel and only serves to bolster the ego of the clinician involved, and it may not necessarily best serve the needs of the client.

Most clinicians in SGID clinics see clients for less than 10 hours before they recommend them for surgery, demanding that the client performs tasks that satisfy the needs of the clinician and not necessarily those of the client. I see people for a minimum of 25 hours, over a minimum period of 18 months, before I will recommend them for surgery. At least one year of that period prior to surgery does require the person to live and work in role.

I have never had anyone who has regretted the decision they made after spending time with me but I do have people who drop out of treatment along the way and return to their former identities. The weeding-out of those who are truly intent upon their course can be better done by offering the client sufficient time and space to explore their own issues and mind-sets; it should not be dependent upon their ability to model a dress or a pair of jack boots.

Hormones are readily available on the black market on the streets of London, New York, Hong Kong, Dehli, Barcelona, and all major international cities and to procure them is not hard for the SGID individual. What is needed is more clinicians who will allow their clients to set the agendas, and who will not dictate to them. If the latter happens, it is likely to force the client into acquiring hormones on the black market, where the preparation they consume may be fake, unsuitable or dangerous.

I realise that some factions have criticised this approach by saying it is hormones on demand; however, that is not true. There are many people who I do not put forward for hormone treatment because I believe they have not thought through the issue of their proposed transition.

221

When I recommend someone for treatment I am generally satisfied that they are perfectly serious about what they are doing and have considered it well.

In therapy, during the period prior to surgery, we look at the many pros and cons of what the client is doing but I never use this to prevent hormone treatment being given. A client needs to feel they can trust me to be kind, honest, empathetic, and be working with them towards gaining the maximum amount of happiness from life. I am not judge and jury, but simply the usher.

SGID is an incongruency between body, mind and social role, and the administration of hormones seeks to minimise or eliminate that incongruency. It is not a behaviouralist token economy reward that is given to a client who is good, but a medication that can ethically be administered to a suitable candidate for sex and gender realignment, who may have already suffered quite enough torment. It should never be withheld on the grounds of social role performance.

The Administration of Hormones to the Transgendered Community

Published in *Reflections International*, July 1997

In this paper I am considering the administration of hormone treatment therapy to the transgendered individual who specifically does not identify as being transsexual. In my 1997 book *Trans-X-U-All: The Naked Difference* my co-author Katrina Fox and I distinguish between the transsexual who identifies as belonging to their opposite biological sex and the transgendered person, who identifies as their original biological sex, but wishes to partially alter their body to physically represent their opposite biological sex.

To help the reader more clearly understand the transgender identification I shall also say that in the US, transgender covers the whole of the trans-community. However, I have had difficulty with this definition because it implies that the transsexual has in some way crossed over from one identity to another. The transsexual believes they have simply adjusted their identity to realigning it with their true sex.

The transgendered person is happy to be identified with having crossed some kind of gender barrier, but not the sex barrier. These individuals will exhibit facets of multiple sexes and genders, or in fact they may very well seek self-labelling according to what suits them.

A biological male who seeks to be transgendered may undergo hormone treatment, plastic surgery and electrolysis, living socially and working as a female or transgendered person full or part time. However, this person will still identify during sex and privately through self-image, to a large part, as male. These individuals are not to be confused with the prefemisexual who is a transsexual awaiting vaginoplasty.

A biological female who seeks transgender self-identification may undergo hormonal and surgical procedures, including bilateral mastectomy. This person will not undergo any form of genital surgery, identifying strongly with their female genitals as being the very core of their true identity as a woman living as a male. This category of person is not to be confused with the premascusexual (a transsexual, originally biologically female, awaiting phalloplasty or who has decided not to have phalloplasty because of surgical risks). These individuals do not think of themselves as men but as women with male characteristics.

Furthermore the transgendered person is not a physical hermaphrodite, transvestite, or a person who wishes to represent themselves as being androgynous, because of the clear identification with their original biological sex.

A very important point to put across at this stage is that the transgendered person seeks their identification and is not a victim of misidentification. Of course they could have had other identifications before they aligned their self-image to that of a transgendered person or they could move on from transgendered to another self-identification.

Western culture has had great difficulty acclimatising to

those members of society who identify as not belonging to the extremes of the sex and gender polarity scale of heterosexual male and female. For thousands of years, in many other cultures in the world, the existence of the less statically gendered has been celebrated, tolerated, or seen as benign.

Unfortunately the modern Western culture has developed a distinct phobia against those who are not stereotypical and who are representations of the diversity of sex, gender and sexuality. This hostility has, at times, been taken to a sociopathological extreme. All forms of prejudice are the results of sociopolitical and religious motives that often cite morality, fanaticism or law and order as their reason for persecution of minorities, including members of the trans-community.

The transgendered person is a true sex and gender adventurer and they choose to make their journey out of a sense of exploration of their own experience. They are beyond those of us who are more strongly tethered to the narrow margins of our own sex, gender and sexualities. When they request hormones, providing there are no serious medical contra-indications, they should be allowed to legally imbibe those hormones without moral judgement from the rest of us, including the medical establishment.

It is appropriate that a transgendered person should sign a form absolving the hormone administrator of blame should complications occur due to that administration. It is essential, however, that the administrator of the hormones and any therapists involved need to take sufficient care in advising the transgendered individuals of the advantages and pitfalls of their intended course.

Insufficient research exists to guarantee the transgendered person that there will be no side effects, so it would be unfair of them to hold the doctors and therapists solely responsible should complications occur. It is also the responsibility of any transgendered person who is taking hormones to monitor publicly available information on the research connected with the administration of those hormones.

Every day in our society people are allowed to tattoo, pierce and mutilate themselves, drink and smoke themselves to death and consume copious amounts of narcotics. Drug companies bombard us with products that are addictive and have disturbing side effects, many of which the consumer was warned about. Yet the transgendered person is often refused the hormones they require to continue their lives in the way they choose.

There has been a trend in psychiatry and psychology to judge transgendered people as having a psychopathology, which bears no official diagnosis. Yet it allows the clinician to be abusive by using their own personal moral standpoints to contaminate other people's desired experiences.

There is a great need for those professionals who work with sex, gender and sexuality to re-educate themselves to be empathic to the needs of all the trans-community, and to reserve their judgmentalism. To date many of the sexologists and doctors I come into contact with daily have trouble understanding the dynamics of transsexualism, but when it comes to the trangendered issues they look at me as if I am speaking Martian.

It has been suggested to me that transgenderism is simply a social construct that is the result of our culture's need to accept the diversity of nature. This may very well be true but even so, that still does not give those of us who are not transgendered the right to deny others their desired experiences.

In a free society if the individual has the legal right to commit suicide, then surely they must ultimately be allowed to live their lives as they see fit, without the interference of the moral majority. Transgendered people do not threaten other people's existence or happiness, therefore they should not be denied the hormones they need to explore their own personal identities. A clinician, on the other hand, does need to point out that the course they take may have irreversible physiological, psychological and sociological repercussions.

I suppose the ultimate question that many would like answered about the transgendered is are they sex dysphoric and/or gender dysphoric? Some may be moving towards their developing identity through free will, therefore not being either sex dysphoric or gender dysphoric. The alternative is that some may be moving away from their old identity, unhappy with it, therefore being sex dysphoric or gender dyphoric. The third option may include both scenarios. However, we should remember that each person has the right to make their own journey through life and that there are no correct formats when it comes to the human condition.

Psychotherapy rarely dissuades transgendered people from pursuing the course that they indicate they wish to take. What tends to happen is that they get the hormones on the black market anyway, but are robbed of any kind of reasonable medical supervision. This further takes them out of the caring system, isolates them, stops them from accessing social care should they need it and turns them into what Kate Bornstein calls Gender Outlaws.

I have had several cases of people who have lived as transgendered for a large part of their lives and these individuals have reported that this was the right decision for them. They did not want to be medicalised as transsexuals and neither did they want to live completely as their original biological sex. The ones who have been denied such treatment talk about having miserable lives held back by their unhappiness with their bodies. These people should have access to hormone treatment to change their bodies in order to facilitate their personalities and live a rewarding life.

The Administration of Hormone Therapy to the Cross-Dressing and Androgyne Community

Published in *Reflections International*, December 1997

At the turn of the century the availability of cross-biological sex hormone administration has been around for nearly 80 years. To begin with, hormones were used for people who were diagnosed as being hormonally deficient. They

They were also administered to the intersex categories of people who wished to define or re-define their sex. Later they were used with people who identified as being transsexual and who believed they belonged to their original opposite biological sexes. In the 1980s and 1990s transgendered individuals were taking hormones to appear one sex while remaining and functioning sexually as their original biological sex.

This paper is specifically dealing with the cross-dressing community (also described as transvestites), who may live part or full time in the opposite role to their biological sex. When I talk of cross-dressers I include those who could be categorised as social or fetishistic transvestites. Social transvestites live cross-dressed, dressing in clothes sociologically associated with the opposite biological sex, because that is how they feel comfortable presenting themselves. Fetishistic transvestites wear the clothes, generally associated with the stereotypes of the opposite biological sex, because they experience erotic stimuli associated with that particular kind of clothing.

It is essential for the sake of clarity to distinguish transvestites from drag queens and kings, as the latter dress up in clothing of their opposite biological sex in a kind of social pantomime performance. Their dressing is intended as a parody of what is socially considered opposite gender stereotypes. Such people often earn their living by performing in drag shows on the gay scene or even in straight theatre or cabaret. They are highly unlikely to want to take hormones, but a few do in order to enhance their ability to imitate or perform. I make no moral distinguishments between transpeople in their needs or desires so I also include drag queens and kings as a sub-classification of transvestites in this paper.

I also deal here with other groups that are presently being described as androgyne, that is those who identify as either both or neither sex and gender and those calling themselves the third sex or gender. These are namely androgenons, androgenans, sinandrogenons, and sinandrogenans.

227

I realise at a later date dealing with all these groups together may, on reflection, seem primitive, but I do presently deal with them together because they are, in today's clinical paradigms, considered to be on the cutting edge of hormone administration. Some sex and gender clinics will not administer hormones to these people and many clinicians speak out, suggesting that these people should not be entitled to hormone therapy.

A number of clinicians, when having been asked to assist these individuals with hormone therapy, have attempted to "normalise" their clients' identities, forcing them to comply to the male and female polarity social stereotypes or even to transsexual profiles. This normalisation treatment has been implemented through psychological therapy, psychiatric drugs, aversion therapy, psychoanalysis and various forms of psychotherapy. At times administration of hormone treatment to strengthen characteristics of the original biological sex has been used, against the clients' wishes or knowledge. These kind of treatments administered to individuals, who wanted to retain their sex, gender and sexuality diversities are now considered more widely as being unethical.

For those people who are absolutely convinced that they no longer wish to continue with the more unusual diverse identities, psychotherapy is still acceptable to help them define a comfortable sense of who and what they are. That is not to say this should depend solely on the moral or philosophical ideation of the clinician, but should always first consider the wishes, needs and general well-being of the client.

What are transvestites trying to achieve by taking cross-biological sex hormones?

They are attempting to either feminise or masculinise their identities to a small extent to assist them to be more convincing during the times they take the roles of their opposite biological sex. What they are not trying to do is change their bodies extensively, wishing to hang onto most of the major characteristics of their original biological sex. In ancient cultures this was done by biological males consuming the urine of pregnant mares. Today in most major cities many such people now buy hormones on the black market, imbibing them without any safe form of medical supervision.

What are those self-identified androgyne individuals trying to achieve by hormone administration?

The androgenon and androgenan identities are trying to become more like their opposite biological sex and gender and less like their original, in order to attain an androgynous concept of self, appearing to belong to both sexes and bipolar genders.

In the case of the sinandrogenon and sinandrogenan identities they are attempting to strip themselves, as much as possible, of all traces of bipolar sex and gender identities. In real and logistic terms they are attempting to become neuter, without sex or gender references.

Within the context of this paper it is unimportant why these people try to define themselves in these ways. The nature versus nurture debate looks set to run for eternity since variables are multiple. My clinical and personal codes of ethics follow the ideals that all human beings have the right to define themselves as they so wish providing they do no harm to others or severe harm to themselves.

In such cases minimal doses of hormones must be administered, because should the physiological development move too far in the direction of the opposite biological sex, then the object of the exercise has been superseded. It should also be explained to that person that there may be unforeseen side effects, for which the clinician could not be responsible since such administration is not a science, at the moment.

In biological males there will be a lowering in sperm count, possible change in psychological outlook, and the development of minimal secondary female bodily charac-

229

teristics. There may be a slowing down of facial hair growth, but on such small doses, it is unlikely this will be dramatic.

In biological females there may be facial hair growth, acne, increase in sex drive, lowering of the voice, cessation of periods, and increased danger of polycystic ovaries.

Each client should be told by the endocrinologist involved, that they are responsible to research at their library, the effects and adverse effects of the hormonal preparation they are taking.

I am aware in suggesting that this is acceptable hormonal therapy to administer to individuals that in some cultures my opinions may go against philosophical, moral or religious beliefs. However, such beliefs, when transported out of those cultures, lose their validity.

Human beings are not simply the bipolar stereotypes of man and woman that so many authoritarian philosophies dictate. The nature of sex, gender and sexuality is highly complex and diverse and each individual has the right to explore these concepts within the bounds of well-being. In saying this I would like to point out that prohibition of these developments can cause mental and physical disintegration and ill health.

We now have available to us the contraceptive pill both for men and women. These prescriptions are administered to a person on request and it is considered, within social and medical thought, that an individual has a right to define their own destiny through these drugs. Therefore I propose that such logic is applied to the subjects of this paper, in that a person must have the moral and legal right to define their own identities, without interference or prohibitions by authoritarian archetypes.

However, I would caution that if an individual wishes to take this course they should consult a medical practitioner who is a specialist in the field of endocrinology. They should also spend a number of sessions talking over the pros and cons of the situation with a doctor, psychiatrist, psychologist, psychotherapist or counsellor who specialises in this field of sex, gender and sexuality, since some of the effects of hormone therapy will be irreversible.

General Practitioners Who Exhibit Resistance to Sex, Gender and Sexuality Variance

Published in *Gendy's Journal*, March 1998

In the normal course of events in medicine of any kind the doctor listens carefully to their clients, takes the information that the client is giving and adds to it the doctor's estimation of events. This gives rise to the classic phrase of "in my professional opinion".

Normally a well-trained and empathetic practitioner would then check back with the client to see if the client is happy with the diagnosis. If the client is not, then there is a need for the practitioner to re-examine the facts. In the case of someone who may be considered to be not in full possession of their faculties or in good mental health there is a need for the doctor to guide the client towards the correct course of treatment.

For the most part, a doctor who does not have any or a great deal of experience in dealing with people who have sex dysmorphobia (an unhappiness with the physical sexual constituents of the body), gender issues or varying sexualitys, he or she would be guided by experts' opinions. Here the client should have the right to choose the qualified experts that carry out the kind of examinations or assessments that may be needed to support a diagnosis.

However, we need to consider that clinicians of any sort come from profuse kinds of backgrounds. Some may have religious convictions, be members of a cult or have certain narrow-minded social constructs. In other words, proportionally, there are just as many rednecks in medicine, psychiatry, psychology and psychotherapy as there are anywhere else.

At medical school, on psychology courses, and during training as a therapist, the training in sexuality and sex and gender variance is nothing less than abysmal. Medical students get 20 minutes on Sex and Gender Dysphoria, psychologists try not to go with any opinion that might be considered unsupported by a cacopheny of empirical studies and therapists often wear the hat that is applicable only for their school of therapy.

When it comes to considering the medical and psychological needs of those who are sex, gender or sexuality variant there is no absolute truth to be found in any book, since each person's experience is genuine. Every client must be treated as an individual and the old medical maxim of listening to the client to get the correct diagnosis must apply.

A good clinician will be open to suggestion and will listen to other practitioners who are experienced in the field in which the client's condition falls. Just occasionally there will pop up a doctor who, because of their own beliefs and personal convictions, will dispute the diagnoses or advice of specialists. This does not stop with one specialist – they will also disagree with several specialists who do not come up with the same opinions as the doctor thinks they ought to have.

These doctors not only do not have training in sexuality, sex and gender issues, but are driven by a compulsion to push their clients into convenient boxes that will suit their idealism.

Furthermore they may purposefully be trying to deprive their client of the kind of treatment they so desperately need by suggesting that hip replacements or heart surgery is more important than counselling, therapy, surgery or hormone treatment. Such moves by doctors are an abuse of the doctor-client relationship, but they get away with it because they have the privilege of having MD after their names.

I wish I could say that the opinions of these particular general practitioners of medicine come about solely through ignorance and that further training would help them to understand the issues better, but that would not be correct. For some practitioners of medicine further training will not change their minds because the divisions are based on their own prejudices.

However, it would be unfair to cite only some general practitioners of medicine of being guilty of this abuse of process between the doctor and client process. Psychologists, psychiatrists, therapists and social workers do, at times, exhibit the same behaviour, but my contention here is that the general practitioner of medicine is the primary carer of a client's physical and mental health and therefore this could be considered as the greatest betrayal.

My experience is that these kinds of doctors are rarer than they were some years ago: those who think homosexuality is an abomination, anything other than the missionary position is a slight against God and that gender or sex variance is either a physical deformity or a mental illness. However, they are out there and clients are putting their trust in them, only to be abused and denigrated for asking them for help with their problems.

After due consideration my best advice to clients and specialists is to avoid these kinds of doctors like the plague. It is not always immediately obvious that such doctors are hostile to their clients' causes because they can employ many different delaying tactics for treatment or put obstacles in the clients' way. Eventually though, when such prejudices do come to light, the doctor needs to be confronted and if they do not adjust their situation then another doctor needs to be sought.

I would like to ask the reader to try to educate such clinicians but I think that would be bad advice. If a doctor has a client with a condition that they do not understand then it is up to the doctor to seek to educate themselves; that is part of their job and they have a duty to do that. If this is not happening, no amount of pressure from external sources can force a doctor to conform.

All good clinicians are constantly seeking ways to increase their knowledge, retrain, research and most of all undergo peer supervision. Peer supervision can also mean a clinician pairing up with other professionals who have the same ideas as them, which, of course, would perpetuate more prejudice of the same kind.

Ethical Dilemmas for Gay, Bisexual, Transgendered, Transsexual and Intersex People Considering Human Cloning

Published in *Gendy's Journal*, November 1998

On the cusp of the third millennium, human cloning inevitably appears as a possible reality upon the horizons of our scientific knowledge. After the first publicly cloned sheep, Dolly, in Scotland, scientists now believe they have eliminated many of the difficulties that can occur from deformities as a result of cloning. However, since the thalidomide disaster, as yet unsubstantiated rumours of invitro-fertilisation (IVF) cases of intersexuality, and environmental toxicity-induced hermaphroditism are not behind us but with us, are we really as clever as we think we are? Many of us consider that the scientific progress made so far in cloning claims clarity out of arrogance instead of genuine knowledge.

In many societies across the globe it is very difficult for gay, lesbian, bisexual, transgendered and transsexual people to be parents. This does not happen because they are unable to physically reproduce, although some may be in that position as 10-15 per cent of the population are infertile, but because social conditions do not allow the right atmosphere for the natural processes of breeding. Undoubtedly, as with adoptions from third world countries, surrogacy and IVF, cloning will, whether legally or illegally, be a real option available to many of society's sex, gender and sexuality minorities

It is the legal and social right of every heterosexual couple to breed...and breed...and breed...until the earth is crammed full of mouths to be fed – and even developing countries only pretend to penalise overpopulation. Throughout the world it is regarded as a basic human right to reproduce; however, with sex, gender and sexuality minorities they are often deprived of those rights, legally, socially and medically. Cloning could make available reproduction as never before because it will take only one parent to initiate breeding, although a woman will be needed to carry the foetus, but even that may only be temporary.

Many ethical issues need to spring to mind in those minorities who have experienced oppression and difficulties in their lives. If a person cloned themselves, being a sex, gender or sexuality minority person, would that mean their clone would be the same? Studies of twins have mixed results, having found that although many traits are shared by monzomatic twins (who share the genes and came from the same egg), it is possible for such naturally occurring clones to have differing sexualties. However, other studies have found twins separated at birth who have grown up with uncanny similarities.

Some as yet unanswered questions need to be thought through very carefully by anyone belonging to those minority groups rushing vainly into the pursuit of reproduction. It is not as though there aren't enough children in the world already. In fact, ecologically, there are probably too many. Many children grow into adults who deforest our planet, destroy coral reefs, murder and torture other species, pollute atmospheres, turn arable land into deserts, drive even more motor cars and increase the size of the hole in the ozone layer. Children are, after all, only in short supply for the childless. It could be said that they are a commodity held to ransom by the elitist breeding order, who constantly exclude the childless, demanding unreasonable examinations to join their club.

Professor Ian Croft of the London Fertility Clinic has spoken publicly about how he remembers many members of the public being against IVF when that first became a viable treatment for infertility. He suggests that it would be inappropriate to ban human cloning altogether when it could be a very good way for infertile people to have children, and he finds nothing at all wrong with the idea.

Professor Robert White, the Papal adviser on cloning, says that it is not acceptable because he believes that each human being has its own soul that comes into being during conception and that would not happen with cloning. However, he has no objection to head transplants as he

235

sees that as extending someone's life. He also states that he does not believe that there is anything wrong with cloning technically, once it has been perfected, but his beliefs are based on religious moralisation.

Louise Brown, the first test tube baby, is now a nursery nurse. In 1997, 1500 childless couples in the USA had babies through IVF. All the fears of gross physical deformities and mental retardation that were feared from IVF programme babies have not been borne out.

No one who has had the privilege of breeding could ever, in any circumstances, understand the biological urge that drives the childless to seek any available means of having children. It is ingrained in many of us since childhood and we are trained to become parents in order to fulfil our own destiny; however, perhaps, in the age of sexual, gender and sexuality freedom, the minority childless may not have to fulfil that destiny to become whole. Perhaps a positive identity of the responsible childless person's contribution towards the arrestation of the earth's destruction could be recognised with a Child-Free Award.

Is this truly a world where we actually need to increase our numbers – or do we need, in fact, to decrease them?

What we would get with a clone would be the repeated benefits and deficits of the original host. Genetically engineering a clone embryo could lead to a change of sex, gender performance or sexuality propensities. Perhaps as genetic science progresses, engineered clones may be a way forward; however, we must never forget that the strength in nature always emerges from its purely random chaos. The resistance to end elimination of disease and disaster along the evolutionary chain of any species or sub species is our inevitable safeguard against extinction. As humans we have reached our limits of evolution if we prevent that chaos from offering us new opportunities.

Will we be genuinely a chip off the old block, or will we go shopping for a baby in box for Christmas?

"Triplets, please – preferably a four-month incubation period because my holiday is booked for May...Yes I will rent the incubator space, I don't want to have to bother with gestation at home...No I don't want any Asian genes thank you...Good Germanic speaking abilities and features...I know I look Chinese myself but what has that got to do with it?...Blonde hair and blue eyes and if you don't get it right I shall want a full refund...Yes one girl and one extremely aggressive boy with good business skills...Gay? Certainly not...perhaps you can pop a transsexual in for the other two to play with...What do you mean you don't take American Express!"

Finally, whatever our desires to produce a harmonious empathic and evolving humanity we must never forget it is the sheer violence of contention among our species that propelled us from Africa to Alaska, the moon and beyond. Choice must always be available, not only to the majority, but also to the minorities to repeat their mistakes.

The World Medical Association urging doctors in 1998 to boycott research into human cloning and any institutions involved in such activities makes you think that perhaps they have cloned some ostrich genes themselves by sticking their heads in the sand. They have not made any protestation about experimental mice who were forced to have human ears grown on their backs or pigs whose hearts are destined to tick away inside a human transplant victim.

The first official human cloning experiment is likely to take place somewhere like Japan, due to the lack of official ethical guidelines and the culturally liberal scientific curiosity of that culture. Unofficial attempts have undoubtedly taken place already out of the public eye. The world will watch with disapproval and reserved interest over a period of several generations, since genetic abnormalities can be like timebombs waiting to happen, generically skipping mutations for a series of lifetimes. What legacy the progress in the manipulation of microbiology can leave to our children and grandchildren can only be disclosed by time, and time alone.

Date-stamped methods of lesbians inseminating themselves with kitchen spoons and gay men sending the contents of their sexual fantasies to a friend for nine months are nearly over. Babies to order will be expensive in the first few years of the new millennium, but like everything else, demand always brings the market into line with the common person's budget.

Genital Organ Transplants
April 1999

It seems that the reality of organ transplants could, in the 21st century, become commonplace. Just as the world's first arm transplant was successful in 1998, and Christian Barnard's heart transplant of the 1960s has become standard surgery, so could the transplantation of human genitals. What was once science fiction is now not only science fact but also respected medical procedure.

One of the major problems with the transplant of human organs has been the rejection factor, in that the body's immune system attacks what it perceives to be foreign tissue, since it comes from another host. As genetically engineered drugs arrive, this will enable pharmacology to reduce the body's attacks on the transplanted organs from foreign donors. One of the problems of such drugs is they have the effect of dampening the body's immune system and reducing the effectiveness of white blood cells. This is why surgeons are happier to carry out transplantation in older people because the long-term immune suppressant damage from the drug therapy has less effect than on someone who will live a shorter life.

Even though major organ transplants such as heart, liver, lung and kidneys are more likely to suffer rejection by the new host this could be overcome in future by genetic technology. If the donor tissue could be marked with genetic tags that identify it as the recipient host's tissue, then the body would be fooled into believing that it is naturally occurring tissue, and rejection would not happen. This is already possible in working with viruses but we have not quite yet learnt to apply this to transplant technology.

Skin grafts, however, are becoming easier to transplant,

as skin cultures are now used to grow skin in the laboratory. To the horror of animal rights campaigners, shark skin has also been used to accelerate healing in burns victims. Tissue from inside the mouth is also now being used to form urethral passages in reconstructive genital surgery, and this tissue lends itself very well to being waterproof, with less chance of fistulas and infections occurring.

The transplantation of organs from animals to humans, for example pigs' hearts and even spare parts from primates carry with them the danger of transference of disease from one species to another, let alone the ethical considerations of such procedures. It is a matter of wide conjecture as to whether the HIV virus did, indeed, get transmitted from the primate population into humans by way of our cruel and unreliable experiments. With the UK's outbreak of BSE (Mad Cow Disease) having led to a new variant of Creutzfeldt Jakob Disease (CJD) in humans, it is more likely that cross-species transplantation carries with it a high degree of possible future pathologies.

There is further concern that the eradication of diseases that are transmitted across species might prove impossible in the future, given that the world now faces such highly contagious and obliterating diseases such as Ebola. Should diseases easily transmitted from one species to another become airborne, waterborne or kinaesthetically transmittable, the consequences could be disastrous.

Many major urology departments worldwide are now seriously considering experimenting with genital transplants. There have been rumours that in China this has been a field of investigation for many years; unfortunately the Chinese guard their research very closely and do not release their knowledge easily to the West.

The difficulty in transplanting male genitals to someone of the opposite biological sex is not in the attachment of male organs to the female skeletal type because organs have been reattached over the years in men as a standard procedure after amputation due to accident. In transplantation of male genitals to biological females problems of tumescence (blood flow into the penis) in the member are also not so complicated as the vascular flow to the clitoral area and nerve connections are basically the same as in biological males. Extra blood vessels also can be taken from other parts of the body to form better connections. The problem is in the mechanical activation of the penis.

With the advent of the drug Viagra, the blood flow into the male member causes a stronger tumescence due to chemical and hormonal activation. Many men who previously had great difficulty with erectile function now have sufficient blood flow into the genital region to carry out sexual intercourse. Undoubtedly the use of Viagra in genital constructive and reconstructive medicine will be invaluable although we do not yet know the the side effects of long-term use.

The further dichotomy of the creation of sperm by testicles, however, needs to be considered as once again it is a pituitary gland's initiation of hormones interacting with the testes that allows this process to take place. In people who were initially biological females or males there are brain formations of their original biological sex that control the signals to produce hormones from the pituitary gland. While those signals can be emulated by hormone replacement therapy the side effects of artificial hormones on the testes are as yet unknown. Transplantation from biological male to male may be more likely to succeed than from male to masculinised biological females in the case of transsexual men.

Transplanted female genitals to the biological males in the case of transsexual women produce profound difficulties in so far as the available cavities and room are concerned, when creating a vagina going through the peritoneum. If a penile inversion technique is used for lining the mouth of the vagina it is unlikely to be elastic enough to act as a birth canal. We must also consider the hip size and the restricted room for the birth canal since it is unlikely that male skeletons that have passed puberty could be induced to develop further.

One of the further difficulties in the activation of the

pituitary which regulates hormone levels, and which in females interacts with the ovaries, is to get the right hormonal balance to create the conditions suitable for ovulation and gestation. Not only are women's menstrual cycles controlled by 28-day lunar cycle but the conditions to allow that to take place depend on the physiology of the brain. We must also consider the circadian rhythm that changes a woman's hormone levels every 24 hours on a continuous basis. Even though we are presently mapping the human genome, the science of chronobiology, which monitors the body's natural rhythms, is yet still young.

We already know that the administration of cross-sex hormone therapy changes the form and function of the brain, rebalancing the right and left hemisphere function in the neocortex, and increasing or decreasing the Corpus Colossum. What we do not yet know is to what extent this happens in the limbic part of the brain that controls reproductive hormone function and what effects that would have on possible transplanted cross-sex genitals. One thing we are aware of, though, is that reversion to original biological sex type partially occurs with the removal of cross-sex hormones administration.

There are also the genetic implications to be considered because males are usually XY and females XX chomosome type, and genetic differentials can sometimes lead to the inability to breed. However, since we understand that cross-sex hormones do clearly alter behaviour profoundly, there may be chemical sequences we have not yet discovered, that could trigger breeding cycles with transplanted genitals in opposite-sex host bodies.

One of the possibilities on the horizon is spare part genetically altered cloning where just a part of the body will be grown to maturity under laboratory conditions. If this were to include the growing of something that may even resemble a human being, then we would have to presume that it was a creature with a soul and therefore entitled not to be abused by the rest of us. If, however, we could isolate the genes for growing individual organs and control the timing mechanism of growth, we would be able

241

to clone body parts from our own bodies and avoid much of the problems of rejection by the host, and the ethics and dangers of animal transplantation. In this branch of medicine a bladder has been grown in a Canadian laboratory and it is anticipated that a liver will be next.

Growing our own spare ovaries or testicles and a penis may well be possible under these conditions. Genetic triggers could be used to select exactly what it is that is grown according to need. What also may be possible is the growing of new body parts while they are attached to the host, therefore giving better nutrition and tissue matches for the parts to be encouraged to grow.

As fantastical as this may sound, it is now a very real possibility. Remember, some people are born with extra fingers and toes, or the heart on the right side of the body, so natural variance is available within the scheme of things. Neurologists are presently optimistic that soon they will be able to connect and reconnect nerves – even to the extent of fixing severed spinal cords.

Professor Martin Bobrow, a speaker at the Medical Journalist/Action Research Lecture 98, and an expert in medical genetics for the British government's Genetics Advisory Commission, said: "I don't believe it would be right to allow people to deliberately clone themselves out of fascination to watch their genetic copy growing up in a different environment. That would not be good." Tissue cloning, he believes, however, is nothing to be fearful about.

Dr Austin Smith of the Genome Research Centre in Edinburgh, who is one of the first Britsh scientists to be granted a licence for medical cloning stated: "The potential benefits in human cloning far outweigh the risks; however, I do not see why anyone would want to clone a whole person."

Professor Christine Gosden of the British Human Fertilisation and Embryology Authority commented: "We need to set the standards so that if organ cloning becomes possible, then we do not need to change the law again. Having talked to everybody and looked at all the work going on thoughout the world we are aware that potential might be there."

What we must remember is that science is unfolding all the time and the development of cross-sex genitals and transplantation would be far easier prior to puberty than it would be after the skeleton has matured and the breeding cycle has begun. This could only strengthen the call for diagnosing intersex, transsexuality, and other sex variance in children and giving them the freedom to choose their sex before they reach puberty. Changing sex may, at last, be a very real possibility or at least the transmutation of male and female sex into medically created hermaphroditism.

Transplantation of human genitals carries with it a highly social and moral set of ethical criteria that are not present with other transplants. For many, those moral issues will take them longer to sort out than the development of the technology itself. Medical advancement in this field could be profound in the next 10 years and will be as profound as our modern medicine is to a person from the 19th century.

A Case of Oestrogen-induced Gastric Parietal Cell Auto Antibody Reaction in a Transsexual (Femisexual)
December 1997

For a considerable number of years, the administration of female hormones to biological males in the treatment of Sex and Gender Dysphoria has often been by mouth. In pill form female hormones go directly into the gastrointestinal system and then are absorbed in the blood stream that takes them throughout the body to assist in feminising. This means that dosage is concentrated when it enters the stomach and naturally the stomach enzymes will try to break it down, as with any consumed product. When feminising effects are achieved through certain foods like yams the activity will be different because the feminising agent is part of its whole nutritional structure. Therefore feminising through food ingestion will take place in a different part of the intestines, as opposed to at the beginning of the digestive process, as happens in administration of female hormones in pill form.

Biological women who either have a hormonal imbalance or who are taking the contraceptive pill also take female hormones orally. The levels of female hormones taken in this way have gone largely unmonitored in the general population. Due to environmental toxicity and the chemical pollution that now exists in our water systems and food chain, the intake of feminising agents through eating and drinking is increasing. There have been concerns raised by many scientists who believe that recycled oestrogen from drinking water and gender-bending chemicals in the environment are now changing and feminising the population at large. Evidence for this was found by Dr Ginsberg at the Royal Free Hospital, London, who has monitored falling sperm counts in males.

Professor Louis Smith, the British government's appointed director of the Institute for Environment and Health in Leicester, has attributed the rise in testicular cancer and the lowering of sperm counts and quality in the West to this environmental problem. Research into the consequences of the feminising environmental effects of chemicals has mainly been carried out by environmental pressure groups and naturalists who have found intersex fish, crocodiles and polar bears in larger numbers.

The lack of monitoring of feminising hormones prescribed to transsexual and transgendered people, born biological males, has not allowed for follow-up studies to be carried out. Since this population tends to be very transient and is unlikely, with the possible exception of Holland, to remain with the same hospital or sex and gender identity clinic, the long-term effects of orally ingested feminising hormones is, to a large exent, unknown.

In biological females, after menopause, the possibility of osteoporosis can lead to brittle bones, diminished reproduction of bone material, reduction in height, dowager's hump, and pain in the joints where the body's structure is unable to comfortably support itself. Since transsexual women (who are castrated gonadal biological males) are technically past their menopause then the same effects can occur due to lack of hormone activity.

Transsexual males (originally biological females), who have undergone oophorectomy and hysterectomy, are also vulnerable to osteoporosis since they are again, to some extent, post-menopausal. Therefore in the three populations it is common practice to prescribe Hormone Replacement Therapy (HRT) with orally ingested oestrogen and progesterone. One of the side effects of this type of prescribing is gastro-intestinal disturbances, which include nausea, vomiting, abdominal cramps and bloating.

Here I report the case of a transsexual woman (originally biologically male) of 41 years of age, who had been ingesting female hormones orally for 25 years. It was found during an immunological blood scan that an antibody to the reactive enzymes that make Intrinsic Factor (a hormone that helps the small bowel to absorb vitamin B12 and which is deficient in pernicious anaemia) had appeared in the stomach.

Although little research has been carried out in this field it is possible that this was the immune system's long-term response to the orally administered feminising oestrogen. We are aware, however, that biological women who have remained on the birth control pill for long periods can suffer damage to their ability to digest certain nutrients. In animal research it has been found that males fed oestrogen can develop antibodies of various kinds and there is grave concern among environmentalists that oestrogen pollution of the food chain may trigger the same effect in humans.

Furthermore there have been concerns that orally ingested oestrogen may be contributory to liver disease and endometriosis in biological females. Perhaps this is an area of research that could be investigated in the future. In Holland, the team at the Department of Andrology and Endocrinology at the Free University, Amsterdam has reported a lower incidence of venous thrombosis in transsexual clients who have been administered oestrogen transdermally using skin patches.

In view of the fact that only limited long-term follow-ups into the effects of oestrogen administered orally have been conducted so far, it would be logical to follow the recommendation of Professor Louis Gooren and change transsexual clients to transdermally administered patches. One of the problems with such patches is that they are uncomfortable and crackle because they need to be waterproof in order to cause the hormone to go directly into the skin. The waterproofing also causes heat and moisture retention in the patch area, which has a tendency to cause rashes that can take weeks to disappear. However, considering that this is more than likely a safer way to administer hormones to an individual than by passing through the gastro-intestinal system, transsexuals and other people taking hormones would be well advised to seriously consider it both pre- and post-transition.

Bibliography

Asscheman H, Kesteren P Van, Megens J and Gooren L, *Venous Thrombosis and Pulmonary Embolism in Oestrogen-treated Male-to-female Transsexuals Remains a Major Problem*, The Department of Andrology & Endocrinology, Free University Hospital, Amsterdam, The Netherlands, X1V Harry Benjamin International Gender Dysphoria Symposium, Bavaria, (DR),1995.

British Medical Association and the Royal Pharmaceutical Society of Great Britain, *Contra-Indications and Side Effects of Orally Administered Oestrogens*, BNF 36, London, (UK), September, 1998.

Dumonde Professor DC, *Immunological Screening Tests*, United Medical and Dental Schools of Guys and St Thomas's Hospitals, University of London, (UK), 21 June 1996.

Mindell, Earl, *The Vitamin Bible*, Arlington Books, London and USA 1979.

Not Treating Transsexualism
Northern Gender Dysphoria Conference
Gateshead, April 1997

This may seem a funny title for a paper delivered to the gender dysphoric and their carers or even the ex-gender-dysphoric, if indeed, for some, the issue of the dysphoria is gender, and not a matter of physiological sex. Further to this I shall question the fact that all clients who come into treatment, necessarily experience any dysphoria at all, and who instead may simply be transient and fluid compared with a statistical average that deems itself to be normality.

Over the years I have come into contact with literally thousands of people, who have at some time been unhappy with their sense of gender identity or physiological sex and one thing has become plain. Much of the treatment they received has consisted of two basic axioms: a possible physical metamorphosis and what professes, at times, to a be a form of psychoanalysis to determine the cause of their condition.

Unfortunately, many people who go through such dramatic physical treatment to bring their bodies in line with their own internal images of themselves, receive very little counselling to help them to acclimatise to their new lives after treatment. Just the other day I received a telephone call, from a colleague who is a psychologist. She had a client who had just gone through gender realignment treatment and was extremely depressed. My colleague, who is a well respected clinician in her own field, was horrified that her client had been allowed to receive major surgery and hormone treatment without being prepared for her new role in life.

There are, of course, those clients who present themselves, categorically stating that they do not want any such interference from a clinician and all they want is hormones and surgery. However, from the group that is now post-realignment I have noted that a number of these ex-clients have gone on to live unhappily in their new roles;

some have developed drug or alcohol dependency, others have become obsessional or reclusive with few social skills, and still more common is the ex-client who becomes long-term unemployed.

Further still I have encountered clients who have come to clinicians to ask for help in exploring what may be an appropriate route for them to take through their sex or gender life. After all, not everyone is male or female identified: some people identify themselves as transgendered and others as the third sex, that which is neither male nor female. These people have not been satisfied with the kind of reception they have received from clinicians who have set themselves up as experts in gender or sex issues. They have complained, that since they were not prepared to take a stance of being male or female, they felt they were left out on a limb without any form of collective identity or understanding.

So what is the differential that determines whether a post-operative or ex-gender or sex-dysphoric person will succeed in being happy in their new role or not? Here, of course, I measure success and happiness by the client's own subjective measures.

Well, confidence seems to be the main factor and the confidence not just to be taken as their destination sex, but to be comfortable in the persona that accommodates the fluidity of their sex, gender and sexuality. Many of the most physically convincing transpersons (by heterosexual models) that I have met have not been happy after treatment, so it seems that merely being undetectable or "unread" as Kate Bornstein called it, is not enough.

Some of the most well-adjusted transpersons I have met have been quite open about their sex reaffirment, even thought they actually had no requirements to do so. This openness has now become more permissible due to the public's changing attitudes to those who rightfully should be classified officially under the intersexes. Trans-education has certainly made it easier to transform in 1997 than it was in 1967 or 1977.

However, such emotional re-adjustments generally

come about after much soul-searching and that process can cause a very large dent to a transperson's ego. In short, all people who have undergone such a metamorphosis will openly tell you that, at times, it was hard and very damaging to their confidence. For the well-educated or well-heeled, who may have many resources at hand, the transition can appear easier, but this is not necessarily so. For the economically, educationally or emotionally disadvantaged, managing their condition, identity, confusion and fighting for personal peace can prove devastating.

What is desperately needed both in the private sector and in the British National Health Service, including the major gender identity clinics is an expansion of the treatment they offer to include more counselling to the transient gender-dysphoric. Of course I hear the cry of "where does the extra money come from?" and that is an inescapable and realistic consideration; however, it is not mine, because I am a psychotherapist – not an accountant.

It is plain that the "operate and hope-for-the-best" mentality in treating Gender Dysphoria does not work in a large number of cases. It leaves many of the ex-clients dysfunctional emotionally, socially and in the workplace. Perhaps it is time for those who take on the responsibility of being clinicians to re-evaluate the kind of treatment they are presently offering. To treat cancer by simply cutting off the affected limb is only a portion of the treatment that the clinician can offer and since that would not be acceptable to cancer clients, why has the "operate and hope-for-the-best" approach in transsexualism become accepted as normal?

There can be an attitude among clients whereby they are almost afraid to talk of their worst fears or greatest aspirations. They believe that this might in some way disqualify them from a transformation programme, being perceived as trouble-makers and refused treatment. So these clients stick to the well-known script that neither deviates nor challenges the form of the classical transsexual profile, thereby hopefully guaranteeing them the surgery and hormone treatment they may think they so desperately need. But the price of their not asking for more, for that extra help that they may need to be able to deal with life, post-transition, is sometimes high as they remain dysfunctional and fail to attain the happiness and success they sought.

Too many people are coming out of treatment believing they have either passed or failed as their destination sex. For some transsexuals it may be important to be legally, socially and privately accepted as their destination sex; however, for the clinician to collude in such a trial is to ultimately set their clients up for failure.

Things are hotting up – transpeople all over the world are communicating and comparing notes on treatment standards, political situations and the changes in the law to afford all transfluid people their human dignity. The trans-community is beginning to challenge legislators, authoritarian physicians, and unegalitarian social pressures. So, as the seesaw tips in our favour and we consolidate a community identity of TRANSPRIDE, the psychologists, psychiatrists and psychotherapists need to understand that more ego-strengthening would help the treatment programme be more effective.

The goalposts of male and female are no longer solely the issues that affect the transfluid community. Whatever a client declares themselves to be when they leave a clinic after treatment, they must have the confidence to defend their identity and not have to compromise their inner self to the ideologies of others' outer selves. More counselling for each client who goes through a transformation programme should be an integral part of the treatment to equip them with that confidence.

Just the other day I arrived home from a nice holiday in the sun to find someone had written a derogatory posting about me on the Internet, citing me as being a "self-confessed transsexual". Their aim was to discredit me professionally because they objected to some psychological research I am publishing. And their attempt failed simply because they showed themselves to be ignorant and prejudicial. Fortunately, I have the knowledge and confidence to stand up to their onslaught.

By not treating just the Gender or Sex Dysphoria and by implementing a more holistic approach to the trans-community, clinicians can then hopefully assist clients to become confident in whatever gender or sex role they identify with.

Psychological Development Beyond Sex and Gender Realignment
Gendy's Conference, August 1998

Nearly all the emphasis of gender and sex realignment treatment, in the past, has been placed on the physical changing process. This is often seen by many professionals and clients as reaching its ultimate conclusion with genital surgery. For others, however, post-transition may not include genital surgery but a point at which they have reached a certain partial physical transformation and social change that is comfortable for them. Any psychological or psychiatric interviews that may have been carried out during this process are often seen by many professionals and clients as test procedures which the client will either pass or fail.

If the client passes the test mentality of the interview then the clinician may recommend them to undergo the physical changes they seek through hormone therapy and surgery. A great number of clients feel they are in danger of not passing such interviews and therefore may be hostile to the clinicians and withhold information, edit the truth and even tell a complete lie.

Some of the responsibility for this must be with the clinicians involved, because in the first part of the clinician and client contract there should be an agreement with the client that they can be safe in telling the clinician absolutely anything. However, because clients are in a high state of anxiety when they arrive, apprehensive, and afraid of the test mentality they often seek to tell the clinicians what they think they want to hear.

The danger with clients' truths not being discussed is that the client can then begin to start what it called doing the rounds, where they go to several doctors, not listening to what they are saying for fear of failure.

Just recently I found myself in a room with six other post-transition transsexuals and transgendered people at a party. Into the room came a biological male who knew us all and he asked how come everyone in the room had got their treatment. One person looked at all the others asked if she should tell him and then casually replied: "Oh! It was easy – eventually we all read the same book so we knew what to say."

Post-psychological development is generally the furthest thing from the sex and gender client's mind when they are in the process of transition, which can be a very *now* orientated experience that demands all their attention in coping with the present. You might call it the emergency of the moment because transpeople are generally so unhappy about their physical selves that the drive to remedy the situation takes over their lives.

It would be foolhardy to pretend that life as a transsexual or transgendered person is anything less than extremely difficult as well as glorious, both pre- and post-transition. After having gone through what may be tantamount to a total physical refit you have to deal, from time to time, with what can be devastating prejudice, ignorance, injustice, abuse, violent attacks on you and your right to live as you wish. And that's only to get your tailor to button the blazer on the other side.

Some transpeople choose to be open and public about what they are and others only feel safe enough to live their lives secretly, telling no one of their personal history. Either way can, at times, be precarious and stressful and despite all the successes achieved by a post-transition individual, the lack of humanity displayed by some people can be deeply distressing.

Fortunately the majority of people in life are kind, but the transfluid person also needs to be psychologically and philosophically equipped to deal with the drivers that drive on the wrong side of life's road.

Of the six people that had been in the room at the party with me, two had been alcoholics, one a heroin addict who had spent several years in a monastery, one suffered from chronic depression, one had had three children taken away by the previous partner, and one had had a heart attack through high anxiety, having been shunned by their entire family. Although these people had survived their experiences and triumphed over life's adversities they all agree that with the right guidance their lives could have been much easier.

April Ashley spoke of how she felt she was driven to alcoholism by continual harassment by the press and the injustices of the British legal system. Renee Richards suffered from dreadful attacks from the press, simply because she wanted to play tennis. Stephen Whittle told me how he woke up to find himself in the Sunday newspapers without him even having been contacted by them to ask for a comment, something I have experienced myself. Dana International, after winning the 1998 Eurovison Song Contest, received death threats from extreme right-wing Jewish groups. Brandon Teena, like many others, was killed, simply for what he was – a sex, gender and sexuality fluent individual.

The catalogue of unnatural pressures that can be brought to bear upon the psychological health of the transsexual, transgendered, or sex and gender fluent person of any kind need not unnecessarily effect them severely or long term. For the first generation of high-profile sex, gender and sexuality fluent people who arose internationally in the 1960s there was less specific help available than there is today.

Many of these had to learn their survival and prosper lessons through the hard knocks' school of life and have come through to achieve excellence in their personal life, careers, and intellectual actualisation, in spite of, or because of the obstacles placed in their path. Some never made it as the pressures of society's rejection was too much for them and they committed suicide, had short lifespans due to stress-induced illnesses, low quality of life or were hounded and frightened into a reclusive lifestyle.

Later generations do not now have to work out their paths with such confusion and disadvantages, as modern cognitive behavioural techniques and the learnings of our sisters, brothers and others can help everyone cope with life situations more easily.

Where many people who are post-transition get into trouble is when they adopt the mindset of "I am finished now...and I can live my life just as everyone else and I can stop thinking about what I am and remain where I am." Therein lies the trap of complacency, lack of evolution and road to psychological decline. A person is what they are and to be in denial about that can rob them of valuable resources that they need to survive as a personality.

Men and women think quite differently – that is not segregation or prejudice, it is nature. Men are more small-chunk thinkers, analytical, narrow focused, goal orientated, more aggressive than women, fraternity based, and literal. Women tend to look at the big picture, are more nurturing, long-term thinkers, time givers, less aggressive and are involved in the fight to define their own status in a post-industrial society.

If a person changes their body to match an internal set of feelings about their core identity, then there is also a need to change their psychology to match life expectancy, aspirations, dreams, achievements, social behaviour and mental development. Not to do so can arrest personal development, happiness, contentment and withhold sex, gender and sexuality resolution.

There are only two motions in the physics of nature: one is growth and the other depletion. Maintenance at the status quo is an illusion. Physical, psychological, social and spiritual growth is the road to being a healthy and happy post-transition sex, gender and sexuality fluent person. If the environment, family, work and society does not allow that to happen, then they must be changed.

Each of us as individuals must hold ourselves responsible for contributing towards an ever better self and world.

No matter how small that contribution may be, it is our key to self-empowerment, and a guarantee against suffering the slings and arrows of outrageous fortune. Whatever the drawback the post-transition person encounters they must continue to develop the kind of mindsets that equip them to deal with that situation and move on to a greater and more satisfying sense of self.

There is also the personal journey of discovering what makes a man a man or a woman or woman and everything in-between, and how that relates to the post-transition person. Learning to accommodate and negotiate the differences, which can be seen as blessings or curses, according to perspective.

How to survive in a man's world and to deal with the wimmin-born-wimmin brigade who choose to exclude anyone who even vaguely threatens their separatism. How to live your life as a sex and gender you were not trained for as a child and discovering a sexuality that transcends the "what bunny rabbits do" biology lessons of early school years.

Altering the body to the mind is not the solution for the sex, gender and sexuality dysphoric, but for some people altering the body and the mind can be a way forward that will give maximum pleasure and satisfaction in life. Too many people have come out of gender realignment programmes punch drunk by the process itself and unsure quite what they are supposed to do next. This reminds me of a philosophy adopted by the charity Oxfam: "Give a starving person food and you will feed them for the moment...teach them to farm in a better way and they will feed themselves".

For the vast majority of people who undergo some form of realignment treatment, through choice as well as compulsion, it transforms and changes their lives to such an extent that they achieve a higher quality of life. Those clients can also ask for even more than a vial of hormones and the cut of the surgeon's knife both during and after that treatment, so that they may achieve their own sense of excellence.

The Application of Ericksonian Psychotherapy to Sex and Gender Dysphoria and Realignment Treatment.

The Third International Congress on Sex and Gender
Exeter College, Oxford, September 1998

Throughout the past 30 years the opportunities for people to present themselves to Gender Identity Clinics and private practitioners for gender and sex realignment treatment have increased dramatically. Initially on considering this information you would think that many more of the people who are presenting with Sex and Gender Dysphoria would be taking up the opportunity to have treatment. However, as we now move forward into a new era and set of attitudes towards the availability of such treatments, and shifting social perceptions of sex gender and sexuality change, we need to look more closely at the clinical situation constructs that influence the decisions of those who present themselves as having trans-identities.

With the use of Ericksonian, permissive, personal-centred psychotherapy I have now found the reverse effect to be true with the people who present themselves to my practice. Far from an increase in the percentage of people who present with Sex and Gender Dysphoria going onto full realignment treatments, I have found a decrease.

Examining the way Dr Milton Erickson, the American psychiatrist and hypnotherapist, worked with his clients we are able to move the responsibility of testing for the validity of genuine transsexualism onto the person presenting and away from the clinician.

In reflecting upon the way many clinics and clinicians have attempted to alleviate Sex and Gender Dysphoria, through physical alteration of the body and directed social behaviour, in the past, I am struck by the often authoritative style inflicted upon clients, which has caused many of them a great deal of distress. In speaking to many of those clients years later it has become evident, in retrospect, that a more open and client-led approach could generally be applicable. As times and social attitudes have changed, and knowledge about sex, gender and sexuality has increased, then so the kind of medicine dispensed to the populous at large must change, including sex, gender and sexuality minority groups.

Dr Milton Erickson was one of America's most visionary and successful psychiatrists, psychotherapists and medical hypnotherapists of the 20th century, whose greatest contribution to modern psychotherapy was his client-led approach. Although this is not surprising considering that he practised around the same time as Maslow, Rogers and Laing, what is important about his work, is that his client-led approach culminated in spectacular alterations in his clients' psychology, behaviour and physiology.

When thinking about the way we could change our clinical approaches I am reminded of an early teaching tale of Erickson's about a horse he found wandering along a country lane. Since there was no immediate evidence available of where the horse might have come from he simply climbed onto its back and told it to "go home". As he rode into its owner's farmyard the farmer asked Erickson how he had known who the the horse belonged to. "I didn't", replied Erickson, "But the horse knew exactly where he lived, and I was just the rider."

In structuring psychosocial medicine for treating Sex and Gender Dysphoria it is necessary to constantly construct and deconstruct models of human behaviour and physiology. That process can never be allowed to become complacent or absolute and clinicians need to be in a continual state of development and self-criticism in order to best serve the needs of professional evolution. After all, what we learn from our clients far outweighs any writings on the subject, and as we take on board those learnings we can allow them to change the way we approach the next client.

A couple of years ago I was a guest at a dinner party for 12 people given by a friend of mine who is in commodities – a very creative woman who, with her husband, loves to cook spectacular, exotic dishes. In fact they are such exquisite cooks that it is a great honour to be invited to one of their gatherings. Sat next to me, purposely orchestrated by my hosts, was Jean-Claude, a 40-year-old transman, who also conducted business with my friends. Jean-Claude was two years post-sex and gender realignment treatment, including commencement of hormone therapy, phalloplasty, and chest sculpturing

Jean-Claude had had a considerable amount of facial reconstructive surgery by the most skilled surgeons that money could buy. He had also been on black market steroids under no medical supervision.

I was able to observe, through the starters and main course, that Jean-Claude suffered from a number of behavioural problems. He never asked anyone how they were or what they were doing in their lives; neither did he express an interest in anyone else's point of view during the dinner conversations. Very aggressively he constantly interrupted people to try and put across his own point of view, which he adamantly held as superior, regardless of any counter-arguments. His body language was permanently defensive, even aggressive and as he tried to process information from the conversations his facial expressions were clearly indicating distress, emotional pain, and rejection of other people's intellectual concepts.

Jean-Claude had no sense of humour, only talked about himself, his wealth, new car and various large houses he owned. In short, he seemed to be a very wealthy, commercially successful man with an absolutely wretched life and disposition.

A few weeks later, Jean-Claude consulted me for chronic deep muscular pain, stress, fatigue and depression. On discussing his history it became evident that he had had minimal psychological help during the sex and gender realignment treatment. Although there had been maximum physical intervention he was unable to adjust well to his new role and social behaviour. His attitude had been that there was nothing wrong with him mentally and he did not want anyone messing around with his mind. He had, since the beginning of his transition, developed a profound inferiority complex about his non-male biological origins, and defended himself from possible attacks by attacking others first.

The constant fear of not being thought of as a "real man" had led him to be so extremely aggressive that he had very few friends, almost no social life and suffered from constant feelings of loneliness. A further secondary gain of the aggressive behaviour was that as a commodities dealer that very characteristic of aggression had made him rich and successful.

The first Gender Identity Clinic he had attended for sex and gender realignment had demanded of him that he live in role as a male for one year before the clinician would prescribe hormone therapy. That, he felt, would have been impossible for him due to a high-profile career and the fact he had been living and working as a woman at the time. This so put him off ever going back there or anywhere else again that he had bought hormones by post from Hong Kong and administered them himself. All his surgery had been carried out on the recommendation of a single psychiatrist he had seen only once, who had no experience in the field, but to whom he constantly paid fees for referral letters.

Jean-Claude's treatment with me consisted of one-hourly sessions once a fortnight for a year. During this time he was assured of a safe space where he could talk freely about absolutely anything he wanted, without fear of losing my respect for his defined sex and gender and partly explored sexuality.

Our agreement was that he would continue to keep the appointments even though at times he may disagree with some things I may say to him. Self-hypnosis and progressive relaxation was taught as I do with all my clients in order to install a sense of daily psychological maintenance and self-efficacy. Jean-Claude also had the opportunity to look at his values, beliefs and attitudes and was assisted in reframing these without critical opposition, giving himself permission to change perspective on these in the future should he so want or need to do so.

Ericksonian, indirect hypnotic suggestion was used to help him change his lifestyle and be less subjective and more altruistic, choosing to spend more of his time, resources and wealth helping to reorganise his favourite charity. External focus was to be one of the major psychological shifts that helped him eradicate the deep muscular pain, depression and move his personality towards maturation. The safe space assured within the therapy environment also gave him that opportunity to look at other ways of affirming his masculinity than taking steroids, which he quickly stopped

Hypnotic, psychoimaginary Timeline Therapy was used to locate perceived psychosynthesised resources in his future that would help him deal with his present situation. These resources were then bridged back into his present timeframe and used as memory supplementation in his past to realign his gender and sex misaligned past. Timeline Therapy is based on Erickson's Pseudo-Orientation in Time technique and in Jungian concepts may be said to be consulting the ego ideal of the wise old man or woman archetype.

Jean-Claude now has a full social life, much interest in other people, no muscular pain, reacts well to stress factors and knows how to deal with them in a more constructive way. He has a well defined sense of his own sex and gender identity, is exploring his sexuality in a comfortable way, has open and non-confrontational body language when communicating with people. He is happy and well adjusted and can enjoy pleasant company and breaking bread without his mobile telephone switched on. One of his most proud possessions has become his keen and evolving sense of humour, not only about life itself but about himself too.

Although Erickson himself never treated a case of Sex and Gender Dysphoria his psychotherapeutic teachings can be applied to their treatment and exploration. His client-led approach can help the clinician help the client to show the clinician the way to treat them. This will allow the client going through treatment to have more confidence, trust and rapport with their psychiatrists, psychologists, psychotherapists and counsellors. One of the main focuses of the Ericksonian approach is that no foreign philosophy is perceived to have been introduced into the person's psyche, therefore reducing resistance to change.

Ericksonian indirect suggestion can also be used to assess the client's reality testing mechanisms to see if they have truly thought through the decision to transition, particularly through to surgery, without the clinician being unduly confrontational. The clinical atmosphere that it is the client that sets the parameters of identity gives them more choice to find and identify what they feel will be more suitable for them. This in turn does not force them into stereotypical sex, gender, or sexuality identities and therefore allows applicants for sex and gender realignment to have greater choice over not choosing that route if it is not for them.

Many of my clients form identities and reform their concepts of themselves while being aware that I have no expectation of what is right or wrong for them and am willing to be guided by their needs and desires, therefore they do not feel pressured to become classical transsexuals if that route is eventually not right for them.

Certain clinical judgements may have classified Jean-Claude as having a psychopathology with paranoid characteristics, aggressiveness, overtly macho and having anti-social behaviour that could be considered as a borderline personality, that was caused by or a feature of his sex and gender realignment. Jean-Claude's problems mainly derived from his lack of psychological adjustment and counselling which should have accompanied his sex and gender realignment treatment.

Sex and gender realignment clients need to be considered like flowers in a garden. Some stand in fertile, good soil and some in limy ditches; there are those who may need a lot of fertiliser and others who will flourish regardless. Many will drown in levels of water that will not be enough for others, but one thing is for sure – watering, manure and pruning do not a prize rose make...it's the way you talk to them.

At the end of the day it is ultimately not the clinician who needs to be satisfied that the client is making the right decision, but the client themselves. What professionals need to be asking themselves is not only can the post-gender and sex realignment person survive in the real world, but how can we help the sex and gender dysphoric define themselves now, in the future, and in dealing with their pasts.

Healing a Misaligned Past
Gendys Conference Workshop 1998

In considering this workshop, which was designed for the gender and sex dysphoric (or people who were previously), I started by thinking about the difference between our perceived reality of childhood, and a childhood that never was, but might have been. Some people have memories about a childhood filled with good things, marvellous memories and a nurturing past that led to a blossoming adulthood. There are also people who had childhoods that were less than ideal, traumatic, unhappy; and for the sex and gender dysphoric child a sense of being robbed of the real childhood identity and innocence. For most people their memories of their childhoods are probably mixed and do not disturb them or intrude upon them in the present. When Sex and Gender Dysphoria is present in childhood it can force the child to grow up too soon, without memories of having been a happy little boy or girl.

Here it is also important to state that I do not refer to sexuality because although children are sexual, in that they feel physical sensations and acquire social learnings about sex, they are prepubescent. This, in my opinion, cannot qualify them to have a sexuality because they have not sufficiently developed social awareness and are not yet held fully responsible for their actions in society.

As a hypnotherapist I have observed how important are our perceptions of our pasts, both at a conscious and unconscious level of awareness, in influencing and shaping our present and futures. Good perceptions of our past support our strength of ego, confidence, self-image and sense of who we are in the world. Even though a person may have had a most horrific childhood, it is possible, through hypnotically repatterning of the mind, to change those memories permanently into positive learning experiences, without reliving the trauma.

Sigmund Freud believed that we are shaped forever by our childhood experiences and are subject to those memory patterns laid down in our childhoods for the rest of our days. He believed by recalling those memories consciously through psychoanalysis we could intellectually understand them and thereby achieve relief from those traumas. This, however, has proved to be untrue and many of his clients who went through psychoanalysis for years, simply gave up in the end and went to another therapist.

Milton Erickson, on the other hand, followed Einstein's theory of relativity and subjectivity, in that he believed that we all create our past, present and future in the actions of the present. The relevancy of this is that there is no such thing as objectivity, because all objective constructs are someone's subjective interpretation. In other words – nothing is fixed in the mind forever.

When intrusive memories are really extreme we call it Post Traumatic Stress Disorder and when they are mild and uncomfortable they can produce anxiety, stress-induced neurosis or obsessive compulsive disorders. In the case of the sex and gender dysphoric, who may not have childhoods that correspond with their adult identities, they often find themselves in a situation where they have to lie or withdraw from social conversations about their childhoods to avoid explaining that they have transfluid identities.

This is often not done to deceive, but simply to avoid having to get into yet another explanation of their whole history that can prove time-consuming, unnecessary, and tedious. At the time of having to tell such lies there can be a sense of loss for the transfluid person who wishes they did have such a childhood to talk about.

In looking at how to develop the process of Healing a Misaligned Past I have considered and cross-fertilised other hypnotic techniques, namely Timeline Therapy; Hypnoanalysis; Bridging; Parts Negotiation, Integration and Reintegration; and Inner Child Therapy. Therefore I need to pay tribute to therapists and hypnotists such as Sigmund Freud, Virginia Satir, Milton Erickson, Eugene Bliss, Richard Bandler, John Grinder, Tad James, Christa Mackinnon and Dave Elman. Hypnosis is the strongest and quickest way for those who are or were sex or gender dysphoric to repattern their memories into a more positive past that they can rely on to support a good sense of self in the present and future.

People rely mainly on the central personality, and although many may change their life and personality styles, they still retain a central focus of self. In people who have religious conversions, near-death or life-changing experiences there can often be a sense of before and after that leads them to disassociate from their previous selves. In gender and sex dysphoric people, who feel the need to change their biological bodies to match their internal sex and gender identity, the disassociation of before and after can be profound, because the pre-transformation period is associated with great distress and psychological pain. In the case of the intersexed there may also be a sense of psychological pain in that they may feel they have been cheated in some way, although in some cultures their status is revered, praised and exalted (as every human being should be).

The main purposes of the Healing a Misaligned Past process are to blend and integrate what might have been with what was, change what was into something else, create amnesia for distressing past memories, synthesise new memories that can now be used for the ex-sex and gender dysphoric people to call upon to form the basis of their history. This will enable them to be more sure of their positive pasts, leading on to making positive presents and futures.

Tracie (T). I'm going to ask for a volunteer in a minute and it is to be someone who has been through sex or gender realignment or who has adjusted their identity to a level which is comfortable for them...because I don't determine those levels for anyone in my practice as everyone needs to be able to find their own levels of good experience.

Like my great friend and fellow therapist Dr Napewastewin Schützer I believe in following a client's lead and find that they are my best teachers about what their needs are.

You may have noticed I referred to sex and gender realignment...and that's because I don't reassign people...I see that more as a matter of directing bus routes... people change by realigning the three concepts of sex, gender and sexuality under their own cognisance and generally do not need someone else to tell them what is right for them.

I see treatment as a progressive and dynamic process which, when using this technique, can take one or more sessions...depending on the individual's needs and how unbalanced they feel they are.

When I'm talking about sex and gender realignment I do separate the two. Sex Dysphoria is talking about concepts of a person's physical self and that is what bits go where on your body...Gender Dysphoria, however, is a reference to a person's gender performance in society, or even in private for that matter. In using this hypnotic psychological rebalancing technique I'm not going to be dealing with sexuality because that develops later in life but sex and gender performance starts at birth...besides people's sexuality only truly has a space to develop when they are comfortable with their sex and gender.

Just to let a potential volunteer know what they are in for, what I'm going to use is integration and regression techniques with hypnosis...has anyone read anything about Carl Jung?

Some of the audience nodded knowingly and approvingly and others looked totally mystified.

T. Well Carl Jung talked about polarities and Emma Jung talked about the Animus and Anima...that is the masculine in the female and the feminine in the male. For people who are sex and gender dysphoric then, they have a sense of attraction towards, getting propelled towards or have a desperate need to move towards their biological or gender performance opposites or variants...and here I think it is very important not to get exclusive about our way of thinking, that needs have any kind of superiority over desire.

Some people after transition, however, are a little disturbed when talking about their pasts...because of transpersonal histories it can be very difficult when other people start talking about how they were as children and then the spotlight turns on them. If the transperson has not disclosed, and there is no reason they should have, they find themselves in the position of having to make up an appropriate history in order not to have to go into the fact that they are one of the trans-identities...As only transpeople know, it can be incredibly tedious to have to go into the education and transpolitical history with every Tom, Dick and Harry, especially if you're only buying a vacuum cleaner from them.

It can get dodgy when reeling out an appropriate history for the vacuum cleaner salesperson who you are only going to interact with for a short time in a busy schedule. Along with the storytelling can be a sense of not really being a true woman or a true man, lack of confidence and even perhaps a sense of being a bit of a fraud. Here I'm not saying that you should not bother telling people about your trans-identity, but it can be very wearing to have to go into it all again and just for the sake of a childhood reference...anyone ever had those feelings of doubt?

Everyone went motionless and quiet

T. So you have all been totally absolutely and 100 per cent confident about your own masculinity and femininity both before, during and post-transition?

Everyone shifted in their seats and declared openly

*that they had not and that included most of the
non-transpeople in the room*

T. You are among friends, and honesty can be a great way forward for you at this moment in time...I'm looking for a volunteer who is also willing to interact in a way to change their perceptions of themselves...as I have said before, people get disturbed after transition when they think of themselves as transformed...stuck in the fixed concept of themselves...and you know I remember waking up some years ago after transition and thinking 'Oh my God! I've grown a penis back again!'...Wow did I have to do some ongoing work on myself.

*Several women from the audience volunteered that they
have had the very same nightmare*

T. So people need to gain a higher sense of self...and who and what they are...defining themselves by uniting the polarities of masculine and feminine...boy and girl, of childhood...into a one central focus identity to be relied on in their history to give them the kind of self-assured confidence to declare their trans-history or use metaphors when talking to people to whom they choose not to declare their real history...reality, after all, is only what you believe it to be.

If a transperson says: "When I was a small child of any sex I did so and so..." they can be incongruent in their communication due to their personal internal history...so who would like to come up and be a demonstration volunteer?

Shirley puts up her hand

Shirley (S). Are you looking for someone who is post-operative...I mean they have had genital surgery?

T. That's a really valid question but I'm afraid I can't answer it for you because it depends what is post-transition for you. Each person, you see, needs to look at their own circumstances and decide what they think is post-transition for them and it would be wrong of me to try and decide that for them.

This was obviously the right answer for Shirley as she came forward. Tracie looks at her name badge

T. Hi Shirley nice to meet you and see you out here bravely doing work on yourself in front of all of us. I'm just going to place your feet on the floor, apart and comfortable...your hands resting in your lap as you sit down and relax...knowing that you can hear that you are safe and respected among friends, and people who admire you for being yourself...and of course many people here understand and empathise with what it is to be having or doing a trans-identity...

Tracie is lightly laying her hand on Shirley's right shoulder as she is talking to her, putting down what is called a safety anchor. This is a stimulus-reaction Pavlovian cue that has been suggested to be associated with being safe, among friends, and having good feelings. Later Tracie will fire this anchor by touching Shirley's right shoulder at relevant times during the hypnotic trance, to give Shirley an unconscious association with good feelings. This is also a bail-out anchor to be used should the subject get in trouble during the regression procedure and find themselves in need of resources to deal with any disturbing memories

T. Of course I think we have all had feelings of being doubtful about our masculinity and femininity at times in our histories. Is that how it has been for you at times?

Shirley nods her head and Tracie addresses the audience

T. So for those of you who are counsellors or therapists I would normally use a relaxation technique with many people to help them feel safe and secure in using hypnosis before I attempted to do deep changing work like this with them...But today because of time constraints I'm going to use the quick Elman technique that puts a person straight into trance immediately, so we can start work right away. We are going to use a dissociation, regressive, integration technique to balance the male and female energies in the past psyche to give the person more confidence about who or what they are in the present.

Tracie quickly puts Shirley into a hypnotic trance ready to do the work

T. OK Shirley, we are going to take you to you safe space and I want you to use that fabulous imagination that I know you have used many times before to transport yourself to a safe place...calm, private...known only to you...where and whenever you need to you can go to rest or recover when you are in trouble...and when you are there nod your head.

Shirley nods her head

Good...very good...and I'm going to touch you on your right hand...in future whenever I touch you on that right hand you can automatically transport yourself to that safe space when ever you want or need to...and I'm going to ask you to do something quite outrageous now and go to a laughter place which is full of laughter just like Brer Rabbit and when you're there I'm going to reach over and touch your left hand...of course the corners of your mouth will turn up and the nerve endings of your mouth will stimulate your laughter and happiness hormones.

Shirley smiles

T. Is that it?

Shirley, still in trance with her eyes shut, breaks into laughter. Tracie reaches across and touches her left hand

T. Good...very good...very good indeed...that's great...so I'm going to fire your safe place anchor and you know you can go there whenever you want to...and now I'm going to fire your laughter anchor...yes...that's good...and just for a moment you can come back to the room awake and with us where I know there is an outpouring of love towards you where people are wishing you well with this experience.

As Shirley comes back to the room Tracie fires the good feelings anchor on Shirley's shoulder without telling her. Tracie addresses the audience

T. So we are using a regression technique, taking the person back to the day of birth and beyond...the way a therapist would do this would be dependent on their discipline...and of course something like Timeline Therapy would be fine.

Tracie passes her hands over Shirley's eyes and takes her back into a deep trance

T. All right Shirley, I want you to leave your body and float up to the ceiling. Looking down with your mind at that body sitting safely and comfortably in that chair...and when you are there, nod your head.

Shirley nods her head

T. Good...very good...and I want you to put a glass walkway below you off into the past that you can comfortably go backwards on that will protect you from any unpleasant or painful memories – off backwards, backwards until the day of your birth and beyond...

Tracie is casually and intermittently firing the good feelings anchor on the right shoulder as Shirley makes the journey

T. Good...very good...keep going now to beyond the day

of your conception before your essence...that is the life-force that made you come into this existence...to the place before, knowing that your body is here safe with me...looking down at the body of you as a child beneath the glass screen from a safe distance...taking all the time in your head you need...and when you are there back in the time before...nod your head...

Half a minute passes and then Shirley nods her head. Tracie fires the right shoulder anchor for good feelings and addresses the audience

T. So we are using a deep dissociation technique to give the person new perspectives and protect the integrity of the central personality, by using the glass walkway, from any disturbing memories of a sex or gender dysphoric past...at the moment Shirley is beyond sex and gender at a time before her birth...so Shirley I want you to become aware of an impending event...something very special that a child is going to be conceived...and I don't know how much joy that is going to bring but I know it is...and you know it is...a cause of absolute celebration...ecstatic jubilation...a new child in the world...one of life's miracles.

Tracie fires the good feelings anchor

T. Now I want you to go down into the date of conception and even birth as well as before...and you can see how you were a child of a certain sex and expected gender performance and I want you to put that child over on your extreme left polarity field of reference...and then you can identify a child of a different sex who has a gender performance of preference or exploration and polarise their identity to your extreme right experiential field...and taking all the time you need to do that...nod your head when it's happened.

Shirley nods her head

T. Good...very good...on your left you can find the

extreme of maleness and on your right the polar opposite
of femaleness...yes the entities of self that will contribute
towards becoming Shirley...but only a child.

*Shirley's head moves all the way from extreme right to
extreme left*

T. And you've lost denial...because it's quite a useless
thing to have...as your male and female energies come
together to give you new resources to be a united you with
many qualities and specialness...each extreme can be
so...so...so very important in bringing together all the
qualities of balance that as united you possess...again
identify the male and the female energies, spirit, lifeforce,
aura and combined resources from the past, present day
and soon to be the future.

*Shirley turns her head and looks from right to left,
smiling in both directions*

T. Now I want you to know you are in safe space.

Tracie taps the safe space anchor

T. The space that you are in is so safe that the extremes
of male and female can talk to each other...they can have
a comfortable chat...they can negotiate...appreciating that
feminine qualities are fabulous and masculine qualities
are actually fabulous too...I won't say one is blue and one
is pink...I shall say that one is lime green or purple or
what ever colour you want them to be...reaching out to
each other...joining hands...sharing common jokes...it's
fun to have the different identities within the one person
and treasuring those different aspects of identity.

*Tracie touches the laughter anchor on Shirley's left
hand and Shirley smiles and nods her head*

T. And sometimes people think: "I wish I was more

female or more male", but those parts are, as you know, so very important in forming the whole person...so now Shirley, let magnetic forces pull them together and let divine knowledge assist in integrating them harmoniously forever...in the past, in the time before your conception...through to today and into your future...and let a light come on inside of you to shine for the rest of your life and beyond as the unification happens.

Tracie fires the safe place anchor on Shirley's right hand and the laughter anchor on her left hand, exactly at the same time. Shirley's face lights up with ecstasy and her head tilts backwards as her whole body relaxes more

T. And I want you to find yourself in a cinema screen...maybe somewhere really posh like the one at Leicester Square in London...with the comfortable seats...soundaround experience that comes from every direction...you can see the picture of the integrated you high upon the screen in glorious technicolor...tasting and smelling your experience too.

Shirley looks more focused ahead even though her eyes are closed

T. And I want you to alter and change that experience on the screen to make it just right for you...pressing buttons, twiddling knobs...when you are ready to step in the screen and put on that integrated, resourceful, smiling Shirley like a body suit...stepping inside the experience...just nod your head...will you nod your head?

Shirley nods her head

T. All right, **step into the first screen NOW!**...(*Tracie clicks her fingers*) put on the new Shirley...step inside her...feel the toes, nose ears, way she stands, thinks, speaks, looks, smells and how she tastes the air...experience her experience of having a more integrated central core identity with a confident balance of male and female...good...very good...and I'm impressed at what a brilliant hypnotic subject you are...and when you are ready to step into the second screen and become more integrated into the new you...nod your head.

Shirley gives a small smile and nods her head

T. All right, **step into the second screen NOW!**...(*Tracie clicks her fingers*)...letting the integration become more intense and complete...as you enjoy embracing your male and female energies (*Tracie fires the safe place anchor on Shirley's right hand, and the laughter and joy anchor of her left hand at this point*)...let the effects reverberate into your present, past and future...enjoy your transformation...and nod your head when are ready to progress to the third screen...

Shirley smiles euphorically as she nods her head

T. All right, **step into the third screen NOW!**...(*Tracie clicks her fingers*)...good...very good...good to be good isn't it....and you know you are...(*Tracie turns to the audience*). You can notice that this time the body moved less when Shirley stepped into the third screen. During the first or second screen there may be a slight twitch or jolt to the body as resistance is worked through at an unconscious level. On the third integration, however, Shirley is more comfortable with the integration process; she is more grounded, back in her body and comfortable with who she is becoming...Shirley, please nod when you are ready for the fourth integration.

Shirley looks upwards and nods her head

T. All right, **step into the fourth screen NOW!**...(*Tracie clicks her fingers*)...good...let it happen, make it so...

Tracie fires the two hand anchors again and turns to

the audience as she speaks

T. It's important to direct the person to be using a high visual internal screen so that the body learning is focused more towards the upward direction. People with a sense of depression or dysfunction tend to have collapsed, downward, heavy stances and they focus their gaze towards the floor. Notice that at each stage I am asking Shirley to be the one who confirms that she is ready to move on by nodding her head.

If there had been a refusal or inaction then I would have needed to ask her what she was encountering and working with a way of dissolving such resistance. Only by working in this way can the hypnotist be sure that the changes are actually taking place...and we can see the marvellous changes are really happening with you Shirley both at a deep unconscious level...and at a conscious level as your unconscious lets your conscious mind know what it needs to know on a need to know basis...when you're ready.

Shirley's head goes right back, nods as she breaks into a broad smile. Her body begins to rock slightly from side to side and her toes turn up and she lets out a really big breath

T. All right, **step into the fifth screen NOW**!...(*Tracie clicks her fingers*)...Wow...we are so proud of you and we know that the only person you need to be in your life is...well who is that Shirley?

S. Me!

T. That's right, you can be confident in who and what you are...and if you encounter any times when your history is asked for...you can say what you like...feeling integrated as a person of male and female energies...and you don't always have to tell people everything about yourself, just what is convenient for you...it's your life...even the history is yours to change as you so wish as you have done today...and only when you are ready to fully integrate into the sixth final screen...becoming fully the new, confident self...having so much love you find you can give some away and still have loads left, will you nod your head?

Shirley nods her head.

T. All right, **step into the sixth FINAL INTEGRATION NOW!**...(*Tracie clicks her fingers*)...and you can congratulate yourself for the wonderful journey you have made...but before you come fully back into your body I want you to look high up ahead and see a healing light...I don't know what colour it is...and the audience doesn't know the colour...but I know you do...walk into the healing light...let the colour of love fill your every atom, cell, organs and self...toes, ears, nose and the space around you throughout your life *(Tracie fires all three anchors)*...let it be you.

Shirley's mouth is wide open as her face is relaxed

T. So when someone makes a mistake and uses the wrong pronoun in addressing you...you can laugh (*Tracie fires the laughter anchor and Shirley begins to laugh to herself*)...so much love pouring from the inside outwards...your central personality changed...changing at a deep unconscious level now and continually into the future as well as in your past...and I'm going to bring you all the way back to the room on the count of eight to one...8...having a sense of learning and change here today and continually...7...knowing what it is to feel good and be a valued member of the human race with things to teach others...6...a sense of your own sensuality, sexuality, gender performance and right to be private...5...remembering that you can do whatever work you need to do on yourself throughout your life...4...confident, loving and a source of inspiration to others...3... it's good to laugh even when you least expect it...2...knowing how grateful we all are for you being such a wonderful person here today...1...feeling relaxed, refreshed and loved...wide awake and alert...eyes open and awake.

Shirley opens her eyes, stretches, yawns, moves around in her chair and Tracie writes the words INTEGRATION, REASSOCIATION on the whiteboard, before going back over to Shirley

T. Hi...how are you?

Shirley takes a long time to answer

S. Strange...(*A very large pause as Shirley orientates herself*)...it's as if I could go out and do anything...(*Shirley laughs*)...and not care what people think...well, not letting that stop me from being myself anyway.

Eradicating Remaining Sex, Gender and Sexuality Dysphoria Post-Transition Through Timeline Therapy

The Third International Congress on Sex and Gender
Exeter College, Oxford, Workshop 1998

Timeline Therapy is a hypnotic technique for which the American therapist Tad James is well known. It could also come under the Neuro Linguistic Programming format of Change Personal History as promoted by Richard Bandler and John Grinder. The original modern-day version though was more widely associated with Milton Erickson's Crystal Ball Technique otherwise known as Pseudo Orientation in Time.

Although there are various personal development tapes on the market that incorporate these techniques I would not advise people to use those products. Material in the form of disturbing memories from their past may arise during this process and may need to be dealt with by a professional hypnotherapist, psychotherapist, psychiatrist, psychologist or counsellor.

While I am all for personal development, being a hypnotherapist, I am also too aware that nothing can substitute for professional help in moving a person forward in their thinking towards a stage of resolution. To conduct this kind of therapy it is advisable for the therapist to have had training in hypnosis; to simply have an MD or training in a particular school of psychology, psychiatry or psychotherapy would be insufficient.

I have written before about disturbed psychological conditions in some people who have undergone sex and gender realignment treatment, whether that treatment has progressed to full genital surgery or the person has adopted a more liberal identity. When I say liberal identity that is not a social comment, but an indication that I recognise that there are a profuse number of identities that the gender and sex fluid person can choose from that may suit their needs or desires. Many of these identities may need medical intervention to alter the person's body and will culminate in a physical self that is other than their original biological sex or sociological gender.

Further still within the group that this technique can be used for, I shall include the biological intersex for whom surgery may or may not be an option or who may have had surgery inflicted upon them. I could also include sexuality groups, because although they have not undergone a biological or surgical change, sociological adjustment may have had to occur as they came to terms with their emerging sense of self.

Among the psychologically disturbed conditions that may arise post-transition are Chronic Childlessness Syndrome, repression, poor social skills and social isolation; paranoia about sex, gender and sexuality identity; aggressive-defensive strategies; high anxiety; chronic depression; feelings of deep loneliness and an inability to form personal, intimate relationships; all of which were a direct result of the Sex, Gender or Sexuality Dysphoria. These I cite as being other than psychotic identifiable psychopathologies which would be classifiable and deemed separate from the issues of sex, gender or sexuality identity.

I would also like to add that people may also suffer from psychological disturbances, post-transition, even if they choose to transition rather than feeling that it was a compulsion. People who have undergone transition treatment and do not have psychological disturbances can also go through Timeline Therapy in order to psychotherapeutically help themselves feel even better about their identities.

I, having undergone considerable medical and psychological intervention and social transformation in order to bring my identity in line with my internal self-image, can appreciate how Sex, Gender or Sexuality Dysphoria and transformation can, at times, be very ego damaging. What can also be ego damaging is the kind of reaction a person may get from other people, professionals or the public, that casts doubt upon their right to define themselves as they so wish or need.

Here I will not attempt to define hypnosis, for that would take up too much space and would deviate us from our main focus; however, I have entered into the debate to define what it might or might not be before (O'Keefe 1998). I shall suffice to say that hypnosis is an altered state of awareness that consists of intense concentration as the focus of attention moves within, paying less attention to the external world. The conscious mind moves aside to give access to the vast unconscious mindsets that run our autonomic bodily and psychological functions, that are ordinarily out of our conscious awareness.

Access to changing unconscious psychological mindsets is made easier for the hypnotist, and the individual, because the defence mechanisms that are present in the conscious mind are partially inactive during hypnosis and do not interfere with the psychological shift. Hypnosis can be a profound changing experience that can have the same or a more powerful effect as any drug or preparation and should be treated with deep respect for its potency and ability to change a person's mind.

Timeline Therapy takes place in light to medium states of trance and involves interaction with the person and the hypnotist, continually checking back for the ecology of the psychological shifts. It is a psychoimaginary technique that requires the hypnotist to direct the person to immerse themselves in all five sensory modality perceptions: sight, sound, feelings, smell and taste to create their internal reality. It does not take place in a deep state of somnambulism that may resemble the sleep-like state, although the person becomes a waking somnambulist during the process.

So in conclusion I highly recommend Timeline Therapy as it is one of the most powerful hypnotic cognitive reorganising processes. Because it is not predominantly direct suggestion, but a procedure of self-development, by the client of their psyche, and recognition of their own resources and how to apply them, it allows maximum ego-strengthening of personality.

Bibliography

Andreas, Connirae, Andreas, Steve, *Heart of the Mind*, Real People Press, Utah, USA, 1989.

Bandler, Richard & MacDonald, Will, *An Insider's Guide to Submodalities*, Metapublications, USA, 1988.

James, Tad & Woodsmall, Wyatt, *Timeline Therapy*, Metapublications, USA, 1988.

Rossi, Ernest L, *The Collected Papers of Milton H Erickson on Hypnosis Vols I-IV*, Irvington Publishers, New York, 1980.

A Case of a Morphic Positive Hallucination Through Hypnosis with an Erotic Transvestite
September 1998

I report this case because it is unusual and because it illustrates the diversity of human sexual experience and how resolutions can be attained without drastic measures. It also fascinated me because I have never quite encountered such a request from a client in exactly the same way before.

I received a telephone call at my practice from a man

requiring hypnotherapy and as usual I tried to solicit some information from the caller about what he was trying to achieve by coming to see me. His reply was that he wanted me to hypnotise him into thinking he had breasts when he made love to his wife.

My immediate response was that I was ethically unable to do that and before I could explain to him that his wife could sue me, the telephone conversation was over. To do such a thing would be hypnotically possible but I would be in danger of malpractice because it would be a hypnotic suggestion that could be construed as inducing some form of dysmorphobia or Gender Dysphoria. Professionally that would place me in position of breach of ethical codes of practice that are designed to protect clients from unethical hypnotists or therapists.

Since I presently have two practices it just so happened that he had earlier in the day left a message on the other answerphone and I called him back not knowing it was the person I had spoke to earlier. When I realised it was the same man I explained my predicament about his request but explained I was an expert in the field of sex and gender and offered to see him anyway.

On arriving at my office he was very nervous, extremely embarrassed and could not look me in the eye as I took a personal history. He was 40, had been married for 18 years and had a child. His wife had been aware of his fantasy for the whole of their relationship and had joined in with it, encouraging him to wear bra and panties when they had sex. They also had a non-fetishistic sex life and even during fetishism he did not need to dress in more than the underwear in order to be excited. By all accounts he was an erotic transvestite who suffered from feelings of guilt after the fantasy and ejaculation, and this, I surmised was due to his Christian background and cultural belief systems.

His nipples became extremely sensitive during sex and he told me his wife was quite comfortable with him having the fantasy of having breasts. Sometimes she even made him wear bra, panties and lipstick in bed until the next morning and referred to him by using feminine pronouns.

My first concern when I questioning him was if there was any dysmorphobia or Gender Dysphoria present or whether the desire to have female parts to his body went beyond the sexual fantasy. It seems that the fantasy was confined to the sexual act and preceding time that led up to sexual excitement. I did not try to find out the origins of the fantasy because the client was very evasive when I asked about its inception which he thought had evolved in adolescence. I also believed that I did not have a right to pursue such an avenue of enquiry because the client was not distressed about the fantasy – he simply wanted it to be more real for him.

In order to maintain rapport and assist this man I told him that I could find a way to help him and that he need not be afraid of discussing sex with me because part of my job was talking about sex all day long. Well...not in the supermarket naturally...but then my partner and I have the shopping delivered anyway. This put him much more at ease.

One feature of the case was that he tended to partake in the fantasy and fetishism more often when he was under stress. This is a noted characteristic of many transvestites and does not tend to happen with the transsexual condition; in fact, the reverse can be said to be true.

I taught him self-hypnosis and self-suggestion so that he was first able to relax before the sex act. This would do many things including allowing sex to last longer, inducing a greater awareness of physical pleasure, being able to focus his attention on the positive hallucination of having breasts. By going with his requests I was able to safely teach him to use hypnosis to fulfil his request in an ethical manner. He was also given a large reading list about how to use hypnosis and an audio tape to practise with as well as being encouraged to investigate and read up on Tantric sex, which uses visualisation and a large hypnotic component.

Having not broken rapport with his original request I was also able to tag on a conditional suggestion that allowed him to have control over his hallucinations and stop them whenever he wished. The hypnotic suggestion used was a cognitive behaviour "STOP" self-suggestion mechanism, that was also a cue to come out of trance and return to normal waking functioning.

If I had not agreed to take him as a client there would have been a possibility that he may have simply telephoned the next hypnotist in the book. The chances of them having understood his condition would probably have been very slim. A hypnotist not understanding the dynamics of Sex and Gender Dysphoria and trans-identity positive or negative hallucinations may have installed a cued hallucination with no "STOP" mechanism and thereby actually induced dysmorphobia. I suggest that this could happen because many of the dysmorphobics I see are using self-suggestion to induce their conditions and later during therapy stop and the dysmorphobia disappears. This can also be true with a wide range of body dysphoria identity disorders such as anorexia, bulimia, ugly ducking syndrome and racial auto-degradation.

By designing the hypnotherapy the way I did, we were able to fulfil the client's request for positive hallucination of breasts during sex, not transgressing my professional ethical codes, and adding an extra behavioural bonus of teaching a self-control facility for the client to stop the fantasy, which he may never have had before. I also taught him how to relax more easily, introduced him to a strong form of self-suggestion which he could use for ego strengthening, improved his sex education, and gave him a sense of not being a freak or weirdo.

I realise that there may be some who read of this case who may accuse me of colluding with the delusions of a person with some form of paraphelia, dysmorphobia or Sex and Gender Dysphoria. To those I would say that neither I nor anyone else has the right to judge the rights or wrongs of how another person may direct their sexual libido, if it does no harm to others. Prudishness or moral superiority is counterproductive in sex therapy and a therapist must generally avoid transference of their ideas to the client's psyche, as that could be defined as abuse.

These resources the client now possessed after the session were also more likely to lead to the prevention of the fantasy turning into dysmorphobia, Gender Dysphoria, sexual frustration or relationships outside what seemed to be a monogamous and happy marriage.

The Effects of Covert Behaviour in People with Sex, Gender, and Sexuality Identity Disorders on Partners and Families

Published in *Reflections International*, September 1999

In looking at the issues surrounding this subject I first of all need to differentiate between a developed sex, gender and sexuality (SGS) identity and an SGS identity disorder. The first would involved a person being at one with their sense of self and behaviours or going strongly in that direction and that does not necessarily involve them being overtly public. A sex, gender and sexuality identity disorder would involve the individual being uncomfortable and confused about themselves and their identity, and may lead them to being extremely secretive, depressed, confused and even aggressive when others try to question them on issues of identity and behaviour. When using the word "covert" I am describing behaviour that purposefully attempts to keep knowledge from others or deceive.

In our society, covert is not necessarily associated with badness because governments are covert in order to protect their citizens against threats to the state and individuals. A person arranging a surprise birthday party can also be said to be operating covertly. However, a shoplifter or assassin can be said to be covert by the very nature of their deceptive behaviour.

In this day and age of the COMING OUT it is possible to be anything and find a support group to help an individual fight for their equal rights to be whatever they are. What is often forgotten, though, is the feelings of friends and relatives and in what way the individuals' emerging or secretive behaviour may have on others.

Many gay, lesbian, transvestite, transsexual and trans-gendered people discover their emerging sense of identity during a relationship they may have formed before their coming out. This can often cause the remaining partner to be extremely confused and disorientated about their own identities, and angry at that individual. They may even have feelings of being tricked, deceived or used as a prop or a stepping stone to support the emerging person while they make up their mind. Some partners report feeling left out and forgotten while all the attention is placed on the person coming out. Others talk about the covert behaviour making them feel as if the trans or gay person was having an affair and not disclosing.

What is far worse is when the person discovering or try-ing to hide their gay or trans status truly sets out to manoeuvre the situation to keep the other person in the dark. At the Gendy's Conference 1998, in Manchester Diane Aitchison, one of the speakers told how she had worked on the Beaumont Society's helpline for 10 years where she dealt with many distraught telephone calls from deeply disturbed partners of transpeople who were refus-ing to admit to their trans behaviour. This often caused those distraught partners to think perhaps they were going mad and imagining the transperson's behaviour.

Aitchison said: "I think it's one of those issues where the variables are interchangeable because of the mindset of the partner. Certainly in the case of secondary transsexu-alism with biological males, the subjects often don't declare themselves openly at the beginning and there may be a lot of covert behaviour which the partner will be aware of but won't understand – for instance if someone is covertly taking hormones there will come a time when, in the case of a male-to-female, he won't go to bed unless he is wearing a T-shirt and pants. He will turn his back on his wife, she will feel that as rejection, she doesn't understand why he no longer makes advances and won't let her touch him.

"This situation can go on for several years, amazing as

that may seem, because the wife believes that he is under-going some sort of trauma or breakdown. They often don't know about the crossdressing behaviour let alone the transsexualism. So here they have their spouse who at one time was reasonably loving and sexual, who now rejects them in quite a profound way. The effects on the partner can be initially shock, then she will be very concerned over why she has been rejected then she becomes angry and bitter. She still stays in the relationship because she believes it to be a temporary situation. There's often children to consider. He's not talking to her, he's not telling her what's going on, he's often secretive."

My own partner never revealed her lesbianism to her parents until she was 27 and although she had never had a boyfriend, they never asked her any questions. A strange dance of silence prevailed between all three of them for all those years. She did not declare her sexuality and they never asked her about it, so between them they covertly remained in denial about a young woman who never brought anyone home or talked about her suitors.

Professor Richard Green of Charing Cross Hospital Gender Identity Unit has also spoken at lengths on the subject of family relationships and the effects on children in trans family relationships (Green 1998). He has often appeared in court as an expert witness to testify that it is best for children to retain their links with parents who have come out as transsexual, gay or bisexual. Phobic responses about people with diverse sex, gender or sexualities is one of the main reasons that people often try to keep secrets about the real emerging sense of self.

Sometimes transpeople are secretive for fear of losing the people around them if they came out. Other times, as I have seen in my practice, the person with the covert behaviour is purposefully attempting to control the psychodynamics of the relationship by not revealing the truth about themselves. This is inadvisable and can be very cruel to the partners.

It is important here to say that everyone has a right to a private life and that there are things that individuals do not want to disclose, even to the people nearest to them. In talking about the effects of a person's covert behaviour on others I am not suggesting that everyone has the right to know everything about us.

In the aftermath of the jubilant gay, bisexual or trans person having come out there are those left behind who need to reorient themselves and their sense of identity to a new reality, and they too must be given consideration, caring, counselling and the right to know the true facts of the situation. Many partners or ex-partners have suffered general identity disorders themselves after the coming out – they become depressed, unable to cope, in some cases had psychological breakdowns, and in extreme cases a few have been hospitalised. The people who are coming out must remember that it is not all about them but also about the effects on the people who surround and care for them.

In order to hide their secret the gay or transperson may have been playing the game of the controlling partner by keeping very tight reins on the permissibility of their partner's behaviour. The partner may then be very oppressed by such games and feel exceedingly betrayed when the truth emerges. Honesty, I tell all my clients, is the very best policy and if you are unable to be honest with your partners then there are problems in the relationship that are fundamentally separate from any form of SGS identity disorder.

It is possible that some people with SGS identity disorders may choose partners who are submissive and will not challenge the individual on their covert behaviour. Maybe the partner who takes the unchallenging role sometimes had problems of their own and seeks out an over-dominant partner with something to hide so that they will not have to deal with their own issues.

In playing the psychoanalyst we must always remember that each and every case needs always to be considered separately and that everyone is fallible to the delusions we create for our own needs. However, I maintain that partners of people coming out must never be forgotten and should specifically be offered or have access to their own counselling help so they can deal with what they are having to go through.

Some partners or relatives are left with a wide range of thoughts and questions that plague them before and after the disclosure:

Was it something I did that made the person the way they are?

Is it because I am unattractive or a failure as a man (or a woman)?

Surely I must be in some way at least partly to blame?

If only I had been more attentive to their needs

Perhaps they chose me because there was something wrong with me?

Does my partner have some kind of illness I do not understand?

Is there something I can do to reverse what has happened?

Let us also remember that not everyone is knowledgeable about the diversity of human nature and behaviour and some people may be very shocked at their partners' emerging identity. They may have an enormous and overwhelming amount of information to consume, digest and come to terms with. We do not all have the same beliefs, values and attitudes. Some partners of gay and transpeople with covert behaviour may have been chosen because they have rigid personality types – for example are perhaps overtly religious – so no one outside the relationship has any inkling that covert behaviour is taking place.

Partners, children, immediate family and close friends can feel betrayed and hurt when the truth about the covert behaviour finally emerges, believing that they were deceived in some way. They may also be offended by the fact that the person with the covert behaviour felt they could not trust them with the truth.

Just recently a client of mine, who was a biological male considering transitioning to a transsexual female, was procrastinating for several months about how and when to disclose their future plans to their 16-year-old son. I urged the client to disclose quickly so that the son did not feel kept in the dark and was able to have a good amount of time to adjust to the client's future plans. When eventually the client made the disclosure the son simply said that he had known about it for some considerable time, such a future move by his parent had been quite obvious to him and it was no great surprise.

There are, of course, disclosures that go badly wrong and people react prejudicially out of ignorance and fear. It is inevitable that not everyone is open to their partners or family members changing identities; perhaps they themselves have an investment in things staying the same. However, on the whole when I hold couples or family therapy sessions with clients who are coming out to their families, it is always the families who have open and honest communication who fare the best. Families with poor patterns of communication do not fare well and need to do a great deal of work on the ways they relate to each other, but even those families in time can come to terms with the emerging truth of the situation and work towards a positive future for all concerned.

It must also be remembered that the stress often created by the dynamics of covert or secret behaviour in relationships can lead to the health of parties involved deteriorating.

One of the main factors in motivating a person to be covert in their behaviour is shame about what they are doing or feeling, and eliminating those socially constructed false values is part of the work they have to do on themselves. It would also be reckless to say that everyone who is considering a life change or who has behaviour other than their disclosed behaviours should blatantly disclose everything to everyone. Disclosures need to be stage managed and carefully thought out. Professional, social and psychological help in managing the disclosure and adjusting to the new realities can be used to articulate and maximise the advantages and minimise any damage.

Bibliography

Green, Richard MD, *Transsexuals' Children: Divorce and*

the Implacable Spouse, The Third International Congress on Sex and Gender, Exeter College, Oxford, 1998.

Aitchison, Diane, *Psychological Effects on Partners of Transsexuals*, Gendy's 98, 5th Gender Dysphoria Conference, Manchester 1998.

Interviews

O'Keefe, Tracie, DCH & Novak, Stacy, of TransEssex support group, and *Reflections International* magazine, 1997. Interview conducted by telephone.

O'Keefe, Tracie, DCH & Aitchison, Diane, The Beaumont Society HelpLine, 1998. Interview conducted by telephone.

Covert Prejudice
August 1998

Covert prejudice can disguise itself as many names or not names; like silent selection or deselection, academic preference, or unexplainable indifference. There is also whispering behind thick oak doors that defies the enquiries of logic or reason and does not reveal the results of processes that only partially tell the truth. Covert prejudice can take whatever shape or form its owner needs it to and be supported by point of law, preferential amendment or secret necessity.

I wish I could tell you, the reader, exactly what covert prejudice is but it is so illusive and distant to someone as naive and open as myself that I do not know its name, colour or breadth. Yet I lie to you, because I too, at times, have been its mistress without my conscious knowledge. It is clever enough never to show its face in public or take a form that can be tracked down and eliminated. Only from a later vantage point did I truly understand that I had courted, coveted and fed it of my own accord.

So for those who defy statistical normality by being another sex, gender or sexuality than is common to the average person, there is always a threat of not only being blatantly affronted, but being silently pursued.

Is there never to be a Nirvana, where all whose dimorphism into a butterfly of another colour can taste the nectar in peace, undisturbed by the hunter of differences?

Don't be silly...do you think those that are different would choose to blend into the melange and tapestry of the repetitive furrows of the mass farmer?...Well maybe those who never learnt how to activate the survival instinct to its full potential would prefer to join those who take pride in being the same as the same as the same.

But if...as someone who is a butterfly of a different kind you could activate the survival instinct to not only protect yourself against attacks for difference but also preserve the status quo of those who choose to challenge you...would you choose that? If so then you would be deluding yourself because the inevitability of difference will never be other than the inspiration of nature in each and every one of us...we survive because we are different and in spite of it.

Covert prejudice can be differently dangerous because it can call itself your friend while poisoning your associates' minds against you and making you seem paranoid or delusionary. It can work away silently in the dark, chipping at the foundations of your civilisation until one morning you wake up and find the sun has gone. So you should stay ever vigilant in your sleep lest your right to life is challenged when your back is turned. Set your friends to watch too, not only on your behalf, but on their own, and against themselves waking up with their lights expunged by their own doing.

The nature of life is such that we all must take responsibility for seeking out and dissolving covert prejudice and that search can never end because it is a lifelong job for each generation. Someone's nemesis is always another person's friend, or pretending to be, until they realise that they are being duped too.

For most of us there comes a morning in our lives when we find that we are no longer attached to our mother's breasts. It can happen at seven months, years or even decades after our birth, but it is a time of realisation that if we want a different world then we have to make it happen ourselves. There will always be open battles to be fought in a world with too many people and not enough space never to bump into each other. Parts of those battles will be silent, secretive, unannounced, and covert prejudice can never tell you when it is coming as it does not know how; but if you want to protect the sex, gender, and sexuality different from such prejudice you must also acknowledge you are and can be covert too.

An Attempt to Get Married: Between Katrina Fox & Tracie O'Keefe

Published in *Transgender Tapestry*, Spring 1999

In February 1998 my partner Katrina Fox and I attended Camden Registry Office, London, to arrange a marriage between myself and Katrina, who was born a biological female. We live in London as a lesbian couple. However, I was born and initially brought up as a boy and it states male on my birth certificate, therefore in law I should be entitled to all rights and privileges afforded to males in British society, which includes the right to take a bride.

As a teenager I presented myself socially as a female and have always lived as such with the aid of hormone treatment and corrective surgery. I have never officially applied to any court to have my birth certificate changed to female, knowing that British law would not presently allow this, since my chromosome sex is XY even though I am cosmetically, socially and for all intents and purposes regarded as a female. In the 1970s enquiries were made at the births, marriages and deaths registration office to amend my birth certificate to female but I was told that it was not possible.

British law does not presently give lesbians the right to marry. At no time did I represent myself to the officials at the registry office as a biological female because I was claming my right to get married as a male. The officials were confused because I cannot pass physically as a male in society due to my looks and physiological make-up. I did, however, explain that although I may appear to be female, my birth certificate says male, and I was claiming the right to get married to Katrina. The wedding was duly booked for 11.00am on 28 March at the above mentioned registry office.

I was then asked to attend the head office at Westminster, Marylebone Road, London a few days later to give notice of marriage between myself and Katrina, as required by law. The man I saw was a Mr Richard Beacham, the Superintendent Registrar, who took the information that is normally required, which was to see a copy of our birth certificates. I also supplied a legal document containing a declaration of change of name for myself, which was countersigned by two solicitors who acted as commissioners of oath.

Coincidentally Katrina is adopted and also has a change of name document which was presented and accepted.

However, this man's attitude was only what I can describe as hostile towards me and he asked me if I could provide any further identification. I refused, telling him that I had complied with what was required of me by law in presenting a copy of my original birth certificate, and the legal change of name which I explained was a valid document. I also explained to him that no matter how I may appear to him I was not, in this instance, claiming to be female.

Since male was on my birth certificate, my gynaecology and physiology was my own business and I explained to him that the only thing he needed to concern himself with was my legal documents. Also I stated that he had no right to refuse me the right to get married as a male. I paid £20 as was required of me, took my receipt and left with the expectation that the marriage would go ahead as arranged.

The day before the marriage was due to take place, I turned up at the Superintendent Registrar's office at 3.00pm to collect the licence that was needed to permit us to get married. He refused point blank to issue the licence, saying that he did not believe that the birth certificate I presented was mine and that he wanted more proof I was that person. I explained to him again that I had provided a legal copy of my birth certificate and a legal document of change of name, and that Katrina had presented exactly the same documents, even though he had never seen her.

I also told him that a precedent had been set at the Chelsea registry office on 28 June 1995 when Tracie Ann Scott, who had been born a boy and had a male birth certificate, had married a woman as a male, even though she had a vagina and breasts and wore a full wedding dress. On that occasion she was only asked to produce her birth certificate. I also reiterated that no matter what my physical or biological make-up was, if I had a male birth certificate I was entitled to marry a woman, and whether I had breasts, ovaries or a penis was entirely my own business.

He had never seen Katrina but he accepted her documents. I was sitting in front of him but he would not accept mine. I further telephoned the solicitor who had prepared my change of name document and Mr Beacham spoke to him over the telephone to confirm this had taken place. I challenged him that if he thought I was fraudulently presenting a birth certificate that was not mine, then the matter must be reported to the police. I then called the police and they attended the scene.

I explained to the police that this man seemed to believe that I was fraudulently in possession of someone else's birth certificate and that I was attempting to illegally get married with it. Mr Beacham told the police that he did not believe it to be a fraud, yet he refused to issue me with the appropriate licence of marriage for the wedding to go ahead. He continually stated that he wanted more proof that I was the person on the birth certificate, but would not specify what kind of proof he wanted.

I asked him again in front of the police, if he believed the documents I presented were stolen or fraudulent and he continually said, as far as he was concerned, they were not. The police did not arrest me because they said they did not believe I was in possession of any fraudulent or stolen documents.

I stayed at the registry office until the close of business when Mr Beacham still refused to issue the licence. I also asked him to put his refusal in writing but he would not do so. The wedding was not allowed to go ahead.

I believe I was discriminated against because of the way I look even though I had a right legally to present myself any way I desired. The Superintendent Registrar was hostile and prejudiced and insisted it was his job to ensure that two biological females did not get married. I explained to him time and time again that I was not presenting myself, in this instance, as a biological female and my birth certificate still stated I was male, but he would not accept that.

Our friends had arrived from different parts of the world and England to attend a legal wedding that the Superintendent Registrar prevented from taking place. We suffered grave disappointment, inconvenience, embarrassment and injury.

I personally was publicly humiliated, embarrassed and discriminated against while trying to pursue my legal right to marry Katrina. She was also discriminated against because she was a lesbian living with a transsexual woman, unable to be married as a lesbian, but was also refused to be married to me as a male.

When considering what happened it is important to clarify certain salient points:

1. Two people presented themselves for marriage, I legally male by virtue of a birth certificate declaration and Katrina legally female by the same criteria.
2. British law does not presently permit a transsexual to change the sex on their birth certificate therefore I should legally not be discriminated against for appearing female.
3. Two people presented exactly the same kind of documents: one birth certificate and one change of name document.
4. Katrina, the biological female, was not seen by the Superintendent Registrar and had her documents accept-

ed as valid.

5. I, the transsexual woman, whose birth certificate still stated male, had been seen by the Superintendent Registrar and was discriminated against because of my looks.

6. All documents presented by both parties were legal and valid.

7. The Superintendent Registrar overstepped his requirement to ascertain a person's identity and right to participate in a legal wedding ceremony and allowed his personal prejudices to perpetrate discrimination against me on the grounds that I am a transsexual woman or transgendered person.

8. Having a male birth certificate prohibits me from getting married to a male in British law.

9. Having a male birth certificate, I was still prevented from marrying a female by a representative of the Crown.

10. Discrimination based on sex, gender or sexuality undoubtedly took place.

Three day later myself and Katrina awoke to find there was a story about us in the tabloid rag the *News of the World*. It was obvious to us that someone at the registry office had sold the story to the press and given them our private and confidential details. Of course the registry office denies this but there is no doubt that is what happened. The only people to be aware, at the time, of both my father's and Katrina's father's details and addresses were those at the registry office and the very next day, which was the morning of the proposed wedding, a reporter visited both our parents' homes.

Not only did the *News of the World* print incorrect and defamatory statements about us but they also stole a photographic image from one of our books and reprinted it without the publisher's permission. The story told how I had turned up at the registry office the morning of the expected wedding all dressed up and ready to go and had gone berserk – even though this had not taken place. In fact, because we knew the wedding could not take place we had attended a large "Legalise Cannabis" march that the broadsheet newspaper the *Independent on Sunday* had organised. And I can assure you we had a much more mellow time than the *News of the World* reported we did.

What did come out later is that I have been married to two men previously, using my dead sister's birth certificate and never sought a divorce before attempting to marry Katrina. However, at the end of the *Corbett vs Corbett* judgement, which is the precedent used in British law to prevent transsexuals changing their birth certificates or getting married to members of their originally registered biological sex, it says: "There is no need for someone born biologically male to get a divorce from a biological male they have married because by British law the marriage was not recognised." I married both men because I was in love with them at the time and I have invited the British government to prosecute me for that, but they have declined my offer.

It took several months until November for Katrina and I to get permission from the British government to get married as two women, one with a birth certificate that said male, and was by British law unable to be changed to female. I had to get my mother to write a one-page handwritten letter to say she had given birth to me, which could have been a forgery because they never interviewed her or clarified the facts. Nor at any time was any medical evidence provided to determine what my true sex is. The whole affair was undoubtedly a fiasco driven by homophobia, transphobia and the untenable position that the British government had placed itself in by determining a person's sex by virtue of gonadal and chromosomal criteria only.

We released the following statement to the press on the week that it become apparent in the British newspapers that there were at least three gay men in the Cabinet, yet the British government still dumps pre-election promises for equal rights for all. It seemed that Blair's government turned out like the Clinton administration – full of wind, down on its knees to get voted in, but does not deliver the goods or stay faithful to many of its promises.

LESBIANS WIN EQUAL RIGHTS BY MARRYING

A lesbian couple wed on Tuesday morning (10 November) at Camden Registry office at 10.30am.

Earlier this year Dr Tracie O'Keefe, 43, a psychotherapist, and her partner Katrina Fox, 32, a journalist, hit the headlines when the chief registrar of Westminster refused to marry the couple, even though O'Keefe's birth certificate records her as male. The original ceremony was cancelled at the eleventh hour by the registrar who said he could not allow two women to marry.

It has taken eight months for the government to concede and allow the couple to marry as man and wife, even though Dr O'Keefe, a transsexual, has lived as a female since the age of 15.

O'Keefe and Fox are angry that they have to suffer the humiliation as a gay couple of going through this ceremony in order to secure pension, inheritance and other rights automatic to heterosexual couples.

O'Keefe says: "It is insulting, after having lived all my adult life as a woman, to be forced to stand in front of bureaucrats and be referred to as 'he', 'Mr' 'the groom' and 'husband' just to protect our financial and contractual futures. It is nothing less than abuse and an attack on my core identity as a lesbian woman. Many other countries no longer allow this kind of discrimination against transsexuals."

Fox adds: "We feel let down by the Labour government, which has delayed on all its pre-election promises to gay people – to lower the age of consent for gay men to 16, the decision not to overturn Section 28 which prohibits the promotion of homosexuality in schools, or support the Sexual Orientation Discrimination Bill, which would outlaw discrimination against gays in the workplace.

"All Tracie and I want is the right for our relationship to be recognised in law – but for what it is – a lesbian relationship, not a heterosexual one. It is ludicrous that we have to go to these lengths and Tony Blair should be ashamed of himself."

In once again being very public about the intimate

details of my life I seek to educate and inform, even to the extent of using myself as a human protest. I am aware that there are many healthcare professionals that think, because I am a professional healthcarer, I should stay quiet and behave in a manner that would become tweed skirts, woolly jumpers and contrived images of respectability. This will never happen as I always keep in my mind the immortal words of Mother Teresa: "I march for peace, not against war".

Gay, lesbian, transsexual and transgendered people are often cited as being miscreants when they expose the prejudice perpetrated against them. I never expect to become mainstream or aligned with a sect, cult or distinct trend because therein for me lies the danger of complacency. Katrina and I live our lives on the edge of reason in order to push forward the boundaries of acceptability – that is our life mission and being married does nothing more than give us pension, inheritance rights and the permission to switch off each other's life support systems when our proletariat spirit has flown – rights that we did not have as an ordinary gay couple.

Having this ridiculous piece of paper called a marriage certificate that now sets us apart from our other lesbian friends only makes us more determined to educate people to become aware of bigotry, sexism, and the shortcomings of the artificially constructed bipolar model of sex, gender and sexuality.

The Genesis of Aunty Jenny's Criminality
Published in *Reflections International*, 1999

In telling you about Jenny, who I first encountered in the late 1960s, I am sharing with you my thoughts on one of the people who I have found most fascinating in my life. I do not judge, mock or seek to analyse her from an authoritative point of view, simply to relay how I see that for some, life is much more complicated than simply the right or wrong ways of going about things.

I remember as a child going ice-skating on a Saturday

afternoon with my skates slung over my shoulder, expenses in my pocket and the freedom of the rink beckoning to me many miles away. As I sauntered along dreamily pursuing my destination I always recalled there was a tall blond woman, with a beehive hairdo, wearing a nylon overall, and smoking a cigarette standing outside the Bingo hall opposite the ice rink. Like clockwork she would smile as I went past, and although she never spoke to me, her image was one of the regular occurrences that documented the time of the day and day of the week.

Some years later when I was 17 I met Jenny in a local gay pub where all the most outrageous of the local society felt safe to gather together and be what they considered normal. It was only then that I discovered that the 35-year-old woman, who called herself Aunty Jenny and had smiled at me on Saturday afternoons during my childhood, was in fact a male transvestite. I was not shocked that a person was a transvestite, for I am myself a transsexual, just that such a person had been there throughout my childhood without me even noticing.

After our introduction I got to know Aunty Jenny very well, and she told me her whole history from cradle to date. I continued to see her in different parts of the country over the next 20 years and followed her life, triumphs and tribulations. She (and I use this pronoun as a mark of respect for how Jenny wished to be addressed) had started dressing as a woman, when she was 19 years old in the late 1950s in Liverpool, her home town. Although this was a place where there had been a large mixed-race population of nearly a hundred years, racism was still rife, and sexism and homophobia were ingrained in the psyche of traditional English working-class life. Jenny was a social transvestite who lived all the time dressed in women's clothing and presented herself as female although she was a biological male and had no desire to be anything else.

In order to survive when her parents had thrown Jenny out of their home in disgust she had become a low-rent prostitute, shoplifter, long-time unemployment claimant and social security fraudster. It had been very difficult for her to find work and if she did secure employment sooner or later it seemed that someone made enough trouble in order to get her sacked. In English society it was very difficult for her to be accepted and she was often beaten up and thrown out of various lodging houses when landlords found out about her true identity. Neither the 1950s, 60s 70s or even 80s were kind to or even safe for her.

Education had eluded her as such people in society at that time had no expectations of even working unless it was the most menial of tasks, never mind aspirations of having a career. She told me how she had been arrested thousands of times for just coming out of her front door every evening dressed in female clothing. Each night she was charged with breaching the peace and lewd conduct. The police used to wait outside her front door and remain there until she eventually emerged to earn her living on the streets. Jenny never expected anything other than the bad lot she had got and the humiliations which had been thrust upon her during her whole adult life because she was a transvestite in a transphobic society.

The borders of where Jenny's persecution and criminality began and ended had been blurred by her socially inferior and vulnerable status in life. Jenny was a frontier person who waged a war to survive in an atmosphere of cruel castigation and discrimination. Like an immigrant, leper or publicly identified child molester authority had listed her among the affronteries to common decency and a perversion of people's morals, burning fury upon their eyes.

Once she had robbed the safe of a nightclub she worked in at 3.00am and then hitched a lift 200 miles on the back of a coal lorry in the previous day's make-up. The next day when I saw her spending her booty on a pier at the seaside she was celebrating for once having the kind of money that most people kept in the bank for a rainy day, but which she had never dreamed of having. Drunk, ecstatic and quite deranged she danced up and down the pier with the police trying to catch her, fully aware of who she was and the treasure she had purloined. Even two years in a men's prison never took away the triumph she felt at prospering

301

over poverty even at the expense of the nightclub owners and her own liberty.

The last time I saw Aunty Jenny was in the early 1990s when she was working in the West End collecting glasses at a gangsters drinking club. She told me she was trying to get promoted to working behind the bar so that she could steal enough money from the till in order to buy herself a new gas cooker. I don't know if she got her wish or her cooker as I have not seen her for five years now and although I send a Christmas card to an old address, I don't get a reply.

Aunty Jenny has been a hopeless criminal always involved in petty scams to survive in a world where other people got jobs much more easily than her because they were considered to be superior. I could not say that if she had not been a transvestite and insisted on living as she did that she would not have been that kind of person. However, I think if I have even a shred of human decency in me I can understand that her lifestyle contributed considerably to the depth of depravation and desperation she experienced. I do not mean to say that such people as transvestites are inherently criminal, only that many societies criminalise people because they present themselves as being gender and sexually different.

What sticks in my mind most of all is when I was 17 years old, homeless, jobless, penniless and suicidal it was Aunty Jenny that offered me the hospitality of her humble bedsit, the food on her table and an alternative to the respectable society of the day that scorned and denigrated my transsexualism.

Institutionalised Sexism, Gender and Sexuality Discriminations
January 1999

To say that people of sex, gender and sexuality variance were the only ones who suffered institutionalised discrimination would be untrue. In 1999 the Stephen Lawrence enquiry showed how the British police force failed to investigate that young man's murder properly because he was black. Asians find themselves set upon by racists in the East End of London. Arabs are kept from fully representing their society in Israel because of institutionalised racism, and Jews suffer the same plight in many other countries. Disabled people are largely ignored or their contributions to our society undermined by prejudice which purports that perhaps they do not do such a good job as an able bodied person could do. Women find it very difficult to climb the political ladder because of exclusions created by misogynists, and men suffer deprivations of contact with their children through matriarchal exclusion.

Were these prejudices restricted to the public at large then the establishment might be a safe place for those suffering from discrimination to appeal to for justified redress. However, since we all ultimately make up the establishment, then underlying social trends towards victimising certain sectors of society permeate into the establishment structure and become the cornerstones of the attitudes with which minority groups are treated.

All establishments have a tendency to restrict their investigations about themselves to bodies set up by and involving themselves and rarely are truly independent. The interests that such bodies have in not finding those establishments at fault often outweighs any reasonably non-biased investigation taking place.

I have recently been acquainted with a case of a young gay drag queen in south-east London, who at 16 years of age, found his parents' house had been pelted with eggs. Threats of violence were made against him and he was constantly heckled by neighbourhood gangs. Each time a crowd gathered around his house he telephoned the police but the police took so long to get there that the crowd had finished their fun and disappeared by the time they arrived. The police told him that they could only give the perpetrators first a slap on the wrist warning, then a caution and eventually a charge, but only if the harassers had been caught by the police performing threatening behaviour, violence or damage.

The police, however, were always too slow to ever catch anyone and in the meantime the boy and his family suffered terrible harassment. In such cases laws that work on the drawing board do not translate into real-life situations, and are not only impotent but are institutionally supportive of discrimination.

I was also involved in a case with a prostitute who had been assaulted by a client who had broken her arm. When the matter came to court the man was not sent to prison because the judge was a member of the same yacht club as the defendant. This was a fact that only came out later, but the judge was not reprimanded for not declaring his common interest with his fellow yachtsman. The young woman, who could not work for a long time, lost her house because she was unable to pay the bills. Here the law operated via funny handshakes and nods in the right direction. The woman's interests, even though she secured a conviction, were not addressed, as the financial compensation and justice she received were pitiful.

What's more, such prostitutes operate outside the law because generally laws only tolerate their existence by default. In such a profession where healthcare professionals urge sex workers to use condoms, no tax allowance is allowed for the purchase of those goods or many others involved in their trade. It is very much a "dammed if you do and dammed if you don't" situation in these sort of professions in that many members of society use their services and then seek to persecute – or prosecute them for operating.

The British Psychological Society only formed a lesbian and gay section in 1999. The opposition to its formation was that it would be giving special treatment to that particular sector of society and its critics did not seem to realise that positive discrimination is sometimes the only way to redress oppression. Furthermore it is necessary for lesbian and gay people to have a particular field of psychology which pertains only to them since they have issues that do not relate to the rest of society.

In 1999 the Bank of Scotland announced that it was to enter into a joint venture with the right-wing American evangelist Dr Pat Robertson, who controls Robertson Financial Services, and is founder of the Christian Broadcasting Network. This caused much condemnation from many equal rights organisations because he has publicly self-identified as being homophobic and holds sexist beliefs concerning the rights of women.

Dr Robertson was reported in *Axiom*, a gay newspaper in the UK, to have said on American television in 1993: "Many of those people involved with Adolph Hitler were satanists, many of them were homosexuals – the two seem to go together." Much talk was aired in the public arena about many of the bank's investors and clients withdrawing from its services, including a large number of gay and HIV charities.

The British House of Lords rallied many of its life peers and prominently Baroness Young to oppose a bill that was to equalise the age of permitted sex between consenting adults for homosexuals as well as heterosexuals. In 1998 the bill had failed to reach royal assent to become law, even though it had overwhelmingly been approved by the House of Commons. A right-wing Newcastle-based evangelical charity called the Christian Institute had provided the baroness with a full-time research assistant to work on her campaign for the past year. However, she had failed to declare this to the House of Lords Register which requires that peers declare fully all gifts, financial interests and assistance involved in influencing the work to be carried out in that chamber.

In March 1999 a transsexual woman had a victory when the Equal Opportunities Commission ruled that West Yorkshire Police had contravened the Sex Discrimination Act by refusing to offer her the post of a constable because of her sex and gender. She commented: "I believe that a police force should reflect the diversity of the community it serves. As a member of a minority group, I am sensitive to equality and prejudice. By nature, I have tolerated attitudes to gender, sexuality and ethnic cultures – and I believe that my personal experiences would be a valuable resource in policing West Yorkshire's diverse communities."

Gays, lesbians, transsexuals, transgendered, transvestites and androgyne people often find it difficult to survive in a society that is built on the foundations of institutionalised prejudice against their right to express themselves as they please. When they stand up to be counted they are often lambasted as being perverts, social deviants, anarchists and subject to threats, according to the perpetrators' need to identify an enemy. Social pressures and tensions determine that there is always a need for a figure in any society to find a target or the victim to vent aggression upon.

What is plain to see is that many people who implement, practise, and support institutional sexism, genderism and sexuality prejudice most of the time have no idea that they are doing it. They have never considered the semantics, humanitarianism or damage that their attitudes can do to other human beings. Other supporters of such prejudice do so because, not to do so, puts them in danger of being persecuted for not running with the crowd and such individuals can be castigated, causing people to lose their jobs themselves or be in contradiction of institutional policies.

Evidence exists of institutional prejudice taking place when one person or group of people is not attaining the advantages and rights automatically given to others freely. Fighting and redressing such prejudices is a dynamic process that never reaches a solution but must be a continuous development.

The equal opportunities agenda need to be constantly examined and re-examined throughout the 21st century and beyond because with each generation there arises new issues.

The law, medicine, psychology and philosophy all support institutionalised prejudice when they alone become mono-disciplinary and choose to support their paradigms in the face of logical contradictions. They also become institutionally prejudiced when they act upon a plethora of

306

expert evidence without considering the subjects' perspectives of the individual themselves or discount that perspective because it is not objective.

Since the nature of our lives is now changing to being transglobal with the event of the Internet, there is an opportunity to tackle such prejudices on two levels. From a micro perspective an individual needs to charge themselves with the agency to monitor their own behaviour and their environment. We are, after all, the guardians of our own souls, and whatever we believe in, ultimately we are the ones who, at the end of the day, have to account to ourselves for our own actions.

On a macro level, however, our new shared global consciousness can collectively produce the kind of resources that can balance the needs of the individual against the mechanics of the oppression in any form. Even though there are moves by many governments to monitor, police, sanction, edit, and control the new medias, technology is now too liberated and developmental to stop the sex, gender and sexuality equality movements forming power bases that are beyond the control of any institution.

The individual who allows themselves to be discriminated against without taking action is guilty of supporting institutional prejudice. Those who stand by and watch such prejudices taking place without attempting to intercede and change the equation are guilty also. Turning a blind eye in order to save your own neck has to be the worst kind of hypocrisy because no matter how much that person may agree later that the person was discriminated against, they supported it by their silence.

The Danger of Disintegration in Transglobal Political Movements for Sex, Gender and Sexuality Freedom
Published in *Gendy's Journal*, September 1998

Throughout history we can look at the kind of social and political change that has occurred in different societies regarding sex, gender and sexuality. Patterns can be clearly defined which show that movements responsible for the changes were propelled by certain groups or individuals who had common causes and motivation.

Emmeline Pankhurst remains in British history as a key woman who persevered and lobbied for women to get the vote and formed an organisation called the Women's Social and Political Union.

Kate Millett was an American feminist bisexual who wrote and pushed forward ideas about women's right to define their own sexuality. Barbara Castle, the British politician, stood shoulder to shoulder with women in the 1960s as they went on strike in order to get equal pay and respect from men in the workplace.

Quentin Crisp, through his notoriety and book *The Naked Civil Servant*, caused a shift in the ideas of many people for the open and honest portrayal of the prejudice that he suffered as a gay man in the 1930s and throughout his life.

John Shirley is lobbying in England for the rights of fathers to be awarded custody of and access to their children.

Madonna, the singer and actress, desensitises Hollywood to public displays of bondage and bisexuality.

Dr Tuppy Owens in England formed and promotes an organisation called the Sexual Freedom Coalition, campaigning for the rights of each individual to define their own sexual tastes and the abolition of archaic and prejudicial laws against sex workers.

Rosalind Miles, in her book *The Women's History of the World*, writes about how our histories since the commencement of the written word have been formed through the eyes of men. Her point is that we do not have a true record of events but only those seen through men's eyes, which have been coloured by the nature of their own sex, gender and sexuality perceptions. During much of history women were considered as chattels and property of lowly intellectual ability; therefore their ideas were not recorded. History is now being rewritten in many quarters by women to rebalance and redress the distortions that have accrued. Undoubtedly the physical strength and violence of men was used against women to divide and conquer them and their political power was, by the nature of segregation, diluted.

It is also important to note that the political and social emergence upon the world's stage of the transsexual, trangendered, intersexed, and sex, gender and sexuality fluid individual is also causing history to be written differently now.

Jane Sasson wrote the books *Princess* and *Daughters of Arabia* about life for a woman in Saudi Arabia, who is considered the property of the males of her family and how she is unable to be a person in her own right in society. Her portrayal of imprisonment was so complete that the manuscripts had to be smuggled out of country and the author lived in fear of male retaliation against her for revealing the truth about her life. The stories tell of the imprisonment of women at the hands of their male captors from birth to death and how women are subject to the whims and fancies of the perpetrators of such slavery.

Muslim women are covered from head to toe in garments that disempower them by taking away their presence in society, and most of all their sexual power, which has often been women's strongest defence against male aggression. While such women are herded together in their own family units under the pretence of protection, their economic and political power is culled and stolen by them being prevented from working, being independent or even simply running naked in the rain, for fear of being stoned to death.

For maximum political and social change it is always a matter of judging the right time and place to assert ideas, protestations and ride on the crest of a wave of social change. Some movements may continue for centuries to try to get the change required and others may be fortunate in capturing the mood of public events and achieve their goals in a very short time.

More than anything though it is the unsung heroes who

toil away in a very perfunctory manner, sending out leaflets, lobbying politicians, giving talks, constantly writing letters and organising the movement that are the ones who truly make change happen. Strong and powerful movements do not necessarily have to have enormous amounts of people behind them, but they do need clear, concise, efficient and well-executed communications taking place within their ranks and with the general public.

Such movements need to present a public front suggesting solidarity. Fighting among the members of any political organisation undoubtedly undermines the public's confidence in that movement knowing what it is talking about. In-fighting and disagreement between members while trying to present a united front is no less than the kiss of death for any political and lobbying movement, as the radical feminist movement of the 1970s found to its cost. Division and subdivision into splinter groups or alternative pressure groups also weakens the structure and momentum of any political power that the original movement tried to assert upon the law-makers.

Although the occurrence of division and substructures is a natural process that takes place as any political lobbying movement gains momentum and grows, it can never be emphasised enough, that division will greatly weaken momentum as well as sometimes being a strength. It should be remembered that the force of political change is generally driven in a democracy by the pressure of the many and not the aspirations of the few. What can also be said to be true, however, is that splinter groups bring new contributions to help the development of ideas and philosophies that are unable to grow and flourish within the structure of larger movements. Indeed subversion, at times, has as much of an honoured place in the structure of political change as unity does.

Historically, change of laws and social attitudes only becomes possible under the guidance of those who know how to create unity, for whatever reason, and can circumnavigate dissent from within. Moses, Alexander the Great, Jesus, Boadicea, Genghis Khan, Mohammed, Elizabeth I of England, Oliver Cromwell, Robespierre, Abraham Lincoln, Lawrence of Arabia, Mao Tse Tung, Lenin, Golda Meir, Winston Churchill, Gandhi, Martin Luther King, Mother Teresa, John Lennon, Timothy Leary and Oprah Winfrey all possessed or possess qualities that led and motivated people together in common causes.

The ability to politically persuade not only led these people to be apart from previous ideas, but also to distil a consensus of opinions, ideals and aspirations of the masses at that particular moment in time. Such kinds of leaders are experts in backwards communication where an individual can lead a group of people to proffer a set of ideas that the individual has suggested to them, even though the group believes they are their own ideas.

While many of the above moved social change and attitudes towards sex, gender and sexuality in their own way and preferred direction, they were always challenged and opposed by sects with differing philosophies. Such is the nature of evolution and survival of the fittest when one set of human beings finds fault with another to knock the opposition out of the food chain. No matter how sophisticated we may think we have become as a species, we are still always subject to primal, base instincts of marking and protecting territories, whether they are a metre or a thousand square miles.

Movements that attempt to change social, political and legal attitudes to sex, gender and sexuality can have hidden, adjunctive or alternative agendas that both aid or sabotage their cause. Therefore it is imperative that those who structure such movements are ever vigilant for fractures in solidarity and do not allow personality clashes to cause rifts that will weaken the central political strength of numbers that can be the movement's greatest ally. The primary rule of any general going into battle is to divide and conquer and that is also the rule by which fascists, bigots, racists, homophobes, transphobes and the ignorant operate too when faced with calls for personal freedom.

Finally, as important as constantly guarding against

splits in solidarity, movements should also continue to seek and strengthen alliances, remembering that in a democracy it is generally numbers that count. The wooing of the masses needs to be constant, ever sweetening and a relentless attempt to educate and enthral the general public about the kind of philosophies the movement is putting forward. Liberty to define oneself is only liberty until it becomes someone else's prison, and having gained that liberty we should also remember it can so easily be eroded by those with different agendas.

A Holistic Approach to Sex, Gender and Sexuality Dysphoria and Exploration
May 1999

Sex, gender and sexuality has undergone countless changes of direction during the 20th century – from the Burlesque bars of New York, sex scandals of politicians, arrest of the Mayflower Madam, liberation of many gays and lesbians, to the surgical rights of the intersex being rewritten by themselves over the Internet. But still many social orders, work sectors, class systems, religions, laws and sciences demonise and pathologise sexual freedom, often resulting in misery.

Freud and the biological determinist medical model of sex, gender and sexuality, during the past hundred years, suffocated more often than liberated the human condition. Jung and sociologists, on the other hand, sought to look further afield for explanations of sexual behaviour within their natural evolutionary environments in varied cultures. What is natural and what is not between consenting adults ought to be the business of those with the agency to safely carry out such acts, and not subject to the preying eyes of the suits, surveillance cameras and cardinals in denial.

The nature verses nurture debate has often turned into a scrum between the pseudo-intelligentsia of singular disciplines and the rest of us. From a scientific perspective it has become a war of the ratings to see who can come up with the ultimate definition of how to make a sex influence a gender performance or possibly prohibit certain sexualities.

The American republicans in 1998-1999 used a semen stain on a young woman's dress to try and blackmail America into putting the country's vast wealth into their hands. Lawyers and evangelical capitalists together passed moral judgement on the untried President and Monica Lewinsky in the name of economic greed. Damage reaped upon their lives and reputations by constant press harassment is surely a reflection upon the distance we all have to travel in moving towards a more humanist way of running our societies. The plot which the republicans so carefully and viciously executed backfired on them and consequently damaged their ratings in the polls instead of bolstering them.

Privacy and personal freedom must be our prime objective when considering how to deal with people who suffer from distorted, painful internal images of their own sex, gender and sexuality, regardless of how they came by those images. Choosing your identity should be as valid an experience as being forced to be something through compulsion or other people's ideals of dysfunction and resolution.

Someone once said a little education can be a dangerous thing and as far as the human race is concerned we still have only a little education. Teachers in school could teach children to celebrate gay pride day; all judges and magistrates ought to have at least a degree in sociology; medical practitioners need to be trained philosophers; and politicians have to be accountable for their decisions on sexual freedom after public office.

It is often social attitudes and public opinion that is pathological, demented, and out of step with nature at large, though only a fool would confront a crowd in their moment of anger. Fools and deviants, however, are the people who change the world because it is they who see things from a different angle. The escalating motion of sex, gender and sexuality freedom movements that has gathered pace throughout the 1900s can, with thought, help the considerations of the world's interdisciplinary academics, guiding us towards a greater acceptance of people's personal choices.

I don't want to live in a new millennium of hate, persecution, ridicule, harassment and crimes against the sex, gender and sexuality diverse. Unfashionable as it may seem I actually like the white, middle-class, heterosexual male just as much as the queer, dyke, trannie, androgyne or trisexual goldfish. If I told you the new millennium will hold no prejudices then I would be like the proverbial ostrich with my head in the sand, and you would not believe me anyway – but what we can all do is daily reinvent humanitarianism in our actions, writings and life.

No single discipline has the only answers to the social discord or personal unhappiness that arises as one group of sex, gender and sexuality orientated people fractiously encounters others of differing compositions or persuasions. Societies rise and fall and with them their feats of great achievements, thinkers, poets, stories of human experience and sexual rituals. Within the spectrum of existence it is a good time to realise that a thousand years is but a drop in the ocean for our species.

It is now well recognised that the reductionist medical model desperately needs redeveloping beyond the science of cause and effect. The 21st century can be an opportunity for changing social attitudes, philosophies and scientific research and application. The intellectual importance of psychologists, sociologists, anthropologists and historians in reaching new understandings of human behaviour can be recognised and respected. Descartes is dead and holistic medicine should not only shape our healing arts but educate new generations to be more tolerant. All the genetics in all the world could not even start to explain the complexities, mechanics and wonders of the human spirit.

We are the children of the new millennium and the greatest monument we can leave at this juncture in time is to mark our presence here, now, with the humanitarianism that supports each individual's sex, gender and sexuality choices.

Vive la difference and remember to do a little drag now and again just for the fun of it...holistically of course!

Caring Systemics for Sex, Gender & Sexuality Evolution and/or Realigment.

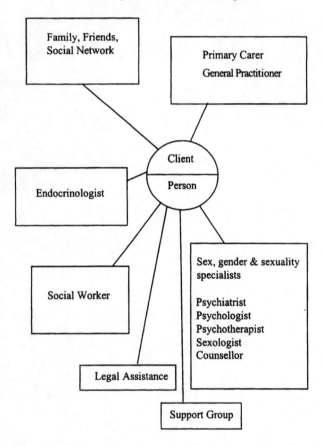

Afterword

For the large part of the 20th century many cultures estranged, ostracised, demonised, disowned and psychopathologised intersex, gays, lesbians, bisexuals, transsexual, transgendered, androgyne and other diverse sex, gendered and sexuality groups. This was done in the name of superior medical, psychological, philosophical and moralistic assumptions that those who passed such judgements know better about people's experiences than the people themselves.

Intersex children were often mutilated by surgery that was unnecessary and performed without their permission or that of their parents. Little psychological help has been given to these people in order to help them cope with their human conditions. Furthermore education still deprives the general public of the whole truth about sex and its anatomical concomitants and diversity.

Gay and lesbian youngsters in many schools are still today made to think that they have done something wrong. Teachers, rather than confront bulling and harassment, turn a blind eye, or choose to collude in the persecution in order not to stick out themselves. In adult life gay people often are not afforded the same legal equality as heterosexuals or "normals" as moralists would choose to label them.

Transsexual children and adolescents are denied the kind of treatment they need in order to live their lives in a pain-free way. The excuse for denying such treatment is that they are told it is for their own good, in case they should change their mind at a later date. In the meantime they suffer profound depression, depleted egos, danger of suicide, and are made to feel like freaks. There are no excuses, because the kind of knowledge we now possess shows that sex and gender realignment treatment in transsexuals is more than 95 per cent effective and produces contributing members of society.

The transgendered and transvestites are denied a place

in society and only tolerated as a party act. They have been forced into gender stereotypes and brutalised because they venture to push back the boundaries of artificial social constructs of the male/female bipolar models of their societies.

Laws and bureaucratic inflexibility robs androgyne people of their rights to label themselves in a way that is most comfortable to them at absolutely no loss to the rest of us. Often language has not even provided the kind of pronouns, nouns or adjectives that we need to address their experiences. Even if you never meet people like this in your life, you have the duty to guard the sanctity of their freedom of choice, if choice is what they have.

As I finish this book the war in Kosovo has produced hundreds of thousands of displaced, hated and abused Kosovan Albanians, leaving them starving to death as exiled refugees. Before that, millions died through the civil war in Somalia. Back further is a similar scenario of fleeing Jews of the Second World War. And back still further was the persecuted Christians of Rome. It seems, at times, that man's inhumanity to man will never cease and that the barbarian in all of us will never find peace or show permanent kindness.

However, now having read this book, I hope you have a greater understanding of the constructs of sex, gender and sexuality. In many cultures, such diversity is treasured and honoured for the gifts they bring to us all. You then, the reader, now possess a greater sense of clarity that can help you be kinder to your fellow human beings, speak more kindly of those who are different from you, and most of all join in the debate to value human life and not debase it...BE SILENT NO MORE...I charge you to be a guardian and prophet of the knowledge you have gained...make good fortune...CHANGING THE WORLD IN THE 21st CENTURY.

STOP PRESS! *On 5 June 1999 the Bank of Scotland announced that their planned merger with Dr Pat Robertson, the homophobic evangelist, was cancelled, due to pressure from their customers.*

BIBLIOGRAPHY

ATKINS, DAWN (Ed)
Looking Queer, Harrington Park Press, New York, 1998.

BERG, CHARLES & KRICH, AM
Homosexuality, George, Allen & Unwin Ltd, London, UK, 1958.

BERNE, ERIC, MD
Games People Play, Penguin Books, London and New York, 1964.

BLAND, JED
The Gender Paradox, The Derby TV/TS Group, Derby, UK, 1993.

BLISS, EUGENE L
Multiple Personality, Allied Disorders and Hypnosis, Oxford University Press, Oxford and USA, 1986.

BORNSTEIN, KATE
My Gender Workbook, Routledge, New York, USA, 1998.

BROWN, MILDRED L & ROUNSLEY, CHLOE ANN
True Selves: Understanding Transsexualism, Jossey Bass Inc, California, USA, 1996.

BURNS, JK
Birth Defects and Their Causes, Stress Books, Galway, Ireland, 1994.

CALIFIA, PAT
Sex Changes: The Politics of Transgenderism, Cleis Press Inc, California, USA, 1997.

CAMPBELL, LADY COLIN
A Life Worth Living, Little Brown & Company, UK, 1997.

CHOMSKY, NOAM
Language and Mind, Harcourt Brace Jovanovich Publishers, London and New York, 1968.

CIVIL, JEAN
Sexuality at Work, BT Batsford Ltd, London, 1998.

COOKSON, WILLIAM
The Gene Hunters, Aurum Press Ltd, London, 1994.

CORINNE, TEE
Dreams of the Woman Who Loved Sex, Banned Books, Texas, USA, 1987.

CORINNE, TEE
Cunt Coloring Book, Last Gasp, California, USA, 1981.

CROWLEY, VIVIANNE
Thorsons Principles of Paganism, Thorsons, London and USA, 1996.

DANA, MIRA & LAWRENCE, MARILYN
Women's Secret Disorder, Grafton Books, London, UK, 1988.

DEVOR, HOLLY
Female-to-Male Transsexuals in Society, Indiana University Press, USA, 1997.

DI CEGLIE, DOMENICO
A Stranger in My Own Body, Karnac Books, London, 1998.

DICKSON, ANNE
The Mirror Within, Quartet Books, London, 1985.

DOUGLAS, NIK
Spiritual Sex, Pocket Books, London and New York, 1997.

320

DREGER, ALICE DOMURAT
Hermaphrodites and the Medical Invention of Sex,
Harvard University Press, London and USA, 1998.

EDMUNDS, VANESSA & HOPKINS, MARTIN & WILLIAMS,
AUDREY
Harassment at Work, Jordan Publishing, Bristol, UK,
1998.

EKINS, RICHARD & KING, DAVE
Blending Genders, Routledge, London and New York
1996.

ETTNER, RANDI, PHD
Confessions of a Gender Defender, Chicago Spectrum
Press, USA, 1996.

FARRER, PETER
In Female Disguise, Karn Publications Garston,
Liverpool, UK, 1992.

FELLOES, TRACI
A Fellow No More, Gary Allen Pty, NSW, Australia, 1997.

FRIDAY, NANCY
My Secret Garden: Women's Sexual Fantasies, Quartet
Books Ltd, London and New York, 1975.

GATHORNE-HARDY, JONATHAN
**Sex: The Measure of All Things: A Life of Alfred C
Kinsey,**
Chatto & Windus, London, 1998.

GRIGGS, CLAUDINE
S/He, Berg, Oxford and New York, 1998.

GRIFFIN, SUSAN
The Eros of Everyday Life, Double Day, New York,
1995.

Bibliography

HEIMAN, JULIA R & LOPICCOLO, JOSEPH
Becoming Orgasmic, Piatkus Publishing Ltd, London, 1987.

HOOPER, CAROL ANNE, MANNING, BERNADETTE, & PECK, JENNIFER
Sexual Violence, the Reality for Women, The Women's Press, London, 1984.

HORLICK, NICOLA
Can You Have it All? Macmillan, London, 1997.

HUNTER, IAN
The Which? Guide to Employment, Which Books, London, 1998.

JAY, MONICA
Geraldine, Mandarin Paperbacks, London 1985.

JAMES, TAD & WOODSMALL, WYATT
Time Line Therapy and the Basics of Personality, Meta Publications, California, USA, 1988.

KANE, SAMANTHA
A Two-Tiered Existence, Writers & Artists Plc, London, 1998.

KATES, GARY
Monsieur d'Eon is a Woman, Basic Books Ltd, New York, 1995.

KIRK, KRIS & HEATH, ED
The Art of India, The Phaidon Press, London, 1954.

KRAMRISCH, STELLA
Men in Frocks, GMP Publishers, London, 1984.

LANGLEY SIMMONS, DAWN
Dawn, A Charlestone Legend, Wyrick & Co, USA,

1995.

LEARY, TIMOTHY
Design for Dying, Thorsons, London and USA, 1997.

LEE, VICKY (ED)
The Tranny Guide 98, The Way Out Publishing Co. Ltd, Enfield, UK, 1998.

LEE, VICKY (ED)
The Tranny Guide 99, The Way Out Publishing Co. Ltd, Enfield, UK, 1998.

LEVINE, STEPHEN B (& others)
Harry Benjamin International Gender Dysphoria Association's Standards of Care for Gender Identity Disorders, Symposium Publishing, Düsseldorf, Germany, 1998.

LEWINS, FRANK
Transsexualism in Society, Macmillan Education Australia Pty, South Melbourne, 1995.

LYNN, STEVEN JAY & RHUE, JUDITH W
Dissociation, Clinical and Theoretical Perspectives, The Guilford Press, London and New York, 1994.

MADONNA
Sex, Martin Secker & Warburg, USA, 1994.

MAHLSDORF, CHARLOTTE VON
I Am My Own Woman, Cleis Press, California, USA, 1992.

MANN, AT & LYLE, JANE
Sacred Sexuality, Element Books Ltd, Dorset, UK, 1995.

MASTERS, WILLIAM H & JOHNSON, VIRGINIA E
Human Sexual Inadequacy, Little, Brown, Boston, USA, 1970.

MIDGLEY, RUTH (THE DIAGRAM GROUP)
Sex: A User's Manual, Hodder & Stoughton, London 1981.

MILES, ROSALIND
The Women's History of the World, Michael Joseph Ltd, London and New York, 1988.

MILLER, CASEY & SWIFT, KATE
The Handbook of Non-Sexist Writing, The Women's Press, London, UK, 1988.

MONEY, JOHN
Gay, Straight and In-Between, Oxford University Press, Oxford and New York, 1988.

MONEY, JOHN
Gendermaps, Continuum Publishing, New York, 1995.

MONEY, JOHN
Lovemaps, Irvington Publishers, New York, 1986.

MONEY, JOHN & EHRHARDT, ANKE A
Man & Woman, Boy & Girl, Jason Aronson Inc, New Jersey, 1996.

MONEY, JOHN & WAINWRIGHT, GORDON & HINGS-BURGER, DAVID
The Breathless Orgasm, Prometheus Books, Buffalo, New York, USA, 1991.

MONEY, JOHN
The Destroying Angel, Prometheus Books, New York, 1985.

MONEY, JOHN
The Kaspar Hauser Syndrome, Prometheus Books, Buffalo, New York, USA, 1992.

MONEY, JOHN

Venuses Penuses, Prometheus Books, New York, 1986.

MONRO, MAROUSHKA
Talking About Anorexia, Sheldon Press, London, 1992.

MUIRHEAD-GOULD, JOHN, (ED)
The Kama Sutra of Vatsyayana, Panther Books, London, 1963.

NEWTON, HELMUT
Sleepless Nights, Schirmer Art Books, Munich, Germany, 1991.

O'KEEFE, TRACIE & FOX, KATRINA
Trans-X-U-All: The Naked Difference, Extraordinary People Press, London 1997.

O'KEEFE, TRACIE
Investigating Stage Hypnosis, Extraordinary People Press, London 1998.

O'RIORDAN, MARIE (ED)
Men's Secret Confessions, Emap Elan, London, UK, 1995.

PAGLIA, CAMILLE
Vamps & Tramps, Penguin Books, London and New York, 1994.

PALMER, FR
Semantics, Cambridge University Press, Cambridge and New York, 1976.

PARKER, K LANGLOH & LAMBERT, JOHANNA (ED)
Wise Women of the Dreamtime, Inner Traditions International, Vermont, 1993.

PEASE, ALLAN
Body language, Sheldon Press, London, 1981.

Bibliography

PITTMAN, FRANK, MD
Man Enough, Berkley Publishing, New York, 1993.

PURNELL, ALICE
A Guide to Transsexualism, Transgenderism, and Gender Dysphoria, Gendys Network, London, 1998.

RAMET, SABRINA PETRA (ED)
Gender Reversals & Gender Cultures, Routledge, London, 1996.

Roscoe, Will
Changing Ones: Third and Fourth Genders in Native North America, Macmillan Press, London, 1998.

SADE, MARQUIS DE
Juliette, Arrow Books Ltd, London, UK, 1991.

SADE, MARQUIS DE
Justine, Philosophy in the Bedroom, Eugene de Franval and Other Writings, Arrow Books Ltd, London, UK, 1991.

SANDERSON, TERRY
Making Gay Relationships Work, The Other Way Press, London, 1994.

SPRINKLE, ANNIE
Post Porn Modernist, Art Unlimited, Amsterdam, The Netherlands, 1991.

SPRY, JENNIFER
Orlando's Sleep, New Victoria Publishers Inc, Australia, 1997.

TAYLOR, TIMOTHY
The Prehistory Of Sex, Fourth Estate Ltd, London, 1996.

TRIMMER, ERIC J, DR (Ed)
The Visual Dictionary of Sex, Macmillan, London, 1977.

TRUDGILL, PETER
Sociolinguistics, Penguin, London and New York, 1974.

TULLY, BRYAN
Accounting for Transsexualism and Trans-homosexuality, Whiting & Birch Ltd, London, 1992.

VOLCANO, DEL LA GRACE & HALBERSTAM, JUDITH "JACK"
The Drag King Book, Serpent's Tail, London, UK, 1999.

WHITTLE, STEPHEN, (ED)
The White Book, Press For Change, London, UK,1998.

WILCHINS, RIKI ANNE
Read My Lips, Firebrand Books, New York, 1997.

WOODHOUSE, ANNIE
Fantastic Women: Sex, Gender and Transvestism, Macmillan Education Ltd, London, 1989.

ZUCKER, KENNETH J & BRADLEY, SUSAN J
Gender Identity Disorder and Psychosexual Problems in Children and Adolescents, The Guilford Press, London and New York, 1995.

PAPERS

COHEN-KETTENIS, PT
Children and Adolescents with GID, Presented to the Third Leicester Symposium on Gender Identity Disorders, Leicester, UK 24 September 1998.

DIAMOND, M
Paediatric Ethics and the Surgical Assignment of Sex,

Journal of Clinical Ethics, 9(4),1998.

DIAMOND, M, PhD & SIGMUNDSON, K, MD
Management of Intersexuality,
Archives of Paediatrics and Adolescent Medicine,
151:1046-1050, 1997.

GORSKI, RA, GORDON, JH, SHRYNE, JE & SOUTHAM,
AM
**Evidence for a Morphological Sex Difference within the
Medical Preoptic Area of the Rat Brain** Brain Research,
issue 148, 1978.

GRIMSHAW, ROSEMARY
**A Reflective Account of the Research Process: What it
Was Really Like,**
Presented to the Third International Congress of Sex and
Gender: Transgender Agenda, Oxford, UK, September,
1998.

GREENBERG, JULIE A
**Law's Failure to Recognise Intersexuals and the
Transgendered: A View Through the Lens of
Therapeutic Jurisprudence,**
Thomas Jefferson School of Law, San Diego, USA,
1998.

O'KEEFE, TRACIE, BA
**General Practitioners Who Exhibit Resistance to Sex
Gender and Sexuality Variance,**
Gendys Journal, Gendys Network, BM Gendys, London,
UK, 1998.

O'KEEFE, TRACIE, BA
**What is Hypnotherapy & How Can it Help the
Transsexual or Transgendered Community?** Gemsnews
20, Gender Trust, London, UK, June 1995.

O'KEEFE, TRACIE, BA

A Big Thank You to Anyone Even Vaguely Gay,
Gemsnews 25, Gender Trust, London, UK, Autumn, 1996.

O'KEEFE, TRACIE, BA
Three Weddings and a Gender Reassignment, Gemsnews 22, Gender Trust, London, UK, December 1995.

O'KEEFE, TRACIE, BA
Unnecessary Links Between Transsexualism and Stress,
Gemsnews 21, Gender Trust, London, UK, September, 1995.

O'KEEFE, TRACIE, BA,
A Review of the XV Harry Benjamin International Gender Dysphoria Association Symposium 1997, Gemnews 30, Gender Trust, London, UK, Winter 1997.

O'KEEFE, TRACIE, DCH,
An Attempt to Get Married, Transgender Tapestry Issue 86, IFGE, Waltham Massachussetts, USA, Spring, 1999.

PFÄFFLIN, FRIEDEMANN
X1V Harry Benjamin International Gender Dysphoria Symposium, Program & Abstracts, Ulm, Germany, 7-10 September, 1995.

PURNELL, ALICE (ED)
Gendys 98: The Fifth International Gender Dysphoria Conference Report,
Gendy's Conferences, Derby, UK, 1998.

SWARTZ, LOUIS H, PHD
Legal Implications of the New Ferment Concerning Transsexualism, Third International Congress on Sex and Gender: Transgender Agenda, Oxford, UK,18-20

September, 1998.

MAGAZINES AND NEWSPAPERS

CONNER, STEVE
Scientists Cast Doubt on 'Gay Gene' Theory, The
Independent, London, UK, 23 April, 1999.

BINDER, SARAH
Man Wins Sex Change On Birth Certificate, Canadian
Press, 24 March, 1999, (Via UKPFC News).

DICKINS, TOM
Lesbians, Gays and Social Constructionism,
The Psychologist, Vol 12, No 3, Leicester, UK, March,
1999.

GRIFFITHS, RAZA
Out and Down, The Big Issue, London, UK, No 336, 24-30
May, 1999.

HANNAH, MICHAEL
GBLT News, Newsletter of the AIUK Gay, Lesbian,
Bisexual & Transgender Network, Issue 10, London, UK,
March 1999.

HARDY, FRANCES
You've Come a Long Way Baby (Louise Brown), Daily
Mail Weekend, UK, 1 May, 1999.

JEFFS, DAVID
Lesbian Art Book Shocker, Sunday Sport, 21 July,
1991.

NORTHMORE, DAVID,
Lords Approve Asylum Rights, Pink Paper issue 577,
London, UK, 2 April, 1999.

NORTHMORE, DAVID
Revealed: Gay List Held by Religious Right, Pink Paper issue 575, London, UK, 19 March, 1999.

NORTHMORE, DAVID
MI5 Warned Gays Could be Next: Soho Bomb Edition, Pink Paper issue 582, London, UK, 7 May, 1999.

RUFFORD, NICHOLAS, & ROBBINS, TOM
Bomb Suspect Arrested as Third Victim Dies, Sunday Times, London, UK, 2 May, 1999.

STEIN, PHYLLIS
Boys Own,
FTM Network London Edition, No 27, London, UK, December, 1998.

O'KEEFE, TRACIE, BA
The Ethical Administration of Hormone Replacement Therapy in the Treatment of Sex/Gender Identity Dysphoria,
Reflections International, Issue 14, TransEssex, Essex, UK, October, 1997.

O'KEEFE, TRACIE, BA
The Administration of Hormones to the Transgendered Community, Reflections International, Issue 15, TransEssex, Essex, UK, 1997.

O'KEEFE, TRACIE, BA
What Made Her The Way She Is?
Reflections International, Issue 17, TransEssex, Essex, UK, 1999.

TV QUICK MAGAZINE
Hayley's Big Day, UK 17-23 April, 1999.

WALKER, MARTIN
Ellen High Water, The Guardian, 30 April, 1997.

WALSH, ABBIE & WHITESIDE, ANDY
What A Banker! Bank of Scotland Beds Down With Notorious US Bigot, Axiom News, London, UK, 11-24 March, 1999.

WILSON, JAMIE
'Grow Your Own Eyes' Operation to Save Sight, The Guardian, London, UK, 18 March, 1999.

LETTERS

BROOKE, PETER, (MP)
Acknowledgement of 1998 Letter of Protest Regarding Consultation Paper on Legislation Regarding Discrimination on Grounds of Transsexualism in Employment,
London, 9 March, 1998.

DEPARTMENT FOR EDUCATION & EMPLOYMENT
Consultation Paper: Legislation Regarding Discrimination on Grounds of Transsexualism in Employment,
London, UK, 16 January, 1998.

DUMONDE, PROF DC
Immunological Screening Tests, London, UK, 26 July, 1996.

JONES, LYNNE, (MP)
Summary of Proceedings from Parliamentary Forum on Transsexualism,
London, UK, 13 February, 1998.

JONES, LYNNE, (MP)
Summary of Proceedings from Parliamentary Forum on Transsexualism,
London, UK, 23 December, 1998.

NEWENS, STAN, (MEP)
Consultation Paper on Limiting Discrimination Against Transsexuals, London, 12 March, 1998.

SIEDLBERG, SOPHIA,
Letter on Intersex Treatment, 1999.

INTERNET POSTINGS

MCNAB, CLAIRE
Police Cannot Bar Transsexual Recruit, Rules Employment Tribunal, UKPFC-News, UK, 19 March, 1999.

MCNAB, CLAIRE
American Senate Hate Crimes Bill, UKPFC-News UK, 23 April, 1999.

MCNAB, CLAIRE
A Victory So Far...But This is only the Beginning, UKPFC-News, UK, 19 April, 1999.

FILMS AND VIDEOS

The First International Transgender Film & Video Festival, Alchemy and Transmutation Productions, London, UK, 1997.

The Second International Transgender Film and Video Festival,
Alchemy and Transmutation Productions, London, UK, 1998.

The Thirteenth London Lesbian and Gay Film Festival, The NFT, London, UK, 1999.

LECTURES

O'KEEFE, TRACIE, DCH
Gender & Linguistics, Université de Toulouse-Le Mirail, France, 3 May, 1999.

O'KEEFE, TRACIE, DCH
Self-Image, London School of Economics, Summer, 1997.

RESOURCES

<u>UK</u>

DR TRACIE O'KEEFE DCH, BA, N-SHAP ADV.DIP.THP, MCRAH
Clinical Hypnotherapist, Psychotherapist and Counsellor
The London Medical Centre, 144 Harley Street, London W1N 1AH
Tel: 0207 935 7920 Fax: 0207 486 5998,
E-mail: katfox@easynet.co.uk
Website: http://easyweb.easynet.co.uk/~katfox/

ANDROGEN INSENSITIVITY SYNDROME SUPPORT GROUP
PO Box 269, Banbury, Oxon, OX15 6YT, UK
E-mail: orchids@talk21.com
Website: http://www.medhelp.org/www/ais

AXIOM
Gay newspaper
73 Collier St, London N1 9BE

BEAUMONT SOCIETY
TV/TS support group
BM Box 3084, London, WC1 N3XX, Tel: 01582 412220
Website: http://members.aol.com/bmontsoc/

BOYS OWN MAGAZINE
See FTM Network

CHANGE
Trans support group
BM BOX 3440, London, WC1N 3XX
Website:
http://members.aol.com.ts1change/homepage.htm

DIVA
National lesbian magazine
Worldwide House, 116-134 Bayham St, London NW1 0BA
Tel: 0207 482 2576 E-mail: diva@gaytimes.co.uk
Website: http://www.gaytimes.co.uk

EQUAL OPPORTUNITIES COMMISSION
Customer Contact Point, Equal Opportunities
Commission, Overseas House, Quay Street, Manchester
M3 3HN
Tel: 0161 833 9244 Fax: 0161 835 1657
E-mail: info@eoc.org.uk
Website: http://www.eoc.org.uk/

FTM NETWORK
Male trans support group
BM NETWORK, London WC1N 3XX
Website:
http://ourworld.compuserve.com/homepages.ftmnet

GAY AND LESBIAN HUMANIST ASSOCIATION
Website:
http://ourworld.compuserve.com/homepages/bretth/gal
ha.htm

GAY TIMES
Worldwide House, 116-134 Bayham St, London NW1 0BA.
Website: http://www.gaytimes.co.uk

GAY TO Z

Directory of lesbian and gay businesses
Website: http://www.gaytoz.com/

GBLT NEWS
Newsletter of the Amnesty International UK Gay, Lesbian, Bisexual & Transgender Network, 99-119 Rosebery Avenue, London EC1R 4RE

GENDYS NETWORK
Trans support group
BM Gendys, London WC1N 3XX
E-mail: gendys@mcmail.com
Website: http://gendys.mcmail.com

GENDER TRUST
Trans support group
BM Gentrust, London, WC1N 3XX
Website: http://www3.mistral.co.uk/gentrust/index.html

IRELAND'S PINK PAGES (ONLINE)
Website: http://indigo.ie/~outhouse/

LESBIAN AND GAY EMPLOYMENT RIGHTS
Unit 1G, Leroy House, 436 Essex Road, London, N1 3QP
Tel: lesbians – 0207-704 8066, Gay men – 0207-704
6066 between 12 noon & 4pm
E-mail: lager@dircon.co.uk
Website: http://www.lager.dircon.co.uk/

LONDON LESBIAN AND GAY SWITCHBOARD
PO Box 7324, London, N1 9QS,
Tel: 0171 837 7324
Fax: 0171 837 7300
Volunteer Recruitment: 0171 837 7606
Website: http://www.llgs.org.uk/

MERMAIDS
Resources for young transpeople, BM MERMAIDS, London, WC1N 3XX

Website:
http://www.geocities.com/WestHollywood/Village/2671/

NORTHERN CONCORD
TV/TS group in the North of England, PO Box 258, Manchester M60 1LN
Website: http://www.northernconcord.org.uk/

OUTRAGE
Gay pressure group
PO Box 17816, London SW14 8WT. Tel: 0208 240 0222.
E-mail: outrage@cygnet.co.uk
Website: http://www.outrage.cygnet.co.uk

PINK PAPER
Gay newspaper
Cedar House, 72 Holloway Rd, London N7 8NZ
Tel: 0207 296 6000

PRESS FOR CHANGE
Trans pressure group
BM Network, London, WC1N 3XX
Website: http://www.pfc.org.uk/

QUEER IRELAND
Website: http://www.clubi.ie/queer/

REFLECTIONS INTERNATIONAL MAGAZINE
See TransEssex

SEXUAL FREEDOM COALITION
PO Box 4ZB, London, W1A 4ZB.
Email: info@sfc.org.uk
Website: http://www.sfc.org.uk/

STONEWALL
Gay pressure group, 16 Clerkenwell Close, London, EC1R OAA, Tel: 0207 336 8860 Fax: 0207 336 8864
E-mail: info@stonewall.org.uk

Website: http://www.stonewall.org.uk

THE TRANNY GUIDE
International resources directory
Way Out Publishing Co Ltd, PO BOX 70, Enfield, EN1 2AE
Info Line, 0207 363 0948,
Vicky Lee Direct, Tel: 0378 157290,
E-mail: vickylee.wayout@virgin.net
Website: http://www.wayout-publishing.com

TRANSESSEX
Support group for TV, TS, TG. Publishes *Reflections International*
PO Box 3, Basildon, Essex, SS14 1PT
Tel: 01268 58376I
E-mail: stacy@transessex.nildram.co.uk

TRANSSEXUALITY IN THE WORKPLACE,
Training video for employers, Task Force, The Medicine
Wheel, Manor Farm, Winestead, Hull, HU12, ONN.
Tel/Fax: 01964 630 235
E-mail: napeWasteWin@medwheel.co.uk

TV/TS NEWS
London newsletter
Box 2534, London WC1N 3XX,
Tel: 0207 609 1093,
E-mail: news@crag.co.uk

VEGETARIAN AND VEGAN GAY GROUP
c/o 50 St. Paul's Crescent, London NW1 9TN
Tel: 0208 690 4792
E-mail: vvgg@freeuk.com

WOMEN OF THE BEAUMONT SOCIETY
Support group for TVs, wives, and families
BM WOBS London, WC1N 3XX,
Tel: 01223 441246
Website: http://members.aol.com.bmontsoc/wobs.htm

INTERNATIONAL

THE ADVOCATE
US gay news magazine, PO Box 541, Mount Morris, IL
61054-0541, USA
Website: http://www.advocate.com/

AUSSIE GAY WEB DIRECTORY
http://www.geocities.com/WestHollywood/Park/2576/

AUSTRALIAN LESBIAN AND GAY ARCHIVES INC
Victorian AIDS Council, 6 Claremont Street, South Yarra,
Vic 3141 VIC
Postal Address: PO Box 124, Parkville 3052 VIC
Tel: (03) 9429-4699
Fax: (03) 9421 2778
Email: jjoyce@silas.cc.monash.edu.au

BC, FTM NETWORK
PO Box 10, 1895 Commercial Drive, Vancouver, BC V5N
4A6, Tel: 604-254-7292,
E-mail: bcftmnet@hotmail.com
For information, E-mail: lukasw@direct.ca

BOYS WILL BE BOYS
Male trans support group
BWBB, PO Box 5393, West End, Brisbane, 4101, Australia

BROTHERSISTER
Australian lesbian and gay newspaper
Suite 33A, 1st Floor, 261 Bridge Road, Richmond VIC
3121, Australia
Tel: 61 3 9429 8844 Fax: 61 3 9429 8966
E-mail: brosisv@webtime.com.au
Website: http://www.brothersister.com.au/

CARITIG
Transgroup, BP 756, 75827 Paris, Cedex 17, France,
Tel/Fax 1 43 42 28 58

Website: http://www.caritig.org

CURVE
US lesbian magazine, One Haight St, Suite B, San Francisco, California 94102, USA
Tel: 415 863 6538   Fax: 415 863 1609

DANISH ORGANISATION FOR GAYS AND LESBIANS
Landsforeningen for Bøsser og Lesbiske, Teglgårdsstræde 13
1452 København K
Website: http://www.lbl.dk/

EUROPEAN LESBIAN AND GAY MAILING LIST
For activists all over Europe to communicate
Website: http://home6.swipnet.se/~w-66936/e-q.htm

FTM INTERNATIONAL NEWSLETTER,
Male trans support group
1360 Mission St, Suite 200, San Francisco, California, 94103, USA
Tel: 415 553 5987
E-mail: TSTGMen@aol.com

FTM NIPPON
Male trans support group
Contact: Masea Torai, Adachi-Ku, Adichi-Nishi-Post, Office Dome, Tokyo 123, Japan.

FWH
Gay and lesbian organisation in Sweden
Website: http://www.fwh.be/

GAY AND LESBIAN INTERNATIONAL LOBBY
Website: http://inet.uni-c.dk/~steff/glil.htm

GAY AND LESBIAN NETWORK OF NORWAY
Website:
http://2000.glnetwork.no/magazine_glnetwork_no.html

GAY AND LESBIAN PARENTS COALITION INTERNATIONAL
PO Box 50360, Washington DC, 20091, USA

GAY TEENS RESOURCES ON THE WEB
Website: http://members.xoom.com/gayzone/

GAY WORLD SWITZERLAND
Website: http://www.gayworld.ch/

GENDER CENTRE
Trans support group
Publishes *Polare* magazine, 75 Morgan St, Petersham, NSW, 2049, Australia Tel: 02 9569 2366
E-mail: gender@rainbow.net.au

GENDERSTICHTING
Trans support group
Belgian Gender Foundation, Pluimstraat 48, Belgium, B-8500

GIRLFRIENDS
US lesbian magazine, 3415 Cesar Chavez St, Suite 101, San Francisco, California 94110, USA
Website: http://www.gfriends.com

GLPGI NETWORK
The newsletter of the Gay and Lesbian Parents Coalition, PO Box 43206, Montclair, NJ 07043, USA

HARRY BENJAMIN INTERNATIONAL GENDER DYSPHORIA ASSOCIATION
For professionals involved in sex and gender medicine, psychology and sociology
Bean Robinson, Executive Director, c/o The Program in Human Sexuality, 1300 South Second St, Suite 180, Minneapolis, Minnesota 55454, USA Tel: 1-612-626-8311
Website:
http://www.tc.umn.edu/nlhome/m201/colem001/hbigda/

INTERNATIONAL FOUNDATION FOR ANDROGYNOUS STUDIES
c/o Delphine McFarlane, University of Western Australia, Hackett Drive, Crawley, WA 6907, Australia.
Tel: 61 089380 2271

INTERNATIONAL LESBIAN AND GAY ASSOCIATION
ILGA Administrative Office, 81 Kolenmarkt, B 1000, Brussels, Belgium
Telephone & Fax: +32-2-5022471, Admin Office (Brussels) E-mail: ilga@ilga.org
Website: http://www.ilga.org/

INTERSEX SOCIETY OF NORTH AMERICA
PO Box 31 791, San Francisco, California 94131, USA
Website: http://www.isna.org/

INTERSEX SUPPORT NETWORK CENTRAL EUROPE
c/o Heike Susanne Spreitzer, MA, Rheinstrausse 2, 50 676 K LN, Germany

IN YOUR FACE
Journal of political activism against gender oppression, c/o Riki Anne Wilchins, 274 W.11th St #4R, NY 1004, New York, USA

LAMBDA LEGAL DEFENSE AND EDUCATION FUND
120 Wall Street, Suite 1500, New York, NY 10005-3904
Tel: 212-809-8585 Fax: 212-809-0055
Website: http://www.lambdalegal.org/

LESBIAN AND GAY COMMUNITY SERVICES CENTER
Also incorporates Gender Identity Project, One Little West 12th Street, New York, NY 10014,
Tel: (212) 620-7310

LESBIAN AND GAY RIGHTS IN RUMANIA
Website:
http://www.geocities.com/WestHollywood/1811/

THE LESBIAN NEWS
PO Box 55 Torrance, CA 90507, USA

LITHUANIAN NATIONAL LESBIAN AND GAY ORGANI-SATION
Website: http://www-public.osf.lt/~lgl/

LSVD
Gay and lesbian organisation in Germany
Postfach 58 04 13, D 10419 Berlin, Tel: 030 440 082 40
Fax: 030 440 082 41
E-mail: berlin@lsvd.de
Website: http://www.lsvd.de/index.html

MANNENGROEP HUMANITAS AMSTERDAM
Transgroup
PO Box 71, 1000 AB, Amsterdam, The Netherlands
Tel: 020-6262445. Fax: 020-6227367.

NATIONAL LESBIAN AND GAY TASK FORCE
1700 Kalorama Road, NW Washington, DC 20009-2624
Tel: 202-332-6483 Fax: 202-332-0207
Website: http://www.ngltf.org/

NEW ZEALAND QUEER NEWS
Website: http://nz.com/NZ/Queer/QNA/

NIVHCOC
National organisation for lesbians and gays in the
Netherlands
Postbus 3836, 1001 AP Amsterdam, bezoekadres:
Rozenstraat 8, 1016 NX Amsterdam,
Tel: 020-623 45 96 Fax: 020-626 77 95
E-mail: info@coc.nl
Website: http://www.xs4all.nl/~nvihcoc/

OUT MAGAZINE
New Zealand's national gay magazine, 92126, Auckland
1, New Zealand

Tel: 64-9-377-9031 Fax: 64-9-377-7767
Email: out@nz.com
Website: http://nz.com/glb/OUT/

PLANETOUT
Online lesbian and gay news, updated daily
Website: http://www.planetout.com/

SONTAGSCLUB
TS group e U, Rhinower str 8, Berlin 10437, Germany

SWEDISH FEDERATION FOR LESBIAN AND GAY RIGHTS
PO Box 350, SE-101 26 Stockholm
Website: http://www.rfsl.se/indexeng.shtml

TRANSGENDER TAPESTRY
Trans magazine
IFGE, PO Box 229, Waltham. MA 02454-0229, USA, Tel: 781-899-2212, Fax: 781-899-5703, E-mail: info@ifge.org
Website: http://www.ifge.org.

TRANSSISTERS
US magazine of transsexual feminism
c/o Davina Anne Gabriel, 4004 Troost Avenue, Kansas City, MO 64110, USA

TRIKONE
Publication for, by, and about, lesbian, gay, bisexual and transgendered people of South Asian heritage.
c/o 37 Melbourne Ave, Toronto, Ontario, M6K 1K4, Canada Tel: 416-537-7742
Website: http://www.trikone.orgj

DR TRACIE O'KEEFE DCH
SEMINARS AND LECTURES

Tracie is a qualified and registered clinical hypnotherapist, psychotherapist, counsellor and trainer at the London Medical Centre, Harley Street. She trained with the National School of Hypnosis and Advanced Psychotherapy in London. Her degree, as well as her doctorate in Clinical Hypnotherapy was earned at the American Institute of Hypnotherapy in the USA and issued in co-ordination with the State of California.

Further to this she has trained at other colleges and schools and constantly spends a lot of her time on developing her skills as a therapist. For over 20 years she has been helping people empower themselves and achieve their goals.

With a wealth of experience in the field of personal and sexual identity, she both writes and speaks on the subject. She is the internationally successful author of the book, **Trans-X-U-All: The Naked Difference**, and teaches in the field of sex, sexuality and gender in the National Health Service (UK) as well as teaching communication skills to sexual health workers.

Her special project has been the development of the **Pan-identity Model of Sex, Gender and Sexuality**, and her work has been reviewed in several international academic publications, including *the European Journal of Clinical Hypnosis* and *The Psychotherapist*. Far from being a stuffy lecturer she is a vibrant and engaging speaker who is fascinated and devoted to human development through therapeutic approaches combined with hypnosis. Tracie is also the author of **Investigating Stage Hypnosis**.

Tracie is available for talks, seminars and workshops. For further details or enquiries, please contact her on:

Tel. 0207 935 7920 Fax. 0207 486 5998
E-mail katfox@easynet.co.uk
Website: http://easyweb.easynet.co.uk/~katfox/

TRANS-X-U-ALL

The Naked Difference

By Tracie O'Keefe and Katrina Fox

Foreword by April Ashley

Please send me..........copies of the above book, which is a comprehensive overview of the transsexual experience. I attach payment totalling.............Cheques made payable to **EXTRAORDINARY PEOPLE PRESS**, which includes postage and packing.

NAME . . . .

Address . . . .

. . . .

Town . . . . **Zip/Post code** . . . .

Country . . . .

If you are paying by credit card please fill in the following details:

Name of card holder . . . .

Card no. . . . .

Statement address . . . .

Town . . . . **Zip/Post code** . . . .

Country . . . . **Date of card issue** . . . .

Date of expiry . . . . . **SIGNATURE** . . . .

Only VISA/DELTA/MASTERCARD CARDS ARE ACCEPTED.
Please allow 28 days for delivery. Mail to Extraordinary People Press, 1B Portman Mansions, Chiltern Street, London W1M 1PX. Prices: UK £13.99/Europe £14.99/ USA &overseas £16.99. Payment can be made by cash in £Sterling or $US and £Sterling only by UK Cheque, Eurocheque, UK Postal Order, IMO, Credit cards. This form can be faxed to 0207 486 5998 for credit card orders only, or by telephone on 0207 935 4490.

Information at:
http://easyweb.easynet.co.uk/~katfox/

Reviews

"**An absolutely fascinating book**" – April Ashley

"**A very detailed and well researched book**" –
The Tranny Guide 1997

"**The most thorough and practical guide to Gender
Dysphoria**" – Gems News

"**The most important book on earth**" –
TV/TS London News

"**Fascinating and eminently readable**" –
TransEssex/Reflections International

"**Every time I put it down, somebody pinches it**" –
Luisa Dillner, Health Editor, The Guardian and British Medical
Journal

"**An excellent book**" – Press for Change

"**An enlightening layperson's guide to the transsexual
experience**" – Gay Times

"**Useful reading, particularly for teachers of Human
Development and therapists dealing with clients
questioning their identity**" –
The Psychotherapist (Journal of the United Kingdom Council
for Psychotherapists)

"**A fascinating, useful resource on an interesting subject,
accessible to all**" – Nursing Times

"**Very readable sound information given with some
humour**" – European Journal of Clinical Hypnosis

INVESTIGATING
Stage Hypnosis
By Tracie O'Keefe
Foreword by Margaret Harper

Please send me..........copies of the above book, which is a comprehensive overview of stage hypnosis. I attach payment totalling.................Cheques made payable to **EXTRAORDINARY PEOPLE PRESS**, which includes postage and packing.

NAME . . . .

Address . . . .

. . . .

Town . . . . **Zip/Post code** . . . .

Country . . . .

If you are paying by credit card please fill in the following details:

Name of card holder . . . .

Card no . . . .

Statement address . . . .

Town . . . . **Zip/Post code** . . . .

Country . . . . **Date of card issue** . . . .

Date of expiry . . . . . **SIGNATURE** . . . .

Only VISA/DELTA/MASTERCARD CARDS ARE ACCEPTED.
Please allow 28 days for delivery. Mail to Extraordinary People Press, 1B Portman Mansions, Chiltern Street, London W1M 1PX. Prices: UK £11.99/Europe £12.99/ USA &overseas £14.99. Payment can be made by cash in £Sterling or $US and £Sterling only by UK Cheque, Eurocheque, UK Postal Order, IMO, Credit cards. This form can be faxed to 0207 486 5998 for credit card orders only, or by telephone on 0207 935 4490.

Information at:
http://easyweb.easynet.co.uk/~katfox/

Reviews

"This is a very important book. I congratulate the author for her courage and hard work" –
Dr Basil Finer, MD, PhD Journal of European Society of Hypnosis in Psychotherapy and Psychosomatic Medicine

"A powerful and revealing exposé" –
Margaret Harper (Campaign Against Stage Hypnosis)

"This is a controversial book, which deserves to be read by every hypnotherapist" –
Dr Morris Berg PhD, National Association of Counsellors, Hypnotherapists, and Psychotherapists

"Well put together and easy to read" –
Derek Crussell, South London Hypnotherapy Practice

"It's about time someone wrote a book like this" –
Dr Prem Misra, psychiatrist and past president of the British Society of Medical and Dental Hypnosis, Scotland

"A very comprehensive book" –
Steve Jones, LBC Radio

"An astounding piece of work" –
Dr Miller, American Institute of Hypnotherapy, on the thesis that formed the basis of this book

SEX, GENDER & SEXUALITY
21st Century Transformations
By Dr Tracie O'Keefe DCH

Please send me..........copies of the above book, which is a comprehensive overview of the world of the sex, gender and sexuality diverse. I attach payment totalling..........................Cheques made payable to **EXTRAORDINARY PEOPLE PRESS**, which includes postage and packing.

NAME . . . .

Address . . . .

. . . .

Town. . . . . : . . . **Zip/Post code** . . . .

Country. . . . .

If you are paying by credit card please fill in the following details:

Name of card holder . . . .

Card no. . . . .

Statement address . . . .

Town. . . . . **Zip/Post code** . . . .

Country. . . . . **Date of card issue** . . . .

Date of expiry. . . . . **SIGNATURE**. . . . .

Only VISA/DELTA/MASTERCARD CARDS ARE ACCEPTED.
Please allow 28 days for delivery. Mail to Extraordinary People Press, 1B Portman Mansions, Chiltern Street, London W1M 1PX. Prices: UK £15.99/Europe £16.99/ USA &overseas £18.99. Payment can be made by cash in £Sterling or $US and £Sterling only by UK Cheque, Eurocheque, UK Postal Order, IMO, Credit cards. This form can be faxed to 0207 486 5998 for credit card orders only, or by telephone on 0207 935 4490.

Information at:
http://easyweb.easynet.co.uk/~katfox/

INDEX

Aborigines 9
Acromegaly 41
Adam and Eve 6, 11, 116
Amazonians 7
Amnesty International 164
Androgen Insensitivity Syndrome
  36, 48
androgenon 111
  androphile 111
  bisexual 111
  gynophile 111
androgenan 111
  androphile 112
  bisexual 112
  gynophile 112
androgynes 30, 34, 47, 66, 67, 78
androgynophile 79
androgynous 11
androgyny 192
Aphrodite 7, 116
Artemis 116
asexual 114
Astarte 7

Bifid Scrotum 42
bisexual 72
bisexuality 17, 66, 70-71
Benjamin, Harry 21-22, 218
  International Gender
  Dysphoria Association 21
Blumenstein, Rosalyne 182
body
  facism 49
  Dysmorphobic Disorder 51
Brigit 8
Buddhism 13
Burns, Christine 196

Caligula 6
candalini 13
Cane, Christie Elan 118
Carlos, Matthew 161
Casanova 6
Catholicism 10-11
celibacy 114
Christianity 11, 99
chromosomes 28, 46
Churchill, Winston 97, 311
Clarke, Steve 189

Cleopatra 6
Cloacal Exstrophy 42
cloning 234, 242
complisexual 108
Congenital Virilising Adrenocorticism
  41, 48
constructionists 89, 92, 93
Cybele 7

Dakini 7
Darwin, Charles 100
deconstructionists 92-93
Demeter 7, 116
drag kings 84
Druids 8
Durga 7
dysphoria 247
  sex, 21, 52, 251, 256, 277
  gender 21, 53, 68, 251, 256, 277, 312
  sexuality 53, 277

earth mother, 6, 7, 8, 12, 14
Ericksonian psychotherapy 256
Erickson, Milton 256-257, 263, 264,
  277
Eros 11

Feinberg, Leslie 6, 173
feminisation of males due to genital
  damage 39
feminising of male foetus 35
feminism 22, 65
femisexual 108
  primary 109
  secondary 109
5 Alpha-reductase deficiency 38, 48
Freud, Sigmund 16, 190, 263-264, 312
fused labia 39, 48

Gaia 7
gender 56
  dysphoria 53, 68, 251, 256, 277, 312
  identity disorder 212, 284
  exploration 212, 312
  genetics 30, 36, 46
  genital organ transplants 238
Gnosticism 11
gonadectomy 39
Gooren, Louis 32, 220, 246

Index

Great Goddess 6, 7
Greer, Germaine 68
gynophile 78

Hanson, Pauline 83
Hathor 7
Havelock Ellis, Henry 17
Hera 116
hermaphroditic 12
hermaphrodite
  true 44, 107
  pseudo 107
hermaphroditism 36, 234, 243
hijra 13
hindu religion 12-13
hir 115
Hirschfeld, Magnus 17, 158
homosexuality 4, 14, 15, 17, 66, 84
Hypertrophied Clitoris 43, 49
circumcision
  male 43
  female 43
castration 43
Hypospadic male 42
  cryptorchid 45
  cryptorchid with feminising
  testes 45
hysterectomies 44

Idiopathic Adolescent
  Gynaecomastia 43
intersex 20, 30, 33, 39, 46, 47-48,
  66, 108
Ishtar 7
Isis 7

Johnson, Virginia 20
Jung, Carl 18, 265, 312

Kali 7, 8, 13
Kama Sutra 12
Kilda-Kele 8
killifish 28, 38
Kinsey, Alfred Charles 19
Klinefelters Syndrome 38, 48
Krafft Ebing, Richard von 17
kundalini 13

Lakshmi 12
language 102
Leary, Timothy 90, 311
lesbianism 10, 14, 15, 66-67, 91

Lotus 12
Mao Tse Tung 14, 311
masculinisation of female foetus 35
masculinisation through
  administration of steroids
  in females 41
Masters, William 19
Mayer-Rotikansky Kuster
  Hauser Syndrome 37
McFarlane, Delphine 192
Mechanical Failure of the Renogenital,
  Intestinal or Reproductive Systems 40
medicalisation of sex, gender and
  sexuality 15
Mills, Theresa 164
model building 93
Money, John 20
  criteria for intersex 44
Muslim 14, 15, 80, 309

Napewastewin-Schützer,
  Marjorie Anne 220, 265
Nataf, Zach 152

Odin 8
Origen 10
ovo-testes 39

Padma 12
Paganism 7, 8, 98
Pallas Athena 7, 116
pan-identity
  model 100-102, 115
  wheel 105
Pankhurst, Emmeline 308
pansexual 107
Pavlov, Ivan Petrovich 17
Persephone 116
phallophile 78
Pneuma 7
polycystic ovaries 40
Potnia 7
Prakriti 11
Prana 7
prefemisexual 108
premature puberty 41
pseudo-hermaphrodite 107
  female with hyperadrenocorticism 44
  female with phallus, ovaries and
  normal mullerian structures 44
  male with well defined mullerian
  organs 44

pseudo-hermaphroditism 38, 39
pseudo-menses 40
psychoanalysis 16, 18, 21
Purnell, Alice 219

Ramsey, Philip 47
Reich, William 18
Rhea 7

Sanger, Margaret 18
Schrenck-Notzing, Albert
  Freiherr von 17
science 88
Selene 7
sex 28, 30, 54
  determining characteristics 31
  dysmorphobia 51, 52
  dysphoria 52, 251, 256, 277, 312
  chromosomal 28
  cosmetic 34
  exploration 212, 312
  fantasy 33
  gonadal 31
  historical 33
  identity disorder 212, 284
  legal 34
  linguistic 34
  psychological 32
  social 33
  spiritual 33
  third 31
  variation 35
sex-change 103-104
sexuality 70, 83, 97
  dysphoria 53, 277, 312
  exploration 212, 312
  identity disorder 212, 284
Shakti 7
Shiva 12
Sibyls 8
simulant females with feminising
  testes 45
sinandrogenon 111
  androphile 112
  bisexual 112
  gynophile 112
sinandrogenan 111
  androphile 112
  bisexual 112
  gynophile 113
sinandrogynes 30, 34, 79
sinandrogynophile 79

sinhir 115
Skopsy Syndrome 10, 13, 113
Sophia 7
Stopes, Marie 18
Stryker, Susan 157

tantric
  sex 12, 13, 282
  yoga 24
testicular cancer 40, 244
Timeline therapy 260, 264, 270, 277-
  280,
trans
  bisexual 109
  heterosexual 109
  homosexual 109
  lesbian 110
  man 109
  woman 109
transgenderism 81
transgenderist 30, 34, 73, 77, 96, 110
  bisexual 110
  heterosexual 110
  homosexual 110
  lesbian 110
transsexual 13, 21, 30, 33, 34, 66, 103-
  104, 107
transsexualism 17, 47
transvestism 17, 81
transvestite 30, 66, 67, 96, 113, 280
Turner's Syndrome 37, 49

Uro-genital Sinus 41

Vatican 4, 10
Vatsyayana 12
Vestal Virgins 8
Virgin Mary 10
Virilising Adrenal Hyperplasia 36
Vishnu 12
Volcano, Del La Grace 84

Whittle, Stephen 170, 253
Wilde, Oscar 6
Wisecraft 8
witchcraft 8
Witschi, Emil 38
Woolf, Virginia 6, 15

XX males 38
XYY males 37